The Cult that Hijacked the World

HENRY MAKOW PhD

SILAS GREEN

ILLUMINATI

The Cult that Hijacked the World

All Rights Reserved © 2009 by Henry Makow PhD

For information address:

Silas Green
PO Box 26041
676 Portage Ave.
Winnipeg, MB
Canada
R3G 0M0

hmakow@gmail.com

www.henrymakow.com
www.cruelhoax.ca

ISBN: 1-4392-1148-5
Printed in the United States

"My flock has become a prey...because there was no shepherd, nor did my shepherds search for my flock, but the shepherds fed themselves..."

Ezekiel 34:8

"The goyim are a flock of sheep, and we are their wolves. And you know what happens when the wolves get hold of the flock?"

Protocols of the Elders of Zion, 11

Table of Contents

Overture – Based on a True Story?

Forward – The "Jewish" Conspiracy

Introduction – The Cult that Hijacked the World

Book One – Bankers, Jews and Anti-Semitism

26 - The Banking Cartel is the Cause of Humanity's Woes
28 - Making the World Safe for Bankers
31 - Bankers Demand We Obey Them
34 - The "Jewish" Conspiracy is British Imperialism
37 - Is the New World Order "Jewish"?
40 - The Imperialism of Jewish Capital
43 - The Jewish Century
46 - The Riddle of Anti-Semitism
49 - Best Picture "Chicago" Celebrates Jewish Power & Duplicity
52 - Communism-A Ruse for Illuminati Theft and Murder
56 - Soviets Spared Synagogues, Razed Churches
59 - The "God" That Serves Elite Jews
62 - The Real Cause of Anti-Semitism

Book Two – Illuminati, Sabbateans and Protocols

66 - The Conspiracy is Against God
69 - The Root Problem: Illuminati or Jews?
73 - Highest Illuminati Defector: "Rothschilds Rule with Druid Witches"
77 - Illuminati Sex Slaves Paint Horrifying Picture
81 - An Illuminati Primer
85 - Humanity is Under Occult Attack
89 - The Satanic Cult that Rules the World
92 - Why Do the Illuminati Hate Jews?
94 - What Every Jew (and Non-Jew) Should Know
97 - Independent Historian Unveils Cabala Conspiracy
100 - The Cabalist Plot to Enslave Humanity
103 - Is Plan for Racial Strife Also a Hoax?

106 - Historian Demands Action Vs. Powerful Doomsday Cults
108 - Protocols Forgery Argument is Flawed
113 - The Protocols of Zion – Introduction and Synopsis
124 - Protocols of Zion Updated by a Jewish Zealot
128 - Illuminati Bankers Seek "Revolution" by Economic Means

Book Three – Zionism and the Holocaust

132 - British Jewry Tried to Stop Zionism
136 - The Worst Anti-Semites Are Zionists
138 - War and Depression are Forms of Extortion
141 - Communism- Zionism's Twin Brother
145 - Zionism-A Conspiracy Against Jews
149 - Zionists Made a Deal with the Devil
151 - The Zionist Roots of the "War on Terror"
154 - Zionism: Compulsory Suicide for Jews
158 - Jews Worst Enemy- Illuminati Jews
161 - The Holocaust as Mind Control
164 - Are Jews Being Set Up for Another Holocaust?
167 - The Other Side of Holocaust Denial
170 - Israel's Descent into A Moral Abyss
174 - Zionists "False Flagged" Iraqi Jews

Book Four – Hidden History

177 - Illuminati Murdered at Least Two Other Presidents
181 - Are World Wars Orchestrated?
183 - Bankers Extended World War One by Three Years
186 - The U.S. is a Crown Financial Colony
190 - The 1933 "Banker's Coup" Was a Ruse
193 - Was Victor Rothschild an Illuminati Agent?
196 - The Illuminati Tricked Hitler With "Appeasement"
199 - How the Bankers Frog-marched the U.S. Into WW2
203 - "I Was Hitler's Boss"
207 - Was Hitler an Illuminati Agent?
211 - Did the Illuminati Hire Hitler to Start World War Two?
214 - Hitler Used Rothschild Banker's Typewriter (to Write "Mein Kampf")
217 - Did Bormann Run Hitler for the Illuminati?
220 - Winston Churchill, Illuminati
223 - Lester Pearson, Illuminati Tool
228 - Be Afraid. The New World Order's Fascist Pedigree
231 - The "Ugly" Secret of World War Two

Epilogue - Surviving the New World Order

Addendum

238 - Jewish Convert, Richard Wurmbrand Defined "Spiritual War"
243 - Illuminati Reveal Crazy Apocalyptic Agenda

Based On a True Story?

If this were a movie treatment, it would be rejected as implausible. Our leaders are not chosen for their intelligence or achievement but rather because they are able to win the peoples' trust and willing to betray it. They are chosen by a small Satanic cult –Cabalistic bankers and Freemasons--that controls the world's finances and media. Our "leaders" are junior members of this international cult, called the Order of the Illuminati.

"We replaced the ruler by a caricature of a government," their Master Plan chortles, "by a president, taken from the mob, from the midst of our puppet creatures."

Many "leaders" are kept in line by having them indulge in horrifying occult rituals including human sacrifices, sexual orgies, pedophilia, rape, torture and murder. (See "Illuminati Sex Slaves Paint Horrifying Picture" and "The Root of the Problem: Illuminati or Jews?" within.)

The Illuminati goal is to degrade and enslave humanity, mentally and spiritually, if not physically. This group's influence is like a cancer that extends throughout society. It has subverted many seemingly benevolent organizations (like charities and professional associations) and most political movements, especially Zionism, Communism, Socialism, Liberalism, Neo-conservatism and Fascism. This is why society seems to be run by soulless men with pinched faces who spout platitudes and exude evil.

The Illuminati have subverted all religions and institutions including one group that fancies itself "chosen by God." In fact, leaders of this group figure prominently in creating this Satanic dispensation. But whenever critics suggest that the "Chosen" are being misled and betrayed, they are accused of "racism" - a clever way of quashing resistance.

Thus, attention to the most pressing problem of all time is dismissed as "prejudice." And the Chosen continue to be pawns, scapegoats and human shields for their diabolical and deceitful "leaders."

Like a security beam, Illuminati tyranny is invisible until you cross it. Then, doors silently close and positions of influence are denied. If you persist, you are slandered, bankrupted or even killed. In the future, truth tellers and dissenters will be denied access to credit and trade. It is amazing how easily we have succumbed to tyranny.

Public success is determined by acquiescence - witting or unwitting - in this diabolical conspiracy. The people of the West are blinkered, leaderless and feckless. Our material and technological achievement is great, but culturally and spiritually we are impoverished and enchained.

The "Jewish" Conspiracy

Recently, on his internet radio show, Alan Stang asked me if there is such a thing as a Jewish conspiracy. He gets e-mail from people blaming Jews, Jesuits, the Vatican, Freemasons etc.

I replied that the central banking cartel is the only group with both the motive and the means to take over the world. Consisting mainly of Cabala-believing Jews and Freemasons, it is the head of the octopus. Zionism, Freemasonry, organized Jewry, Imperialism, Jesuits, Vatican, Intelligence agencies, mass media, etc. are among countless octopus arms.

The "motive" is to protect its priceless but fraudulent private monopoly over public (government) credit (money creation.) They need a "world government" to ensure that no nation prints its own money or defaults on the "loans" the bankers spun out of nothing.

The "means" of course is their unlimited wealth funneled through their network of cartels, which allows them to own the government, mass media, education, etc. Anyone who succeeds in public life is their puppet or unconsciously serves their agenda. Their Zionist-Freemason-Communist-Socialist-MI-5/6 etc. networks allows them to exercise covert control.

The ideology of world tyranny, Illuminism, derives from the Jewish Cabala which preaches that man (i.e. the bankers) can usurp the place of God and redefine truth.

About 1770, a syndicate of bankers led by Mayer Rothschild started the "Illuminati," a Satanic cult designed to subvert society. According to Edith Starr Miller, the Rothschild syndicate included Jewish financiers such as Daniel Itzig, Friedlander, the Goldsmids and Moses Mocatta. ("Occult Theocracy," p. 184.)

According to Miller, the goals of the Illuminati (Communism and the NWO) were the destruction of Christianity, monarchies, nation-states (in favor of their world government or "internationalism"), the abolition of family ties and marriage by means of promoting homosexuality and promiscuity; the end of inheritance and private property; and the suppression of any collective identity in the spurious name of "universal human brotherhood," i.e. "diversity." (p.185)

Naturally, they are trying to suppress this kind of information. The Canadian Jewish Congress has complained to the Canadian "Human Rights" Commission demanding Jewish references be removed from my website, www.henrymakow.com. As of March 2009, the CHRC is holding a "Tribunal" to investigate my writing. The excuse that I promote "hatred" is the tired pretext.

In my mind, this confirms everything I am saying. I am not a great prophet but Isaiah, Ezekiel, Jeremiah and Amos also criticized Jewish "leadership" and would have been treated the same way today.

The CJC doesn't want Jews to know that the Jewish enterprise has been hijacked. Jewish leadership has perverted the ideal of a holy people chosen to advocate for morality into an elite self-chosen to take God's place. The bankers use this Jewish Messianism as an instrument to consolidate their material, spiritual and cultural hegemony. Judaism (with Communism & Zionism) are systems to control Jews, and through them the human race.

The world government tyranny is the only conquest to take place without the knowledge of the conquered. In the "Protocols of the Elders of Zion," the author repeats, our "countersign" is "Force and Make-believe." By "Make-believe," he means deception which is their "magic." (Protocol 1)

When alien bankers control the purse strings, inevitably the State becomes synonymous with these bankers. The State is a ruse used to manipulate the masses, "public" in name only. This is the truth behind the "make-believe" face of the Communist NWO.

This tyranny is also the first in history which cannot be mentioned for fear of being branded "anti-Semitic" and a "hater." Trust me, the hatred is entirely on the Cabalist side.

This ruse is achieved by blaming all Jews for the machinations of a relative few. It's as though all Italians were blamed for the activities of the Mafia. Blaming all Jews naturally makes them run interference for the Rothschilds, thus confirming suspicions. Talk about walking into the line of fire! What would we think of Italians if they defended Al Capone and organized crime?

Organized Jewry uses "anti-Semitism" and "hate" like a witch doctor's curse from which all shrink in horror. To neutralize this voodoo, we should wear the badge of anti-Semite with pride, asserting that it stands for opposition to the disproportionate Jewish (and crypto-Jewish) role in advancing the New World Order. (No one is advocating or condoning genocide.) Thus, anti-Semitism will become a legitimate political (not racial) movement directed against specific Jewish (and non-Jewish) Illuminati pawns and policies.

WHAT BEING JEWISH MEANS TO ME

For me, being Jewish is a matter of spirit, mind, blood and culture. I have a strong sense of God as an immanent moral dimension. I believe man's purpose and duty is to manifest this dimension. I won't ever impose my idea of good on you. But in a society that had its bearings, questions of what is true, just or beautiful would be a focus of constant debate.

I am an assimilated Jew. I identify with the human race first, my countrymen second, and Jews third. I have had no Jewish education and don't regularly associate with Jews. So far, except for the Ten Commandments and a few parts of the Old Testament, the "religion" doesn't attract me. "Know them by their fruits," Jesus said.

In contrast, I can see the civilizing effect Christ's Gospel of Love has had on society. The first baby steps in human spiritual evolution is considering others before oneself and recognizing that all men (not just Jews) are brothers.

In his book, "Jewish History, Jewish Religion" (1994) Israel Shahak confirmed my suspicion that Judaism is not a religion. "Faith and beliefs (except nationalistic beliefs) play an extremely small part in classical Judaism. What is of prime importance is the ritual act, rather than the significance which that act is supposed to have or the belief attached to it." (p.35)

The next step for me was concluding that Judaism is a pagan racial creed at best, and a Satanic secret society at worst. The nature of a secret society is that the membership is fed idealistic platitudes and isn't told the real agenda.

Most Jews are unaware that Judaism largely eschews the Old Testament in favor of the Talmud and Cabala. Very few Jews read these books. If they did, they might realize that the Talmud is full of hate and contempt for non-Jews. They would discover that the Cabala is the basis of modern witchcraft, astrology, numerology, tarot cards, black magic, androgyny, sex worship and much of the New Age movement. It teaches that good and evil are one and that black is white and vice-versa.

Cabalist Jews tell this joke privately: "An orthodox Jew is interviewing three applicants for a job. He asks them, 'What is 2 plus 2?' The first two applicants answer 4 and 22. He kicks them out. The third answers, "'Whatever you want it to be.' He is hired." This is what we are up against in the NWO, an attempt to reshape truth itself according to self-interest.

The Cabala is the basis of the cult of sex worship that has engulfed the world. Conjugal sex is a required ritual for Cabalist Jews on the Sabbath. Physical desire supposedly "increases a man's love for God," and intercourse is "an instrument for uniting with God." (This, of course, is rubbish. You unite with God by serving Him seven days a week. Sex is a natural instinct like eating, not a sacred act.)

The arc of Western Civilization has gone from (ascent) belief-in-God to (descent) belief-in-Satan. The apex was the so-called "Enlightenment" when the money men decided they could take over from God. Typically, the decline into moral darkness is represented by Luciferians as light, sunrise (eg. Barack Obama's logo.)

According to Texe Marrs, the Cabala teaches that the "holy serpent is the true God; that all the evil that a person does, through alchemy is magically transformed into righteousness; and that yes, Lucifer is Lord. Satan is the true and only god. That is the essential doctrine of Cabalism." (Codex Magica p. 426.)

I suspect the Cabala is the blueprint of the post-Christian era, the reason we are drowning in media-generated occultism, pornography, violence and fear.

As a youth, I was told that Jews always have been hated for no reason. (This is how the leadership controls and manipulates Jews.) My grandparents died in the holocaust and my parents bore the scars of passing as non-Jews in Nazi Europe. I was told Israel was the answer to centuries of persecution. I saw my fellow Jews in America as a small and vulnerable community.

I now realize anti-Semitism is caused by a complex variety of reasons. The main one is that, unknown to most Jews, Judaism contains an ideology of supremacy and domination. The Illuminati Jewish leadership regards itself as God. Leon Trotsky put God on trial in Moscow in 1923 before 5000 men of the Red Army. God was found guilty of various ignominious acts and convicted in absentia. ("Berliner Taegeblatt," May 1, 1923.)

The "Jewish World" announced Feb. 9, 1883 that, "The great ideal of Judaism is that the whole world shall be imbued with Jewish teaching and that in a Universal Brotherhood of Nations -- a greater Judaism in fact -- all the separate races and religions shall disappear."

This sentiment plays an important part in the New World Order. It provides a support system for the central bankers and diverts blame away from them. If your ethnic or religious group is secretly being used for evil, you had better distance yourself or you will be left holding the bag.

This applies to almost everyone, not just Jews. As an ethnic Jew, I ask, does the Jewish god represent a universal moral order or a primitive tribal egregore (i.e. projection of group psyche?) Is the Jewish egregore now Lucifer? (See within, "The God that Serves Elite Jews.")

We may be approaching a crisis. Organized Jewry and their Masonic allies are following a script based on End Times Biblical prophesies (which they may have written or modified.) This script calls for a Third World War and mass destruction of all people including 2/3 of all Jews. The New World Order is supposed to rise from the debris.

The human race is entering a Dark Age. As the New World Order is enacted, anti-Semitism inevitably will grow. Now is the time for Jews to awaken and take a stand. Now, there is no reward for such a courageous act, only scorn. Later if anti-Semitism becomes rampant, Jews will have to circle their wagons. It will be too late.

Two final and unrelated comments: Many Jews are alienated from the concept of a loving God represented by Jesus' teaching. These Jews are metaphysical outcasts. They feel they have to "earn" love by overachieving. Like a woman who overeats to compensate for lack of love, they seek money and power. In extreme cases (like the Rothschilds,) their quest for limitless wealth and power, their need to own and control everything, define Satan's dominion.

I used to look askance at the ability of Christians to enjoy ordinary life. "Normal" and wholesome seemed boring and ridiculous. I had to justify my life, find life's meaning. I didn't realize that life has inherent meaning when it is led according to God's loving design.

Finally, people can't discover the truth if they don't know what to look for. The truth – that mankind is controlled by Satanists -- is hard to prove conclusively. But in more than 60 articles, I show that this is the most convincing explanation for mankind's morass.

The Cult that Hijacked the World

Who said the following?

"Instead of agitating for war, the Jewish groups in this country should be opposing it ... for they will be among the first to feel its consequences. The greatest danger to this country lies in their large ownership and influence in our motion pictures, our press, our radio and our government."

Charles Lindbergh delivered these words in Des Moines, Sept. 11, 1941. Exactly sixty years later, the Illuminati Zionist Mossad is a prime suspect in the "false flag" attack on the World Trade Centre designed to foster more war.

Zionists were also behind America's entry into World War One. They made a trade-off. America will enter the war if Britain takes Palestine from Turkey. (See my website for "Americans are Rothschild Proxies in Iraq.")

History repeats itself because it follows a prepared script. The Rothschild banking syndicate did not announce its intention to overthrow Western civilization. It went ahead and did it. The Rothschilds claim to represent the Jewish people but there never has been a vote.

For over 200 years, they have used Jewish groups and Freemasons to foment war in order to advance their world government tyranny. Their Jewish agents admit it. For example, on May 4, 2003, the Israeli newspaper Ha'aretz stated: "The war in Iraq was conceived by 25 neo-conservative intellectuals, most of them Jewish, who are pushing President Bush to change the course of history... almost all of them Jewish, almost all of them intellectuals (a partial list: Richard Perle, Paul Wolfowitz, Douglas Feith, William Kristol, Eliot Abrams, Charles Krauthammer...) ("White Man's Burden" by Ari Shavit)

In a letter to Giuseppe Mazzini dated August 15, 1871, Albert Pike, the Grand Commander of U.S. Freemasonry foretold "three world wars." The first two have transpired as predicted. "The Third World War must be fomented by taking advantage of the differences caused by the "agentur" [agents] of the "Illuminati" between the political Zionists and the leaders of Islamic World. The war must be conducted in such a way that Islam (the Moslem Arabic World) and political Zionism (the State of Israel) mutually destroy each other."

"Meanwhile the other nations, once more divided on this issue will be constrained to fight to the point of complete physical, moral, spiritual and economical exhaustion ... [Thus the nations will be forced to] receive the ... pure doctrine of Lucifer, brought finally out in the public view." (see http://www.threeworldwars. com/albert-pike2.htm)

The stage is being set in the Persian Gulf, Eastern Europe and the Caucuses for a nuclear conflagration pitting Russia, China and Iran against the U.S., the EU and Israel. The Rothschilds control both sides. Jews - all of us - are pawns in a wider game of chess designed to finish Western civilization and build a New World Order on its ashes. On a cosmic level, the plot is to hijack mankind and divert it to the service of Satan and his disciples.

Today, even after the debacle in Iraq, Zionists lobby for an attack on Iran. Zionism is controlled by "the Order of the Illuminati" which represents a group of dynastic families, generational Satanists, associated with the Rothschilds and European aristocracy, united by money, marriage and Freemasonry (i.e. the Cabala.) This cult stems from the Satanic Jewish Sabbatean-Frankist movement described later in this volume.

While it often exhibits disdain for non-Jews, this cult intermarries strategically with other generational Satanists. It monopolizes power, wealth and culture and works to stymie moral and scientific development. It is re-engineering humanity to be serfs in a Neo-Feudal World Order.

What we call "history" is theatre. Our human experience is largely the product of a spell they cast by "education" and mass media. Our political and social attitudes are given to us. For example, currently there is a full-court-press to undermine marriage and family and make us look to promiscuous sex for life's meaning. (See my book, "Cruel Hoax: Feminism and the New World Order.")

THE ILLUMINATI

"Mary Anne" a prominent former member of the Illuminati, said she was told the cult dates back to ancient Babylon and the Tower of Babel, (which not coincidentally resembles the present EU parliament.) When the Cabalists' plans for a tower reaching to heaven were foiled by God, they instigated their centuries-long vendetta against Him and vowed to hijack His Creation.

The Cabalists were relatively few in number so they decided to conquer using Gold, i.e. economic domination. In 1773 Amschel Mayer Rothschild, an orthodox Jew who never changed his underwear and let his clothes fall apart, convened a meeting of 12 prominent Jewish bankers. They refined their programme by baiting the hook with the spurious promise of "liberty, fraternity and equality." The 1848 Communist Manifesto which demands the theft of private property and the destruction of liberty and family in the name of "equality" reflects their Satanic agenda.

In 1776, they appointed Adam Weishaupt to reorganize the Illuminati which merged with Freemasonry in 1782. According to Andre Krylienko, Freemasonry was used "to enlist non-Jews consciously or unconsciously in the service of Jewry." ("The Red Thread," p. 93)

The Cabalistic bankers were behind the revolutionary movements of the 17th- 20th Centuries as well as each respective reign of terror. Throughout history, they have pursued an evil vendetta against humanity. They finagled a monopoly on credit (usurping the government's right to create money) and have used it to conquer the world. Since they create money out of nothing, they think they are God. This meshes with Messianic Jewish and Cabalistic prophesies. Essentially, for co-operation in their diabolical plan, they let fellow Jews and non-Jewish Freemasons in on their lucrative racket.

In a famous statement, Georgetown University professor Carol Quigley, an insider who was Bill Clinton's mentor, said the central banker plan is "nothing less than to establish a world system... able to dominate the political system of each country." ("Tragedy and Hope," 1966, p. 324)

The Illuminati control the Establishment in Europe, America and most of the world. Its secret war against humanity is designed to make us acquiesce in their tyranny (i.e. "world government.") By owning the leaders on both sides and the media, they start all major wars and determine their outcome. They are responsible for revolutions, depressions, and more recently 9-11 and the "war on terror" -- pretexts for more war and a police state. (See the section on "Hidden History" within.)

Jewish groups are one of their instruments. In 1920, Oscar Levy, a Jewish philosopher wrote "there is scarcely an event in modern Europe that cannot be traced back to the Jews...Jewish elements provide the driving forces for both Communism and capitalism, for the material as well as the spiritual ruin of this world."

Levy blames the "intense idealism of the Jew" for the revolutionary havoc. "These revolutionary Jews do not know what they are doing. They are more unconscious sinners than voluntary evil doers...but please do not think I wish to exonerate them on that account...."(Preface to George Pitt-Rivers, "The World Significance of the Russian Revolution.")

This book focuses on how Jews are used. Another volume could be written about how Freemasonry is used. In the meantime, I recommend "Unholy Alliances" (1996) by Dr. James Wardner. I expect that Jesuits have also played an important role but I have not had time to research it yet. I refer you to Eric Jon Phelps whose "Vatican Assassins" is the classic. I emphasize that the Illuminati conspiracy is all-pervasive, has infiltrated every social institution of significance and includes millions of non-Jews.

"ANTI-SEMITISM"

I believe all human beings have a direct relationship with the Creator regardless of their religion or lack thereof. We all have a spark of the Divine within. I judge each person by his response to his Divine calling, not by his ethnicity, religion or race.

Most Jews are unaware of the Illuminati agenda. They are manipulated and compromised like everyone else. For example, all Americans are implicated in war crimes in Iraq by their taxes. But the average American had no say in the inception or execution of this war. Organized Jewry doesn't represent me any more than the U.S. government represents Americans. Both have been hijacked by the Illuminati banksters.

The Illuminati hides behind the skirts of ordinary Jews. The cult that hijacked the world is the tiny nucleus of Cabalistic bankers and Masons based in London and directed by the House of Rothschild.

They govern through their subtle control of large corporations (cartels - especially finance, oil, defence, pharmaceuticals,media); government, mass media, secret societies, intelligence agencies, the military, law, churches, foundations, think tanks, NGO's and education. Chatham House in London (The Royal Institute of Internal Affairs) and Pratt House in New York (Council on Foreign Relations) are two main control mechanisms. Illuminati power is omnipresent yet the masses don't even know it exists.

Recently, Doreen Dotan, a Jewish woman from an Illuminati background, posted a talk on You Tube saying she is tired of taking the blame for the Rothschilds and Warburgs. Unlike this courageous woman, ordinary Jews have been complacent. Professor Albert Lindemann wrote that Jews actually "do not want to understand their past, or at least those aspects of their past that have to do with the hatred directed at them..." ("Esau's Tears: Modern Anti-Semitism and the Rise of the Jews," 1997, p. 535)

Generally, Jews act like people engaged in an enterprise that they don't really care to understand as long as it continues to work in their favor. I rarely hear from Jews one way or the other. This Sept. 2008 e-mail from a British Jew was a pleasant exception:

"Hello, I want to thank you for your very interesting website. Like you, I am of Jewish descent, so I was understandably horrified when I heard about a 'Jewish Plot' etc. But your website has broken it down into more manageable parts, which I appreciate. I also appreciate the way you don't spread hatred, which is common among people promoting the validity of the Protocols. Cheers and Shalom."

Nothing happens without the blessing of money. The Illuminati finance whom they like. Most people "go along to get along" unaware of the big picture. They instinctively embrace ideologies and groups that advance their material interests. Hence the Communist term, "useful idiots."

The masses are "accustomed to listen to us only who pay it for obedience and attention. In this way, we shall create a blind mighty force which will never be in a position to move in any direction without the guidance of our agents...The people will submit to this regime because it will know that upon these leaders will depend its earnings, gratification and the receipt of all kinds of benefits." ("Protocols of Zion" 10)

Virtually every nation, group and religion has been co-opted and ordinary Jews are no exception. (Read within, "The U.S. is a 'Crown' Financial Colony" to learn how this control extends to virtually all organizations, even the Boy Scouts and the YMCA.)

The knee jerk charge of "anti-Semitism" is basically a ruse to keep people ignorant of the Illuminati conspiracy. Nobody is condoning or advocating genocide. The charge is used to stifle opposition.

The issue is really about a monopoly of credit, power, culture, and wealth. The bankers are concerned only with their own supremacy and that of their Sabbatean-Frankist-Illuminati cult. This isn't about the ordinary Jew.

Jewish leaders cannot concede any legitimacy to anti-Semitism because they have no intention of changing course. Thus they pretend it is motivated by "prejudice." Organized Jewry (Neocons, Zionists, B'nai Brith) has the self-consciousness of a snake devouring a mouse. It regards the death spasms of the mouse as "hatred." Increasingly, we are taught to accept the snake's perspective, even if we are the mouse.

"We have already contrived to possess ourselves of the minds of the goy communities...they all come near ...looking through the spectacles we are setting astride their noses." ("Protocols of Zion," 12)

TALMUD AND CABALA

Judaism has been hijacked. Originally Judaism was based on Moses' vision of God as a universal moral force. This is the only Judaism I identify with. I have always intuited that life is neither random nor meaningless but governed by inherent moral and spiritual laws. This led me to invent "Scruples", the game of everyday moral dilemmas, in 1984.

Judaism today is based on the Talmud, which consists of the interpretations of "sages" (Pharisees) during the Babylonian exile 586 BC to 1040 AD. Generally speaking, the Talmud contradicts the spirit of Moses and takes precedence over the Old Testament.

Jesus was in the tradition of Moses. He reproached unbelieving Jews: "If you believed Moses, you would believe me, for he wrote of me." (John 5:24-27) Jesus reviled the Pharisees as hypocrites, liars and a "generation of vipers." He said they nullified God's Commandments "teaching for doctrines the commandments of men." (Mark 7:6-8) He accused them of worshipping the devil: "Ye are of your father the devil, and the lusts of your father ye will do." (John 8:44)

Elizabeth Dilling, (1894-1966), a courageous Christian whose visit to Soviet Russia in 1931 inspired a 20-year study, exposed Judaism's most closely guarded secret -- its supremacism and hatred for non-Jews, especially Christians. ("The Jewish Religion: Its Influence Today." 1964, http://www.come-and-hear.com/)

What follows is very distasteful and shocking. I take no pleasure in presenting Dilling's conclusions. However, I believe they are true and too important to ignore. The devil operates by deceiving and corrupting good people. According to Dilling, the Talmud is founded on the assumption of Jewish supremacy.

"The non-Jew ranks as an animal, has no property rights and no legal rights under any code whatever... 'Milk the gentile' is the Talmudic rule but don't get caught in such a way as to jeopardize Jewish interests. Summarized, Talmudism is the quintessence of distilled hatred and discrimination, without cause, against non-Jews." (p.16)

The Talmud is characterized by "obscenity and more obscenity, a setting up of laws seemingly for the purpose of inventing circumvention, and evasions; delight in sadistic cruelty; reversal of all Biblical moral teachings on theft, murder, sodomy, perjury, treatment of children and parents; insane hatred of Christ, Christians and every phase of Christianity." (4)

It characterizes the Virgin Mary as a "harlot" and adulteress and Jesus as a "bastard" and sexual pervert who was crucified as a "blasphemer of Pharisee Judaism." Jesus' punishment was to be "lowered into dung up to his armpits" and then strangled. Christians in hell are punished by "hot boiling excrement." (14)

Judaism rejects Moses' vision of God as a moral force. Its basic doctrine is that "God is the "En Sof" a nature essence which has no attributes and can neither know nor be known. That is atheism..." (57)

"So called Judaism is nothing but Babylonian Talmudic Pharisaism, which at base is crass paganism, pantheistic atheism, a conglomeration of all the forms of paganism concocted through the centuries. New descriptions concocted for this very old Satanism, such as... [Marx's] dialectical materialism merely [dresses] up old pagan concepts." (38)

The Talmud undoubtedly contributes to anti-Semitism. Dilling writes: "The attitude resulting from such teachings has been resented by non-Jews in all countries and centuries. Such resentment, however, is always portrayed by Jews as 'persecution of the Jews.' " (2)

Michael Wex, the Jewish author of a 2006 book on the Yiddish language confirmed Dilling's finding: "The Jews are not merely out of step with Christian civilization, they hold it in utter contempt." ("Born to Kvetch," p. 24)

I doubt if 10 per cent of Jews today are aware of the Talmud. I certainly wasn't. However I do think the leadership is influenced by these attitudes.

What fault could the Pharisees find with a gospel that preaches human brotherhood and putting others before yourself? Answer: It denies their special claim. They're competing with Christ to be God themselves. Thus the Talmudic hatred of Christ.

Another main book of Judaism (and the central text of Freemasonry) is the Cabala. Dilling writes: "The Jewish Cabala with its non-existence of evil, its deification of man, is a source book of modern 'isms.'" (31)

The Cabala depicts the achievement of universal harmony in terms of facilitating sexual union of male and female deities. It preaches that "arousal below provokes arousal above." It provides the basis for the Illuminati sex cult reflected in the Illuminati symbol, the dot in a circle, symbolizing the penis and vagina. It is also seen in the propensity for homosexuality and pedophilia among initiates.

The Cabala preaches that man influences God, and creation requires destruction. It is not monotheistic; it even includes sacrifices for Satan (the "God of the gentiles") so he won't sexually molest the "divine Daughter," the female principle.

According to David Bay, of Cutting Edge Ministry, the Cabala is the keystone of all Western occult thought and practice today. It is the cornerstone of belief for all Illumined Ones [Masters of the Illuminati] and is hostile to non-Cabalistic Jews.

"Whether an occultist is White Magic or Black Magick, their cornerstone of belief and thought is the Cabala. When Antichrist arises, he shall be basing his practice of the occult on the Jewish Cabala. Thus, the irony is that, when Antichrist strides out of the newly-built Jewish Temple after committing the "Abomination of Desolation" and begins his effort to slaughter every Jew on earth, the Jewish Cabala will have provided the major impetus for his efforts! Indeed, the Cabala formed the cornerstone of Adolf Hitler's occult beliefs, so this terrible irony will strike the Jewish people twice in world history."

JUDAISM IS NOT A RELIGION

Some writers have suggested that the Jewish religion is a ruse. Harold Rosenthal seems to confirm this:

"At a very early date, urged on by the desire to make our way in the world, Jews began to look for a means whereby we might distract all attention from the racial aspect. What could be more effective, and at the same time more above suspicion, than to borrow and utilize the idea of a religious community?" (See "Protocols of Zion Updated by a Jewish Zealot" within)

In my view, Jews are an ethnic or racial group. Talmudic Judaism is not a religion but a racial credo. Jewish holidays celebrate historical events.

Religion by definition means to know and obey God. God's nature is essentially Moral, i.e. Good. Christ taught that God is Love.

God is universal. The Jewish God is really an alter ego for the ambitions of the Pharisaic Jewish leadership. The Jewish God does not represent a universal Moral Order. He serves Jewish leaders, and Jews to a lesser extent, but no one else.

Talmudic Judaism does not renounce wealth, power or lust. It puts little emphasis on eternal life. It is materialistic, naturalistic and regards non-Jews as sub-human.

Talmudic Judaism is a model of totalitarianism. It isolates Jews from non-Jews by enforcing a complex system of laws governing every aspect of life. It was enforced by the rabbi often on pain of fine, beating, death or banishment. Adapted from Plato's political system, it was one of the original models for totalitarianism and kept most Jews in bondage until roughly 1780. This authoritarian Jewish tendency is evident in the attempt to suppress my writing.

The Communist New World Order represents a return to Talmudic tyranny. John Beaty writes: "Since the Talmud contained more than 12,000 controls, the regimentation of Marxism was acceptable, provided the Khazar politician, like the Talmudic rabbi exercised the power of dictatorship." ("Iron Curtain Over America," 1953, p.27)

Goldwin Smith calls the Talmud a vast repertory of "legalism, formalism, ceremonialism, and casuistry. Nothing can be more opposed to the spontaneity of conscience, trust in principle, and preference of the spirit to the letter characteristic of the Gospel..." ("The Jewish Question," in "Essays on Questions of the Day," 1894)

I am not dismissing the whole Jewish spiritual tradition. I expect that there are many valuable veins of truth that can be tapped. Jews like everyone else have a direct relationship to God, by virtue of their soul.

I am saying that the good serves as camouflage for the Satanic, and we need to wake up to that. I am not saying Jews are Satanic. I am saying that organized Jewry is wittingly or unwittingly the tool of a long-term Satanic agenda.

"THE DEVIL AND THE JEWS"

In 1943, the Jewish Publication Society published "The Devil and the Jews." The author Professor Joshua Trachtenberg was puzzled that throughout the Middle Ages, Jews were considered agents of Satan. Their goal was to destroy Christian civilization and mankind. Jews were identified with the use of medicines, drugs, poisons, cosmetics, aphrodisiacs, sorcery, alchemy and astrology. They were condemned as usurers, swindlers, desecrators, infidels and heretics.

"In the Christian world, the Jew was inevitably looked upon as a heretic – indeed, the heretic. ...Jews were generally suspected of inspiring the schismatic sects, and the commonest charge against these heresies was "judaizing"... Everywhere the Church and the people discerned the diabolical hand of the Jews turning simple Christians aside from the true faith..."(174-176)

Trachtenberg lays the blame for these attitudes on church teachings, but there is evidence they predate Christianity.

After narrating the massacres committed by the Jews on the gentiles in Africa and Cyprus, Edward Gibbon expressed in flamboyant terms the hatred of the Roman world for the Jews, whom he designates as the "implacable enemies, not only of the Roman government but of humankind." (Edward Gibbon, "Decline and Fall of the Roman Empire," Chap. xiv.)

Tacitus speaks of the Jews as enemies of all races but their own (Histories, V, v), and Juvenal, in a well-known passage, speaks of them as people who would not show a wayfarer his road or guide the thirsty to a spring if he were not of their own faith.

Prof Goldwin Smith writes, "Those who maintain that there is nothing in the character, habits, or disposition of the Jew to provoke antipathy have to bring the charge of fanatical prejudice not only against the Russians or against Christendom, but against mankind." ("The Jewish Question," 1894)

Before he worked for the Jewish bankers, Winston Churchill wrote, " It would almost seem as if the gospel of Christ and the gospel of Antichrist were destined to originate among the same people; and that this mystic and mysterious race had been chosen for the supreme manifestations, both of the divine and the diabolical." ("The

Struggle for the Soul of the Jewish People," Feb. 8, 1920)

Oscar Levy wrote: "We who have posed as the saviours of the world; we who have even boasted of giving it the 'Saviour,' we are today nothing else but the world's seducers, its destroyers, its incendiaries, its executioners."

"We who have promised to lead you to a new Heaven, we have finally succeeded in landing you in a new Hell...There has been no progress, least of all moral progress ... And it is just our Morality, which has prohibited all real progress, and---what is worse---which even stands in the way of every future and natural reconstruction in this ruined world of ours ... I look at this world, and I shudder at its ghastliness; I shudder all the more as I know the spiritual authors of all this ghastliness..."

It gives me no pleasure to repeat these things. But until Jews scrutinize their affiliations, they will be compromised and blamed. While I believe many Jews as individuals have great warmth, genius and integrity, it has been liberating for me to scrutinize this complex heritage and distance myself.

I am not alone. Many Jews sense something is wrong and are fleeing Jewish organizations in droves. According to a 2001 survey, 25% of the roughly five million American Jews identify with another faith. Another quarter are "secular" leaving just 51% to say they are "Jewish" by religion. One half of all U.S. Jews intermarry and three-quarters of these raise their children in another religion. ("The Jewish Week," November 2, 2001)

THE SECRET SOCIETY MODEL

The "secret society" appears to be the organizational model for Judaism as well as Freemasonry, Zionism and Communism (which are Masonic orders.). Essentially, the leadership deceives and manipulates the membership with idealistic-sounding goals. Only those corruptible (and blackmail-able) are let in on the true agenda and allowed to rise.

This model now applies to the whole world. "Successful" people have often accepted the Devil's Bargain- "Serve me and I will give you the world."

This view of Judaism is confirmed by the author of the "Protocols of Zion" who says: "No one will ever bring under discussion our faith from its true point of view since this will be fully learned by none save ours, who will never dare to betray its secrets." (Protocol 14)

(The "Protocols of the Elders of Zion" is the blueprint of the New World Order and key to understanding history and current events. I examine it and the "forgery" claims later in this volume.)

Edith Starr Miller, an expert on religion and the occult, called Judaism "a secret society posing as a religion," and "a sect with Judaism as a rite."

The real purpose of Judaism and all secret societies, Miller says, is to con people into advancing the agenda of the super rich. "Regardless of their exoteric objects, the esoteric aims of most societies are all directed toward the same end, namely: the concentration of political, economic and intellectual power into the hands of a small group of individuals, each of whom controls a branch of the International life, material and spiritual, of the world today." ("Occult Theocracy," 1933, p.661)

Flavien Brenier compares the goals of Judaism with Freemasonry: securing political power and gradually modifying "the conceptions of the people in the direction of their secret doctrine." ("Occult Theocracy," 80)

The secret aim of Judaism is the same as Freemasonry.

In his Encyclical Humanum Genus (1884) Pope Leo XIII wrote that the ultimate aim of Freemasonry is "to uproot completely the whole religious and moral order of the world, which has been brought into existence by Christianity...This will mean that the foundation and the laws of the new structure of society will be drawn from pure naturalism."

Again, Pope Leo XIII said: "Freemasonry is the permanent personification of the Revolution; it constitutes a sort of society in reverse whose aim is to exercise an occult overlordship upon society as we know it, and whose sole raison d'être consists of waging war against God and his Church." (De Poncins, "Freemasonry and the Vatican," p. 45)

An expert on secret societies wrote that Freemasonry "has been used as ... a net wherein to catch, test and select persons who could be used for subversive ends...the revolutionary directorate [uses] wherever possible, harmless bodies as their cloak, and innocent people as their unconscious agents..." (Miss Stoddard, "Trail of the Serpent," p. 203)

This is confirmed by Illuminati founder Adam Weishaupt who wrote: "The [Masonic] Lodge shall be our nursery garden. All those who are not suited to the work shall remain in the Masonic Lodge and advance in that without knowing anything of the further system." (Webster, "Secret Societies," p.210)

These dupes, "innocents" or "useful idiots" have the added advantage of attacking anyone who dares question their Cause. Innocents cannot conceive they've been betrayed and cling to their precious identity. They prefer a comfortable lie to the bitter truth. Thus Satan fills his ranks.

The holocaust duped Jews into taking Palestine to establish a "national homeland." Israel's real purpose is to be the capital of the Rothschild's one-world tyranny. But how many Jews would have sacrificed their money and lives for that? (See Book Three: "Zionism and the Holocaust" within.)

Deception is Satan's way. The Illuminati literally are his servants. The goal is to compromise people and then let them take the blame. Would it make sense to tell average Jews or Masons the real agenda? Of course not. They would not support it. By the time they find out, it is too late.

Jews are kept in the dark about their history and religion. Between the first and the early 19th century, not a single Jewish history text was written. Afterward, Jewish apologists were the only ones allowed to publish and be heard. Jewish dissidents like Norman Finkelstein are rooted out of positions of influence.

At the same time, ordinary Jews are given a flattering self- image of a people disliked not for their leaders' attack on Christian institutions, or their part in the totalitarian New World Order, but for their superior intelligence, industry and devotion to social justice.

THE REAL CHARACTER OF MODERN HISTORY

"The question of the Jews and their influence on the world, past and present, cuts to the root of all things," Oscar Levy wrote. (op. cit.)

Modern history recounts the overthrow of Christian civilization by Cabalist Jewish bankers and the people they co-opted using Freemasonry, Communism, Zionism, Liberalism, Feminism, Socialism, etc. The Cabalist bankers want to be God, hence the rejection of God, the destruction of the Church, and the trend to "secular" society which is really only a transition stage to something much darker.

Christianity never stood a chance. While Christianity taught people to seek spiritual perfection, Judaism regarded wealth as a sign of divine favour. Like all true religions, Christianity is a spiritual discipline. It posits two orders, 1.) a higher moral order (otherworldly or spiritual) associated with the soul and eternal life, and 2.) a lower material or instinctual order associated with this world and the body.

The essence of all true religions is to raise mankind up by disciplining the lower carnal order (greed, lust, power) in favour of our spiritual aspirations (truth, beauty, peace, harmony, justice.) Just as it is unthinkable for an ascetic to run a brothel, a devout Christian cannot be a trader, i.e. buy and sell at profit. He wishes to serve God not Mammon. Jews happily filled this void and soon dominated many areas of commerce. (See, Werner Sombart, "The Jews and Modern Capitalism.")

Thus while Christianity (and civilization and culture) requires checking our bodily appetites, in many cases the Jewish preference is to regard self-restraint as repressive and unhealthy. Many Jews seem to favor Naturalism, i.e. an embrace of our bodily appetites and functions.

"Do as thou wilt," is the Illuminati watchword. "Let us give ourselves indiscriminately to everything our passions suggest, and we will always be happy... Conscience is not the voice of Nature but only the voice of prejudice," the Marquis de Sade wrote.

I doubt if the Marquis de Sade was a Jew. Obviously, the conflict between the soul and body is universal. Organized Jewry doesn't have a monopoly on self indulgence. However, Illuminati controlled media and education legitimized De Sade just as the "Protocols of Zion" boasted of the "success we have arranged for Darwinism, Marxism and Nietzscheism."

As Leon de Poncins wrote, the Jew always was the "doctor of unbelief," the enemy of faith and a bastion for those in revolt. ("Judaism and the Vatican," pp.111-113.)

The only excuse for self indulgence is to learn that the objects we crave are overrated and don't satisfy our hunger, which is spiritual. Apparently, the Illuminati understands this. Insider Harold Rosenthal illustrates how they literally and consciously do the devil's work:

"Your people never realize that we offer them only worthless baubles that cannot bring fulfillment. They procure one and consume it and are not filled. We present another. We have an infinite number of outward distractions, to the extent that life cannot again turn inward to find its definite fulfillment. You have become addicted to our medicine through which we have become your absolute masters....

We have converted the people to our philosophy of getting and acquiring so that they will never be satisfied. A dissatisfied people are the pawns in our game of world conquest. Thus, they are always seeking and never able to find satisfaction. The very moment they seek happiness outside themselves. they become our willing servants." (See "Protocols Updated by a Jewish Zealot," within. The whole interview can be found online.)

Born in 1949, I have noticed that society has become increasingly money-minded. In my youth, stock market or real estate speculation was not widespread. Mutual funds were considered sophisticated. Today, average people are glued to the stock market, many day trading. In real estate, "house flipping" enjoyed a vogue until the recent downturn.

CHOSEN TO BE GOD

While Christians chose heaven and eternal life, Jews chose the earth and this life. The Jewish Pharisees would make this world a heaven -- for them. They would be God.

This denial and usurpation of the Divine is how I define the Satanic. I also include the denial of what is natural and good, (like love between man and woman, mother and child, i.e. feminism) and the desire to harm or subjugate others. When we seek limitless power, money and sex as a perverse substitute for infinite love, we express the Satanic instead of the Divine. The motivation behind the New World Order is Satanic.

Masonic leader Albert Pike admitted Freemasons worship Satan: "The true name of Satan, the Kabalist say, is that of Yahveh reversed; for Satan is not a black god, but the negation of God. ....Lucifer the Light-bearer! Strange and mysterious name to give to the Spirit of Darkness! Lucifer, the Son of the morning! It is he who bears the light...............Doubt it not!" ("Morals and Dogma" p.102,321)

Rather than the people of God, Flavien Bernier said Jewish teaching makes them the God-people: "The promise of universal domination found in the Law by the orthodox Jew was not interpreted by the Pharisees in the sense of the reign of the God of Moses over the Nations, but in the sense of a material domination which would be imposed by the Jews over the universe." ("Les Juifs et Le Talmud," 1913)

An extreme expression is found in a famous letter from Baruch Levy to Karl Marx quoted in "Review de Paris," June 1, 1928. It also shows how Socialism and

Communism were just devices to usurp power and property.

"The Jewish people taken collectively will be its own Messiah. His reign over the Universe will be obtained by the unification of the human races and through the elimination of frontiers. A Universal Republic will come into being in which the Sons of Israel will become the directing element. We know how to dominate the Masses. The governments of all nations will gradually fall, through victory of the proletariat, into the hands of Judah. All private property will become the possession of the princes of Israel - they will own the wealth of all lands. Thus will be realized the promise of the Talmud that when the time of the Messiah comes the Jews will hold under their keys the property of all the peoples of the world." (See within, "Communism, a Ruse for Illuminati Jewish Theft and Murder.")

Bella Dodd, a former member of the U.S. Communist Party's National Council testified she was told to contact any one of three wealthy capitalists living in the Waldorf Towers in case of trouble communicating with Moscow. What amazed Dodd was that whenever these men gave instructions, Moscow always ratified them. When asked who the men were, fearing for her life, Dodd refused to say. But when pressed to say ultimately who ruled Communism, she replied simply, "Satan." (See my "Communism-Wall Street's Utopian Hoax" on my website.)

ISRAEL SHAMIR

Israel Shamir, an Israeli Jew who converted to Christianity, warns that Judaism wants Jews to replace Christ as the intermediary between God and man. Individual Jews must decide whether they want IN or OUT of this plan. ("Pardes," 2005)

Jewish Messianism (the building of a humanist "earthly paradise" according to Jewish specs) replaces spiritual salvation. The Jewish holocaust replaces Christ's Passion. That's why it takes precedence over the other 60 million people who died in World War Two.

"Israel wants to unite the world under her spiritual guidance," Shamir says. "The Temple of God...is to be located in Jerusalem, the centre of this Jewish-ordered universe and all nations will bring their tribute to it. The Nations will worship God by serving Yisrael..." (72)

Shamir says the deification of Jews requires people have no other God but material gain and sensual pleasure. "In the Jewish reading, the exclusive sacrality [sacredness] of Jerusalem and of Israel calls for the de-sacralization of the nations and the rest of the world. There will be no churches nor mosques, no Christian nor Muslim priests. The world will become a profane desert populated by profaned beasts, the nations, and their shepherds, the Jews." (73)

"It begins with small things: removal of [Christian] religious signs from schools and public places. But our souls interpret this surrender of spirit as the proof of Jewish victory... (78)

"The Jewish universe is being built brick by brick and one of its signs is the lowering of the educational and spiritual life of gentiles.... American films degrade their viewers...For total victory of the Jewish spirit will be reached only when a debilitated, illiterate goy will thankfully lick a Jewish hand and bless him for his guidance."(80-81)

The so-called "Enlightenment" (named for Lucifer, the "Light Bearer") was really a rejection of God's plan for man and a foolhardy assertion of human arrogance. The outcome of this perverse philosophy is that we increasingly live in a Judeo-Masonic solipsism based on defiance of God, nature and truth.

I expect most Jews will respond to this information by asking not, "Is it true?" but rather, "Is it unflattering to Jews?" Increasingly this is the standard of truth in our solipsistic world.

SOLIPSISTIC BUBBLE

As Jewish historian Yuri Slezkine noted, modernity has turned us all into Jews. ("The Jewish Century," 2004.) Modernism is the dysfunction that results from making oneself God. Modern man is the Jew, the heretic, the anti-hero, alienated from God, society and paradoxically himself. He lives in a self-created reality divorced from truth.

Mia Farrow's description of the neurotic, sex-obsessed Woody Allen exemplifies modern man: "Woody lived and made his decisions while suspended in a zone constructed and controlled almost entirely by himself...He did not acknowledge other beings except as features of his own landscape, valued according their contribution to his own existence. He was therefore unable to empathize and felt no moral responsibility to anyone or anything." (Mia Farrow, "What Falls Away," 208, quoted in Jones, "The Jewish Revolutionary Spirit.")

We live in a solipsistic world. Modern Judeo-Masonic culture elevates subjective truth and shuns universals (i.e. our common human experience. What makes us feel good about being human.) Our culture exalts trivia and nothingness. While brilliant and very funny, "Seinfeld" was a TV show "about nothing." It was also about selfishness and self absorption.

The New World Order, any kind of domination, requires a rejection of objective truth. They can't admit they intend to enslave us spiritually and mentally if not physically. So they must annihilate the concept of truth altogether. The truth is unknowable, subjective, they tell us. People have different versions of it but we can never discover the real thing. That's what they want us to believe.

REVOLUTION

The role of organized Jewry throughout history is subversive in the profoundest sense, doing Satan's work by overturning the will of God, ("Logos," the inherent Design, Reason and Purpose of Creation) by hijacking mankind and arresting its development.

The true esoteric meaning of "revolution" is "to overturn" God and replace Him with Lucifer who represents the self-interest of the Illuminati (i.e. central bankers, organized Jewry and Freemasons). The other reasons given for revolution are all window dressing.

This was confirmed by Christian Rakowsky in his KGB interrogation. "Christianity is our only real enemy since all the political and economic phenomena of the bourgeois states are only its consequences," Rakovsky said. Peace is "counter-revolutionary" since it is war that paves the way for revolution. (See my "Rothschilds Conduct Red Symphony.")

Thus, organized Jewry through its Freemasonic arm, has always sabotaged personal and social identity based on race, religion (God), nation and family. They have caused wars (like Iraq, Afghanistan and possibly Iran and World War Three) revolution, division, corruption and sought to normalize dysfunction and deviance.

All to prove that the salutary and natural order represented by Christian ideals is corrupt and hypocritical, and must be replaced by Jewish gods, i.e. Communism, Socialism and their latest utopian test tube tyranny, the New World Order.

Thus, to the mortification of decent Jews like myself, Jews often are on the vanguard of trashing Christian mores and creating dysfunction whether it's undermining gender and marriage or peddling promiscuity, pornography, homosexuality or abortion.

For example, a recent music video of a 50-year-old French Jewish singer and his adolescent daughter normalizes incest. Former French Prime Minister Leon Blum (1872-1950), a Jew, wrote in 1907, "It is natural and frequent for sister and brother to be lovers," ("Marriage" 1907.) As Masonic revolutionary Guiseppe Mazzini said, "we corrupt in order to rule."

Today, hardly any movies set inspiring moral examples. Few are honest and informative. Too many Hollywood movies involving Jews are filthy, vulgar, violent and degrading. (Of course, there are wonderful exceptions like Julie Taymor's "Across the Universe," 2007)

Judd Apatow, the writer-director, recently gave a speech that typified his movies. He talked about, respectively, his 10-year-old daughter's unnatural curiosity about "butt sex," his daughter's vagina, his daughter's budding breasts, his own penchant for masturbation, and, finally, the greying of his pubic hairs. Then came his star actor Seth Rogen, another Jew who talked about his masturbation habits, followed by a learned discourse on his testicles. Because they associate with studio executives, their puerile home movies receive worldwide distribution and media acclaim.

Describing this sickening speech, Michael Posner (a decent Jew) wrote: "You began to get the impression that if sex was not involved in some fashion, none of them had anything to say. Actually, even if sex were involved, they had nothing interesting to say." (Globe and Mail, July 21, 2008)

These movie makers assume they are 'oh so daring and chic.' For them, sophistication consists in trampling on whatever scrap of innocence, decorum or human dignity remains in society. They are perpetually at war with "repression" earnestly indulging every sexual urge and pointing at their toilet accidents like proud toddlers.

Why do adults offer these obscenities as though they were courageous and edifying? They are not just flouting convention, i.e. human dignity and decorum, they are thumbing their nose at God. Their god is Lucifer, whether they know it or not, the symbol of rebellion against the intrinsic natural and spiritual order.

Organized Jewry reminds me of a soldier marching out-of-step in a parade. The other marchers point this out but he has the chutzpah, money and media to convince them that in fact, they are out-of- step. Extrapolate this to a cosmic level and you will understand the New World Order.

FINALLY

The Crucifixion of Christ represents the rejection of the Divine Order which is modelled on absolute spiritual ideals such as Love, Truth, Justice, Goodness, Beauty, etc. God is a spiritual dimension in which these ideals are self evident to us. We were put on earth to manifest these ideals. I don't know if Christ was God but I believe he represented God and these ideals. His message was that all men should follow his example. God is Reality. As we deviate from Truth, we become more unReal, and risk annihilation.

We know food and sex exist because our bodies hunger for them. Similarly, our souls hunger for God, for spiritual ideals. This proves we have souls; indeed, we are souls. However, we will never listen to our souls if we don't believe in them. We will never take spiritual ideals seriously if we don't recognize that they are the ultimate Reality.

The New World Order is an attempt to overthrow God and replace Him with Satan. It says black is white, evil is good. It creates a bogus reality designed to serve the few and enslave the many.

Nobody alive today should be blamed for the Crucifixion. But we are responsible for what we do to upset the spiritual order Christ represented.

Jews live in a bubble, told they are wonderful people persecuted for no reason. Jewish society allows little to no unsanctioned self-criticism. Increasingly the Western world is becoming a closed society like Jewry. Genuine self-criticism is not self-hatred. It is essential to health and survival.

Jews are kept in the dark about organized Jewry's role in the New World Order. Essentially, Zionism (U.S., EU, Israel) is one pincer; anti-Zionism (Iran, Russia, China) is the other. I believe the Illuminati bankers intend for the two to destroy each other. Let us not embrace our destruction like lemmings.

Is the NWO primarily motivated by a political, racial or occult motive? All three are important and complementary but, based on the "Red Symphony," I would put power (the political) in the driver's seat.

Illuminati insider Chaim Rakowsky stated in 1937: "The fact that [the bankers] control unlimited money, insofar as they themselves create it, does not...determine the limits of their ambitions . . .The bankers, have the impulse towards power, towards full power. Just as you and me."

"They created the Communist state as a "machine of total power" unprecedented in history. In the past, due to many factors, "there was always room for individual freedom. Do you understand that those who already partially rule over nations and worldly governments have pretensions to absolute domination? Understand that this is the only thing which they have not yet reached..." (See my "Central Bankers Seek Totalitarian Power").

Although the Illuminati was originated by Jews, it sees non-Illuminati Jews, Jewish Messianism and Freemasonry, all as means to this end.

Louis Marshall's famous letter (Sept. 26 1918) illustrates this point. "Zionism is but an incident of a far reaching plan. It is merely a convenient peg on which to hang a powerful weapon." Marshall was Legal Counsel for central bankers Kuhn Loeb and a stalwart of organized Jewry.

Since many Jews are Zionists, they must be an "incident in a far reaching plan." We can only ignore the truth for so long before it bites us. I reiterate. These bankers created and financed Hitler. Ultimately they are responsible for the holocaust. Paul and Max Warburg were Directors of I.G. Farben when it funded Hitler and built his war machine. (Anthony Sutton, "Wall Street and the Rise of Hitler," 1976, pp. 109, 147.)

Their stated goal is for a third world war; current events are lining up exactly as they foretold almost 140 years ago by Albert Pike.

Henry Kissinger, CEO of the New World Order said: "a people who have been persecuted for 2000 years must be doing something wrong."

Our mistake is trusting our leaders. Jews and Masons are being used to create a veiled totalitarian police state. They are building a sham civilization dedicated to money, sex and violence, a Clockwork Orange burlesque doomed to self destruct.

"Where there is no vision, the people perish." (Proverbs 29:18)

BOOK ONE

Bankers, Jews and Anti-Semitism

The Banking Cartel is the Cause of Humanity's Woes

(Review of "The Secrets of the Federal Reserve" by Eustace Mullins)

"I believe that banking institutions are more dangerous to our liberties than standing armies." ---Thomas Jefferson

In November 1949, Eustace Mullins, 25, was a researcher in Washington DC when friends invited him to visit the famous American poet Ezra Pound who was confined at St. Elizabeth's Mental Hospital as a "political prisoner."

A leading poet and critic, Pound introduced the world to James Joyce, W.B. Yeats and T.S. Eliot. During World War Two, he was charged with treason for Radio Rome broadcasts that questioned America's war motives.

Pound commissioned Mullins to examine the power of the U.S. banking establishment. Mullins spent every morning for two years in the Library of Congress and met with Pound every afternoon. The resulting manuscript, "The Secrets of the Federal Reserve" proved too hot for any American publisher to handle. Nineteen rejected it. One said, "you'll never get this published in New York." When it finally appeared in Germany in 1955, the U.S. Military Government confiscated all 10,000 copies and burned them. The book is available on line.

Why is it so (excuse the pun) inflammatory?

It portrays the United States in a radically different perspective. "Notwithstanding the war of independence against England," writes Mullins, "we remained an economic and financial colony of Great Britain." Between 1865 and 1913, he says London-based Rothschild bankers used agents such as J.P. Morgan and J.D. Rockefeller to gain control of American industry and organize it into cartels.

Where did these bankers get the money? For over 200 years, European bankers had been able to draw on the credit of their host countries to print it.

In the Seventeenth Century, the moneylenders and the aristocracy made a pact. If the king would make paper currency a liability of the state, the moneylenders would print as much as he liked! Thus the Banks of England, France and the Reichsbank came into being but they were all private corporations.

Accordingly, the moneylenders got to charge interest on assets they created out of thin air. The aristocracy all took shares in the central banks plus they got to finance a burgeoning government and to wage costly wars. This clique bought the wealth of the world using our credit. This piece of chicanery is at the heart what plagues humanity.

The bankers have a vested interest in the state (i.e. the people) incurring as much debt as possible. They are behind the Marxist, Socialist and Liberal movements which call for big government and social spending. They are behind the catastrophic wars of the last century.

Naturally if you can create money out of thin air, there is a powerful incentive to use debt to control populations and take over their real assets. This is the essence of the "third world debt crisis." Dedicated to owning all wealth and enslaving humanity, an insatiable vampire has been unleashed upon the world.

Much of Mullins' book is devoted to the subterfuge by which the United States was drawn into this lethal embrace. In 1913, the Owen-Glass Bill gave mostly foreign-controlled banks (posing as "the Federal Reserve") the right to create currency based on the credit of the United States government and to charge it interest for doing so.

To accomplish this, the bankers had to rig the election of 1913 in order to get Democrat Woodrow Wilson elected. (They defeated the incumbent W.H. Taft by getting their lackey Theodore Roosevelt to split the Republican vote.) Then their stooges in Congress passed the new banking legislation on December 22 after their opponents had gone home for Christmas.

"This act establishes the most gigantic trust [cartel] on earth," Congressman Charles Lindbergh said at the time. "When the President signs this bill, the invisible government by the Monetary Power will be legalized. The people may not know it immediately but the day of reckoning is only a few years removed."

Mullins explains that the legislation passed just in time for the American people to finance World War One. The European powers no longer could afford the luxury of another war. But the U.S. was relatively debt free and made the whole thing possible.

Mullins makes a convincing case that every U.S. President since T.R. Roosevelt has been a lackey of the bankers. In 2006, the American people paid over $400 billion in interest on the national debt, most to the central bankers. To maintain this massive fraud, the bankers enforce an iron grip on the political and cultural organs of the nation. According to Mullins, "The New York Times" is owned by the Kuhn Loeb while "The Washington Post" is owned by Lazard Freres. In Europe, the Rothschilds own Reuters as well as the French and German news services.

U.S. publishers, TV networks and movie producers are similarly beholden. Rockefellers, Carnegies and the Fords endow the nations' libraries and universities. Journalists and professors dutifully parrot fantasies about democracy and freedom. Mind control laboratories run by the CIA and the Tavistock Institute dream up ways to control the population. The psychological sterilization of the human female ("feminism") is an example.

At last the cosmic battle between Good and Evil is out in the open.

Making the World Safe ...
for Bankers

International bankers live in fear.

Not of starvation, disease or war. These are the concerns of children in the Third World.

Bankers are terrified we might object to paying them billions each year in interest for money they create out of nothing, guaranteed by our taxes. (The Federal Reserve Board, a private cartel of mostly private foreign banks, finagled this monopoly in 1913.)

The bankers are frightened that, like the homeless man's dog, we might say, "I can do this myself."

They are scared the government might go even further and "default" on trillions of make-believe "debt."

They are frightened of losing control. They toss and turn at night. In order to sleep more soundly, the bankers have taken steps.

These precautions help us to understand the world we live in, why it is becoming safer for bankers but less safe and more bizarre for everyone else.

First, people who own money machines tend to have lots of friends. The bankers helped their friends establish monopolies in oil, chemicals, pharmaceuticals, transportation, media etc. and took a healthy stake. As you can imagine, these people are thick as thieves. Lawyers, journalists and intellectuals all vie for a piece of the action. (Servicing this cartel of cartels is what passes for "success.")

The bankers' first precaution is to buy all the politicians. The second is to buy the major media outlets in order to promote the illusion politicians make decisions and represent our interests. The third precaution is to take control of the education system, ensuring that people stop thinking at an early age.

Then the bankers use the government and media to convince us that religion, nationalism and nuclear family are unfashionable, and we want what they want. These policies are never debated or voted on. They seem to appear out of nowhere and pretend to represent the popular will.

We "want" secularism and the separation of church and state. Even though we were fine with Christianity and Christian values for centuries, the bankers don't want us to have any spiritual reference point that might interfere with their dictates.

We "want" world government ("globalization.") The bankers need to eliminate nation states, freedom and democracy in order to streamline their business and consolidate their power. The UN, NAU, EU, IMF and World Bank -- glorified loan sharks and collectors -- will make the laws.

We "want" diversity. Countries are not allowed to maintain their national identities or traditions. Last Christmas, my provincial Premier tried to rename the Christmas tree at the legislature a "multicultural tree." Diversity is respecting every culture but European Christian. Every nation must be as heterogeneous as a box of Smarties -- no one in a position to challenge the bankers.

We want "feminism." Masquerading as equal rights for women, this ideology is designed to spread lesbian dysfunction. If women focus on finding careers, they give less importance to finding husbands. They have fewer or no children who will be raised by state daycares.

Under the guise of "women" and "gay" rights, we are being re-engineered to be androgynous and behave like homosexuals, who generally don't marry or have families. Psychological and biological differences between men and women are not "stereotypes." But signatories to the latest UN "CEDAW" Convention (passed by the U.S. Senate Foreign Relations Committee) will be required to "take all appropriate measures to modify all social and cultural patterns of conduct of men and women." (Article 5)

This kind of Communist-inspired social engineering is simply persecution of heterosexuals. It is intended to arrest our natural development. Meanwhile the birth rate has halved while the divorce rate has doubled. An army of highly paid lawyers, social workers, psychiatrists and bureaucrats treat the casualties. These self-serving professionals are the bankers' political constituency.

People --stunted, love-starved, sex-obsessed -- without family, religious or national identity, are easy to control. (They'll join anything; they're looking for a family.) But in case of resistance, the bankers have created a bogeyman, "terrorism" to justify a huge security apparatus.

The Office of Homeland Security is designed to control us -- the domestic population. Why would this be necessary? We're "in debt" trillions of dollars and the bankers intend that we pay. One day they will take away our toys. In case that's a problem, an Orwellian police state will be in place. But first, the Muslims must be subjugated and robbed.

Talking about the United States as if it were an independent country is silly. American politicians pawned U.S. sovereignty in 1913. Ever since, U.S. soldiers have been bullyboys for international bankers, and nothing else.

SUPERPOWER AS SUPER GO'FER

The American taxpayer and soldier made the First World War possible. It started just six months after the establishment of the "Fed". Its purpose was to increase debt, cripple the great European nation states, slaughter a generation, and establish two of the bankers' pet projects: Communism (Russia) and Zionism (Palestine.) After the war ended, banker world government -- The League of Nations (a.k.a., "The League to Enforce Peace") was established.

The U.S. didn't enter the Second World War in Dec. 1941 to save Western civilization. England had stood alone against Germany for more than two years. The U.S. entered the war just six months after Hitler attacked Russia. The purpose was to save Communism! [I am indebted to A.K. Chesterton ("The New Unhappy Lords," 1969) for this insight] For the same reason, the U.S.SR got $5 billion in U.S. lend-lease after the war ended.

After the smoke cleared, Communists instead of Nazis tyrannized Eastern Europe. Soviet agents/ U.S. diplomats Alger Hiss and Harry Hopkins established the United Nations on land donated by John D. Rockefeller. One of the UN's first acts was to create the State of Israel.

Ben Hecht (in "A Child of the Century") wrote "the Twentieth Century was cut off at its knees by World War One." Before committing suicide in 1942, Stefan Zweig ("The World of Yesterday") spoke in the same despondent tones about the demise of Western civilization.

The planet has been hijacked. Our leaders are dupes, opportunists, traitors or all three. Almost everything we know about modern history is a hoax. A stench of moral compromise hangs over our public and cultural life. Anything promoted by the media, education or government is suspect. This is what happens when we deny Moral Order, i.e. God.

This is the world our children will inherit, one that is safe ... for international bankers.

Bankers Demand that We Obey Them

Current events are like a "Magic Eye" picture that you have to stare at for a long time. But if you know what to look for, the picture soon emerges.

As incredible and bizarre as this sounds, a Satanic (Cabalistic) occult society has taken control of the planet through the central banking system. It seeks to impose its tyranny through the ruse of the "war on terror" and "globalization." Every war was a trick used to slaughter and brutalize humanity and to increase the wealth and power of this clique, which is based in the Bank of England.

Another confirmation of this disturbing truth is a spine-chilling letter that rewards periodic consideration. The letter, which surfaced on the Internet a few years ago, dispels any illusions that we are free citizens living in a beneficent democracy. Return addressed, "your globalist friend" the letter advises citizens of the world "you are our property" and must accept servitude "for your own good."

"The days of putting a stop to us have long since past," our friend writes sounding like Big Brother.

"We have full control of the earth and its finance, along with the major media propaganda, and there is simply no way any nation or power can defeat us... We can send American or European troops to wherever we like, whenever we like, and for whatever purpose we like, and you dutifully go about our business...How much more evidence do you need? ...Does it not seem reasonable that you simply obey and serve us?"

I caution you material like this can induce cognitive dissonance because the image of reality is so different from the one the mass media provides.

The six-page letter was written in the autumn of 1999 but didn't receive broad circulation. I summarize here but urge you to read it in full on the Net. (Search, "Letter from Your Globalist Friend.")

The letter could be a hoax but I think it describes our present reality. It is consistent with what many conspiracy researchers have discovered independently, yet more vivid and insightful than anything they could fabricate.

THE LETTER

Our globalist friend says he wants to explain political reality to us so we "might know how to behave in the New Order now taking shape on the earth."

Like the author of the "Protocols of Zion," he boasts that he represents a secret force that controls the world yet is invisible to all.

"We run everything, yet, you do not know who to attack. I must say this hidden hand is wonderfully devised and without any known historical precedent on this scale. We rule the world and the world cannot even find out who is ruling them. This is truly a wonderful thing. In our media we present before you exactly what it is we want you to do. Then, as if in a flash, our little servants obey."

But he does identify himself. He clearly represents the central bankers: "Your own money has served to forge the chains we bind you with, since we are in control of all money."

As I have said, the central banking cartel is the mainspring of the New World Order. By giving alien private interests the power to create money based on our credit, our predecessors doomed Western civilization. These private interests naturally bought control of everything and everyone and now want to institutionalize their control globally.

"Our kingdom is the kingdom of money," our globalist friend writes. "We have given you a piece of paper or some numbers on a computer screen that we have termed 'money.' It is backed up by nothing and proven by nothing but what we say it is. We create it from nothing, we print it, we loan it, we give it its value, and we take its value away. All things that have to do with money are in our hands."

Our globalist friend reveals that the bankers have a symbiotic relationship with us. We produce profits by borrowing from them.

"We want you to be in the system. When you are buying a house, we not only receive the tax revenue to use for our purposes, but we gain large increases from the interest on the loan. You may pay for your house two or three times over from the interest alone. The interest is also taxed which is again placed for use in those sectors of influence we choose. We do not want you to escape free and that is why we have made it as we have."

One of those sectors of influence is education. Our taxes pay for "the indoctrination of your children in the public schools we have set up. We want them to grow up well trained into the system of our thinking. Your children will learn what we want them to learn, and you pay for it."

"You are our property. We will not permit you to buy or sell unless you submit to our mark of authority. If you go to court against us, we will wear you out there and in the end you will lose. If you use violence, we will end up having you in one of our labor camps, more specifically called prison industries. You need our money, our entertainment, our fuel, and our utilities to function and if you don't have them, you feel deprived. By this, you are made to yield to our will."

OUR LEADERS

Many political leaders are chosen from the ranks of criminals and perverts because they can be blackmailed. Exposing President Clinton's depravity was "very helpful in adjusting the moral habits of the youth downward."

He scoffs at attempts to impeach Clinton: "He is useful to us and he will not be removed by anyone until we are ready to have him removed...the leader we set up will be there until it serves us to have another. At that time we place our proposed leader before you and you vote for what we want. In that way we give you the vain voting exercise in the belief you had something to do with placing your president in office."

He cites Saddam Hussein and Slobodan Milosevic as leaders who refused to obey. "There is only glory in following our purposes and doing what we say. If one does not, there will be such a sad and tragic result. I would really have you spared of such an end."

As for smaller fry, he says rebellion will merely serve as an excuse for more repressive laws. They can tie dissenters up in court, which they also control. They can destroy people like David Koresh and discredit them at the same time.

He says Liberals and Conservatives "serve with the stamp of our approval but they are not allowed to present the real issues. By creating controversy on all levels, no one knows what to do. So, in all of this confusion, we go ahead and accomplish what we want with no hindrance."

The media occupy the masses with sex and violence so people are programmed to fight mindlessly and "do not have the integrity or brain power to deal with the really important matters which are left entirely in our hands."

China and Russia do not present a challenge: "We have no fear of Russia or China for we are already in full control of their system of things. China knows that we can freeze any number of its corporations in America and all of its capital at the stroke of a pen."

CONCLUSION

We are taught that society is participating in an age of enlightenment and progress but this is a ruse. In fact a primitive predatory beast reaches its claw out of the past to impale mankind.

Sooner or later we will recognize that we are witnessing the culmination of a diabolical conspiracy against mankind. Human events only make sense when we realize disciples of Satan are establishing a global regime dedicated to their evil god. I know this sounds too bizarre to be true. They count on that.

The "Letter from Your Globalist Friend" is consistent with the other great revelations of the invisible government: the Harold Rosenthal Interview; the House Report; the Svali Disclosures; The Soviet Art of Brainwashing; Quiet Weapons for Silent Wars, The Report from Iron Mountain, The Red Symphony and the Protocols of the Elders of Zion.

We are living in a fool's paradise. Unfortunately people won't wake up until they take away the goodies, and then it will be too late.

The "Jewish" Conspiracy is British Imperialism

Conspiracy theorists believe modern history reflects a long-term conspiracy by an international financial elite to enslave humanity. Like blind men examining an elephant, we attribute this conspiracy to Jewish bankers, Illuminati, Vatican, Jesuits, Freemasons, Black Nobility, and Bilderbergs etc.

The real villains are at the heart of our economic and cultural life. They are the dynastic families who own the Bank of England, the U.S. Federal Reserve and associated cartels. They also control the World Bank and IMF and most of the world's Intelligence agencies. Their identity is secret but Rothschild is certainly one of them. The Bank of England was "nationalized" in 1946 but the power to create money remained in the same hands.

England is in fact a financial oligarchy run by the "Crown" which refers to the "City of London" not the Queen. The City of London is run by the Bank of England, a private corporation. The square-mile City is a sovereign state located in the heart of greater London. As the "Vatican of the financial world," the City is not subject to British law.

On the contrary, the bankers dictate to the British Parliament. In 1886, Andrew Carnegie wrote that, "six or seven men can plunge the nation into war without consulting Parliament at all." Vincent Vickers, a director of the Bank of England from 1910-1919 blamed the City for all the wars of the world. ("Economic Tribulation" (1940) cited in Knuth, "The Empire of the City," 1943, p. 60)

The British Empire was an extension of bankers' financial interests. Indeed, all the non-white colonies (India, Hong Kong, Gibraltar) were "Crown Colonies." They belonged to the City and were not subject to British law although Englishmen were expected to conquer and pay for their upkeep.

The Bank of England assumed control of the U.S. during the Theodore Roosevelt administration (1901-1909) when its agent J.P. Morgan took over 25% of American business. (Anton Chaitkin, "Treason in America," 1964)

CLUB OF THE ISLES

According to the "American Almanac," the bankers are part of a network called the "Club of the Isles" which is an informal association of predominantly European-based royal households including the Queen. The "Club of the Isles "commands an estimated $10 trillion in assets. It controls such corporate giants as Royal Dutch Shell, Imperial Chemical Industries, Lloyds of London, Unilever, Lonrho, Rio Tinto Zinc, and Anglo American DeBeers. It dominates the world supply of petroleum, gold, diamonds, and many other vital raw materials. These assets serve its geopolitical agenda.

Its goal is to reduce the human population from over 5 billion people to below one billion people within the next two to three generations, to literally "cull the human herd" in the interest of retaining their own global power and the feudal system upon which it is based.

Historian Jeffrey Steinberg could be referring to the U.S., Canada and Australia when he writes, "England, Scotland, Wales, and, especially Northern Ireland, are today little more than slave plantations and social engineering laboratories, serving the needs of ...the City of London..."

"These families constitute a financier oligarchy; they are the power behind the Windsor throne. They view themselves as the heirs to the Venetian oligarchy, which infiltrated and subverted England from the period 1509-1715, and established a new, more virulent, Anglo-Dutch-Swiss strain of the oligarchic system of imperial Babylon, Persia, Rome, and Byzantium....

"The City of London dominates the world's speculative markets. A tightly interlocking group of corporations, involved in raw materials extraction, finance, insurance, transportation, and food production, controls the lion's share of the world market, and exerts virtual "choke point" control over world industry."

JEWS FROM VENICE

Steinberg, who is associated with economist Lyndon Larouche, has traced this scourge to the migration of the Venetian mercantile oligarchy to England more than 300 years ago.

Although Larouche historians do not say so, it appears that many members of this oligarchy were Jews. Cecil Roth writes: "The trade of Venice was overwhelmingly concentrated in the hands of the Jews, the wealthiest of the mercantile class." ("The History of the Jews in Venice," 1930)

As William Guy Carr points out in "Pawns in the Game," both Oliver Cromwell and William of Orange were funded by Jewish bankers. The English Revolution (1649) was the first in a series of revolutions designed to give them world hegemony. The establishment of the Bank of England by William in 1694 was the next crucial step. Behind the facade, England has been a "Jewish" state for over 300 years. (pp. 20-24)

The Jewish banking families made it a practice to marry their female offspring to spendthrift European aristocrats. In Jewish law, the mixed offspring of a Jewish mother is Jewish. For example, in 1878 Hannah Rothschild married Lord Rosebery who later became Prime Minister. (The male heirs marry Jews although Victor and his son Jacob Rothschild are exceptions. They both married gentiles.)

In 1922 Louis Mountbatten, the uncle of Prince Philip and cousin of the Queen married the granddaughter of Jewish banker Ernest Cassel, one of the wealthiest men in the world. Winston Churchill's mother, Jenny (Jacobson) Jerome, was Jewish.

By the beginning of the 1900s, very few English aristocrat families hadn't intermarried with Jews. When they visited the Continent, Europeans were surprised to see Jewish-looking persons with English titles and accents.

According to L.G. Pine, the Editor of "Burke's Peerage," Jews "have made themselves so closely connected with the British peerage that the two classes are unlikely to suffer loss which is not mutual. So closely linked are the Jews and the lords that a blow against the Jews in this country would not be possible without injuring the aristocracy also." ("Tales of the British Aristocracy," 1957, p.219.)

BRITISH ISRAEL

If they aren't Jewish by intermarriage, many European aristocrats consider themselves descendants of Biblical Hebrews. The Hapsburgs are related by marriage to the Merovingians who claim to be descendants of the Tribe of Benjamin.

In addition, many aristocrats belong to the "British Israel" movement that believes the British sovereign is the head of the Anglo Saxon "Lost Tribes" of Israel and that the Apocalypse will see the full reconstitution of the British Empire.

According to Barbara Aho, Rosicrucians and Freemasons, who believe in British Israelism, have a plan to place one of their bloodline on the throne of the rebuilt Temple in Jerusalem. This positioning of a false messiah whom the world will worship as Christ has been carefully planned and executed over many centuries.

Barry Chamish writes, "there would be no modern state of Israel without British Freemasonry. In the 1860s, the British-Israelite movement was initiated from within Freemasonry. Its goal was to establish a Jewish-Masonic state in the Turkish province of Palestine...Initially, British Jewish Masonic families like the Rothschilds and Montefiores provided the capital to build the infrastructure for the anticipated wave of immigration. However, luring the Jews to Israel was proving difficult. They liked European life too much to abandon it. So Europe was to be turned into a nightmare for the Jews." ("British Freemasonry Covets Israel." online)

In conclusion, the Jewish British elite's goal of world domination took the form of British and American imperialism, and later Zionism and the New World Order.

Is the New World Order "Jewish"?

Let's begin by defining the "New World Order."

The mainspring of the New World Order is the desire of the world's central bankers to translate their vast economic power into permanent global institutions of political and social control.

Their power is based on their monopoly over credit. They use the government's credit to print money, and require the taxpayer to fork over billions in interest to them.

Central banks like the Federal Reserve pretend to be government institutions. They are not. They are privately owned by perhaps 300 families. It is significant that the majority of these families are Jewish, or part Jewish. I am a non-observant Jew who believes this situation is lethal for humanity and Jews alike.

The American inventor Thomas Edison described this colossal scam as follows:

"It is absurd to say our country can issue bonds and cannot issue currency. Both are promises to pay, but one fattens the usurer and the other helps the people."

Central banks also control the supply of credit to businesses and individuals. Robert Hemphill, Credit Manager of the Federal Reserve Bank in Atlanta described this untenable situation:

"This is a staggering thought. We are completely dependent on the commercial banks. Someone has to borrow every dollar we have in circulation, cash or credit. If the banks create ample synthetic money, we are prosperous; if not, we starve. We are absolutely without a permanent money system. When one gets a complete grasp of the picture, the tragic absurdity of our hopeless position is almost incredible, but there it is... It is so important that our present civilization may collapse unless it becomes widely understood and the defects remedied very soon."

In an infamous letter to New York agents in 1863, Rothschild banker John Sherman characterized their proposal for a national bank in these terms:

"The few who understand the system will either be so interested in its profits, or so dependent on its favours, that there will be no opposition from that class... The great body of the people, mentally incapable of comprehending, will bear its burden without complaint, and perhaps without even suspecting that the system is inimical (contrary) to their interests."

ARE "THE JEWS" RESPONSIBLE?

The New World Order is a hydra-headed monster. The bankers work through many fronts such as Communism, Socialism, Liberalism, Feminism, Zionism, Neo conservatism and Freemasonry. Unknown to most members, these "progressive" movements are all secretly devoted to "world revolution" which is a euphemism for banker hegemony and Satanism. (See my "Rothschild Conducts Red Symphony.")

The bankers control the world's major corporations, media, intelligence agencies, think tanks, foundations and universities. They are responsible for suppressing the truth. Jews figure prominently in all of this, a cause of anti-Semitism. Of course, many other people are pursuing "success" as well.

The bankers also work through countries. They are largely responsible for British and American imperialism, whose aim is to monopolize the world's wealth. In his book "The Jews" (1922) British social critic Hilaire Belloc writes that the British Empire represented a partnership between Jewish finance and the British aristocracy.

"After Waterloo [1815] London became the money market and the clearing house of the world. The interests of the Jew as a financial dealer and the interests of this great commercial polity approximated more and more. One may say that by the last third of the nineteenth century, they had become virtually identical."

The confluence of Jewish and British interest extended to marriage.

"Marriages began to take place, wholesale, between what had once been the aristocratic territorial families of this country and the Jewish commercial fortunes. After two generations of this, with the opening of the twentieth century, those of the great territorial English families in which there was no Jewish blood was the exception.

"In nearly all of them was the strain more or less marked, in some of them so strong that though the name was still an English name and the traditions those of a purely English lineage of the long past, the physique and character had become wholly Jewish..."

If the marriage of Al Gore's daughter with Jacob Schiff's grandson is any indication, this mingling of the Jewish and gentile elite extends to America as well.

The British and Jewish goal of world domination was synonymous and used Freemasonry as an instrument. Belloc writes, "Specifically Jewish institutions, such as Freemasonry (which the Jews had inaugurated as a sort of bridge between themselves and their hosts in the seventeenth century) were particularly strong in Britain, and there arose a political tradition, active, and ultimately to prove of great importance, whereby the British state was tacitly accepted by foreign governments as the official protector of the Jews in other countries.

"It was Britain which was expected to intervene [wherever Jewish persecution took place and] to support the Jewish financial energies throughout the world, and to receive in return the benefit of that connection."

If Belloc is right, the New World Order is an extension of the British Empire, in which elite British, American and Jewish imperial interests are indistinguishable.

CONCLUSION: WHAT IS JEWISH?

The majority of Jews would want no part of the New World Order a.k.a. "globalization" if they understood its undemocratic character and how they are being used.

The true Jewish spirit holds that truth and morality are absolute and cannot be trimmed to fit one's perceived self interest. G.J. Nueberger expresses this spirit in his essay "The Great Gulf Between Zionism and Judaism."

"The Jewish people are chosen not for domination over others, not for conquest or warfare, but to serve G-d and thus to serve mankind...Thus physical violence is not a tradition or a value of the Jews. The task for which the Jewish people were chosen is not to set an example of military superiority or technical achievements, but to seek perfection in moral behaviour and spiritual purity.

Of all the crimes of political Zionism, the worst and most basic, and which explains all its other misdeeds, is that ... Zionism has sought to separate the Jewish people from their G-d, to render the divine covenant null and void, and to substitute a "modern" statehood and fraudulent sovereignty for the lofty ideals of the Jewish people."

The bankers obviously aren't concerned about true Judaism or racial purity and were quite willing to sacrifice millions of Jews to achieve their design by creating Hitler. They are sacrificing thousands more Jewish, American and Muslim lives in the Middle East in their Orwellian "perpetual war for perpetual peace."

Does the New World Order serve a "Jewish" racial agenda or a Cabalistic banker elite agenda? I would venture that it serves the latter, and organized Jewry has been harnessed to this agenda like so many other opportunistic or unwitting groups.

By giving private individuals the ability to create money out of nothing, we have created a monster which threatens to devour the planet and with it the human race.

The Imperialism of Jewish Capital

A book published in 1889, "The Red Dragon" by L.B. Woolfolk suggests to me that Western imperialism originated in the need of Jewish bankers and their gentile confederates to translate money they could create out of nothing (thanks to their control of credit), into real wealth (i.e. world ownership.)

When these bankers finagled a credit monopoly in England in 1694, they turned into a monster that now has highjacked humanity. The London-based banking cartel literally has gobbled up the planet, and will not be content until it owns everything, and enslaves mankind, mentally and spiritually, if not physically. This, in a nutshell, is the New World Order.

The last push came from a secret society Cecil Rhodes started for Nathaniel Rothschild in 1891 to, "absorb the wealth of the world" and "to take the government of the whole world."

A recent UN study says 2% of the world's population own 50% of the wealth, while half own barely 1% of the wealth. Needless to say, the richest 2% include the London-based bankers and people associated with them.

Today British, American and Zionist imperialism manifest the banker agenda for "world government" through the destruction of religion, nation, race and family. This imperialism does not express the interests or wishes of ordinary English, American or Jewish people who are being colonized themselves.

THE RED DRAGON

L.B. Woolfolk was an American Baptist preacher who traced the machinations of the banking cartel in the decades after the Civil War. He confirmed his assertions by contacts with members of this cartel during visits to London . He says "the Great Red Dragon" is the symbol of the "Jew London Money Power."

In his book, which is online, he describes how this cartel bought up the U.S. economy through intermediaries, and controlled it long before the passage of the Federal Reserve Act in 1913.

By 1864, almost 150 years ago, Woolfolk claims the wealth of the world already was concentrated in their hands.

"The Imperialism of Capital to which I allude is a knot of capitalists—Jews almost to a man—who make their headquarters in the Money Quarter of London, in Threadneedle Street, Lombard, and other streets in that vicinity, where bankers have their habitat. These Jew capitalists have succeeded in centralizing in their own hands the industry and commerce of the earth. —They own almost all the debts of the world, —the debts of nations, states, counties, municipalities, corporations and individuals, —amounting in the aggregate, it is estimated, to seventy-five billion dollars, on which they are annually receiving about four billion dollars of interest. —They own the manufactories, the shipping, and the commerce of Great Britain, and most of the manufactures, shipping and commerce of the whole world. —They have attained control of the industry and trade of the whole earth; and are rapidly centralizing all business in their own hands. They hold possession of all the great lines of trade and business of all kinds, and they regulate all prices by their own arbitrary methods. This Money Power of the Money Quarter of London is the only grand pre-eminent Imperialism existing on the earth."

Woolfolk traces the beginnings of this cartel to the British East India Company in the early part of the Eighteenth Century.

"In 1764, the British East India Company was the grandest and richest corporation in the world. It was the only corporation which ruled a territorial empire...it came to pass that the greater part of the stock of the East India Company, and of the other companies afterwards organized out of the dividends of that great company, fell into the hands of the Jews. The Jews became the great Money Kings of the world.... History presents no career of conquest, in which fraud, deceit and rapine were so blended as in the conquest of India by the East India Company. It was the first example in the history of the world of a trading corporation becoming an imperial power; and its imperial rule was marked by the rapacity, chicanery and fraud that characterize a great corporation in the soulless and conscienceless pursuit of gain."

After the invention of the steam engine in 1775, only the capitalists of the British East India Company had the means to profit from the industrial revolution. They set up hundreds of joint stock companies—manufacturing companies of all kinds, coal and iron mining, railways and ships, real estate-- which concealed their ownership.

"In commercial crises, often originated, and always manipulated by them, they managed systematically to break down rival companies, and buy them out, and to rob and plunder the minority stockholders; until, in the end, these organized capitalists got into their own hands and very cheap, all, or the greater part of the stock of the various companies, manufacturing, mercantile and shipping, that originated in steam manufactures. They thus reduced to a system and a science the art of crushing rival companies, and freezing out minority stockholders."

Woolfolk speculates that the Rothschilds did not act alone but represented a syndicate of Jewish bankers.

"The rise of the house of Rothschild is memorable as the first grand combination of the Jews in a syndicate, for the transaction of a vast business in which all their capital might be combined. The Rothschilds became the head of the Jew Money Kings, and have ever since been the head of the Jews, acting as a syndicate. That house is probably at the head of the Jew Money Power of the world. The wealth of the Money Power is simply beyond calculation. It cannot amount to less than $160,000,000,000. It is probably nearer two hundred billions.... The Money Power has so much money, now, that it can not find investment for it. In one more double it will about have all the property of the earth. In the beginning of its career, a double of its capital meant $100,000,000. Now a double of its capital means $400,000,000,000. And all the property of the world is less that $600,000,000,000."

According to Woolfolk, the Rockefellers and most great American industrialist-financiers were merely agents of the London Money Power. Standard Oil is a classic example of how it established a monopoly in every enterprise. Owning the railroads needed to transport oil, the Money Power put Rockefeller competitors out of business by raising their prices.

This cartel of cartels kept the business class in line by creating the spectre of Communism:

"It is their policy to keep up a hot agitation for Communism and Socialism in the great cities; so that the businessmen, in their antagonism to those ideas, will keep on the side of the Money Power. It is a significant fact that most of the agitators for Socialism are Jews, who are most probably the agents of the Money Power to keep up this agitation for their own purposes... It is a part of the consummate craft of these Money Kings."

CONCLUSION

"The Red Dragon" is an important reminder that even 150 years ago, wealth and power were concentrated in a relatively few hands. Modern history reflects the hidden machinations of this power. The whole world has been colonized.

We see evidence today that one hand directs all the great multinationals. For example, they all sing from the same songbook of diversity and feminism. All U.S. Presidents are front men for this banking cartel. Their Cabinets are chosen from the ranks of the Rockefeller-controlled CFR. Presidents who defy the Money Power are eliminated. (i.e. most recently JFK and Nixon.) All the Presidential candidates support Israel which was created by the banking cartel to be their world government capital.

I have always thought this cartel was mostly motivated by a desire to consolidate its power, but I now wonder if the Sabbatean Jewish heresy is a major factor in their design. Anyone who creates something out of nothing thinks he is God, and as Satan promised, these bankers have inherited the whole world!

This lethal problem arose because all the nations apparently relied on a network of Jewish bankers to create their money supply. No nation had the power or wit to break away from this worldwide imperialist system.

The Jewish Century

Kevin MacDonald's book "The Culture of Critique" (2002) portrays the 20th Century as "a Jewish century." A hundred years ago, Jews were an impoverished people living mostly in Eastern Europe surrounded by hostile populations. Today Israel is firmly established and Jews have become the wealthiest and most powerful elite in the West.

More significantly, according to MacDonald, the Western world has become Judaized. Jewish values and attitudes now constitute our culture. Because of deep-seated Jewish hostility toward traditional Western (i.e. Christian) culture, the founding peoples "have been made to feel deeply ashamed of their own history, surely the prelude to their demise as a culture and a people." (lxix)

Specifically, Jewish organizations promote policies and ideologies aimed at undermining cultural cohesion while practising the opposite policies themselves. While they promote multiculturalism and internationalism in the West, they insist that Israel remain a racially pure national enclave for Jews.

"The present immigration policy essentially places the United States and other Western societies "in play" in an evolutionary sense which does not apply to other nations of the world," MacDonald writes. "Notice that American Jews have no interest in proposing that immigration to Israel should be similarly multiethnic, or ... threaten the hegemony of the Jews." (323)

THE PARTY OF NATIONAL DECOMPOSITION

MacDonald says anti-Semitism in Weimar Germany was based on a perception that "that Jewish critical analysis of gentile society was aimed at dissolving the bonds of cohesiveness within the society." One academic referred to the Jews as "the classic party of national decomposition." (163)

MacDonald speculates that Jews feel more comfortable in societies without a distinctive national character. He focuses on how Jewish intellectual movements led by authoritarian figures took over modern intellectual life. He discusses Boas in Anthropology, Adorno in Sociology, Freud in Psychiatry and Derrida in Philosophy.

The "Frankfurt School," for example, was a "Marxist Jewish cult" financed by Jewish millionaire Felix Weil. Theodore Adorno's influential book "The Authoritarian Personality" (1950) was actually sponsored by the American Jewish Committee. It portrayed gentile group affiliations (including Christian religion, patriotism, and family) as indications of psychiatric disorder (162) and attributed anti-Semitism to Christian sexual repression.

Society has accepted Adorno's view that there is no objective standard of truth, no common reality. Everyone is isolated and different. Adorno resisted attempts to "endow the world with any universality, objectivity or totality, with any single organizing principle that would homogenize society..." (164)

This philosophy has paralysed modern Western culture. Western civilization was built on the foundation that truth is spiritual, universal, absolute and knowable. Ultimately God is Truth.

Universities today have given up the pursuit of truth and are devoted to Bolshevik-like social engineering and indoctrination. A liberal arts education today is not only a waste of time but toxic. Far from bearers of the Western tradition, universities now are its executioners with the tacit blessing of the government.

A RARE EXCEPTION

Kevin MacDonald, a professor of Psychology at California State University is a rare exception. His courageous indispensable book unveils the subversive character of our time.

A soft-spoken man who approaches his subject with scientific detachment, MacDonald has amassed a wealth of remarkable detail. For instance, did you know that white gentiles are the most underrepresented group at Harvard? They account for approximately 25% of the student body. While Asians and Jews make up only 5% of the U.S. population, they account for at least 50% of Harvard enrolment.

"The United States is well on the road to being dominated by an Asian technocratic elite and a Jewish business, professional and media elite," MacDonald says.

He details the Jewish role in sponsoring Communism, non-European immigration and the NAACP. He documents the stranglehold Jews have on U.S. cultural life and shows how it is used to shape American attitudes.

"For example, [the TV show] 'All in the Family' ...not only managed to portray working class Europeans as stupid and bigoted, it portrayed Jewish themes very positively. By the end of its 12-year run, even archenemy Archie Bunker has raised a Jewish child in his home, befriended a Black Jew (implication: Judaism has no ethnic connotations), gone into business with a Jewish partner, enrolled as a member of a synagogue, praised his close friend at a Jewish funeral [etc].... Jewish rituals are portrayed as "pleasant and ennobling" ... There is never any rational explanation for anti-Semitism...[it] is portrayed as an absolute irrational evil that must be fought at every turn." (lviii)

On the other hand, Christianity is typically portrayed as evil in the movies, and Christians are even depicted as psychopaths. MacDonald cites conservative Jewish critic Michael Medved who complains that he couldn't find one film made since 1975 where Christianity was portrayed positively. (lix)

JEWISH-CHRISTIAN RIVALRY

MacDonald sees anti-Semitism as the result of legitimate conflicts-of-interest. Yet Jewish organizations demonize anyone with the temerity to address Jewish dominance. They suppress the fact that Jewish-Christian rivalry has very deep roots in Western society.

In my view, this rivalry boils down to the fact that Jewish Pharisees rejected Christ's gospel of universal love and human brotherhood. Ever since, Jews have been social and metaphysical outcasts, albeit ones with uncanny powers of self-justification. Jews have been used as pawns by worldly power brokers bent on destroying Christian civilization. The "modernist" trend of the 20th Century can be seen in these terms.

As I have suggested elsewhere, Judaism is more a racial creed than a religion. Jews are told we have a mission to create equality and social justice. In fact, financiers are using Jews as instruments to build a totalitarian world order. A beacon for humanity, we are not. Deceived ourselves, we have deceived others and purveyed personal dysfunction and societal division. Our role in Communism is a disgrace. Israel's treatment of the Palestinians is an embarrassment. Jews need to discover who we really are and rededicate ourselves.

We can begin by reading "The Culture of Critique" and the other books in MacDonald's trilogy, "A People that Shall Dwell Alone" (1994) and "Separation and its Discontents" (1998). MacDonald's publisher sent "The Culture of Critique" to 40 Jewish publications and didn't get one review. Nor has there been any mainstream coverage, a confirmation of his thesis and measure of our captivity.

MacDonald does not suggest remedies. But to combat the "New World Order," Western nations must return to their Christian and national roots. The founding groups should reassert their values and traditions as the common glue. Minorities should be welcomed but they should not be be used as the bankers' excuse to undermine national character and cohesion. Immigrants don't want to do this.

At birth, we each enter a drama already in progress. We may sense something is very wrong but we can't define it. In fact, we are in the advanced stages of a long-term conspiracy to subvert Western civilization. "Modernism" in the 20th Century was a hoax designed to strip people of their familial, cultural and religious identity before enslaving them in a new dark age. Western societies must assert their Christian and national roots or this drama will not end well.

The Riddle of Anti-Semitism

"We're being flooded by Jews," a Canadian immigration officer remarked to his associate.

The year was 1951. He was checking the papers of a young couple with a baby boy. My father understood English. He had narrowly survived the Nazis. This was his welcome to Canada.

Luckily it was not a harbinger. We encountered little discrimination and my family prospered.

Nonetheless, my parents wanted to assimilate. They gave their children English-sounding names and hardly associated with the Jewish community. The extent of our Jewish observance was that my mother lit the candles on Friday and we celebrated the major holidays.

My parents rarely spoke of my grandparents who had perished. They seemed to regard being Jewish as a curse. I did assimilate. It's ironic therefore that my father, now 85, has disowned me because I try to understand anti-Semitism other than in simplistic terms.

The fact that anti-Semitism is not irrational does not justify the Nazi policy of genocide. You would think Jews would want to understand what really happened. How else can they ensure that they will not meet such a fate again?

DEFENSE MECHANISM

Anti-Semitism is not an irrational hatred or sickness in the gentile soul, as Jews imagine. It is a healthy defence mechanism of mainly Christian and Moslem nations, cultures, races and religions that are threatened by a gradual and insidious process of extinction (i.e. feminism, diversity, world government.)

Most "anti-Semitic" books I've seen are remarkably free of hatred and rancor. They do not advocate violence against Jews but present measures to retain national and racial character similar to those practised by Jews in Israel today.

They tend to be reasonable and portray the gentile as a feckless victim of superior Jewish intelligence. Leon de Poncins would even accept Jewish leadership if it were benign.

Competition between "Christian" and "Jewish" world views is the central factor in the development of the western world.

"The advent of Christ was a national catastrophe for the Jewish people, especially for the leaders," Leon de Poncins wrote. "Until then, they alone had been the Sons of the Covenant; they had been its sole high priests and beneficiaries....The irreducible antagonism with which Judaism has opposed Christianity for 2000 years is the key and mainspring of modern subversion...[The Jew] championed reason against the mythical world of the spirit ...he was the doctor of unbelief; all those who were mentally in revolt came to him either secretly or in broad daylight..." ("Judaism and the Vatican," pp.111-113.)

"The Jewish Question" has been a major issue for hundreds of years. As early as 1879, a German writer Wilhelm Marr lamented that it cannot be discussed honestly.

"Since 1848 if we Germans so much as criticized any little thing Jewish, it was enough to have us entirely outlawed from the press. While a sense of delicacy is wholly absent among the Jews [when satirizing Germans], it is demanded of us that we handle them like fine glassware or extremely sensitive plants." ("Anti-Semitism in the Modern World: An Anthology" 1991, p.85)

THEODOR FRITSCH (1852-1934)

Called "the most influential German anti-Semite before Hitler," Fritsch's most influential book "Handbuch der Judenfrage" 1896 ("Handbook of the Jewish Question") went through dozens of printings, and was taught in German schools during the Nazi era. Most copies were destroyed after World War Two.

"Handbook" was translated into English in 1927 and retitled "The Riddle of the Jew's Success" by F. Roderich-Stoltheim, a pen name. It is extremely rare; original copies cost as much as $1000.

Fritsch does not fit the image of hate monger foaming at the mouth. His book impresses me as the work a civilized man with considerable spiritual discernment. His central point is that Judaism does not deserve credit for monotheism because the Jewish God is not universal.

"It is a fatal mistake of our theologians to regard the Jewish God as identical with the Christian. On a closer examination, Jehovah is found to be the exclusive God of Jewdom and not, at the same time, that of other men."

He cites many passages from the Old Testament to demonstrate that the Covenant between Jews and their God "bears a hostile meaning for all non- Jewish people."

For example, "Ask of me, and I shall give thee the heathen for thine inheritance and the uttermost parts of the world for thy possession. Thou shalt break them with a rod of iron..." (Psalms 2.8.9)

As a consequence, the Talmud (the Jewish code of law) distinguishes one system of morality for Jews and another for gentiles who are regarded as cattle or swine. Fritsch cites many references to show it is permitted to lie, cheat or steal from a gentile. (pp. 57-65)

Fritsch concludes that anti-Semitism is a natural reaction to these hostile attitudes which he claims are actually practised by many Jews. Since these beliefs are kept secret from non-Jews, he says Judaism is a conspiracy against non-Jews. Its aim is to fulfill the Covenant, and gain dominion over mankind by controlling wealth.

He claims that all Jews are part of this scheme and none can be excepted. I respect the right of Germans and other non-Jews to a national homeland but I think he is wrong to judge all Jews by one racist standard.

The anti-gentile character of Judaism is news to many Jews who are brainwashed just like gentiles.

How would Fritsch like to be condemned for what other Germans (e.g. Nazis) did or said? Jews are individuals and should be judged by their individual actions. The majority are alienated from Judaism and would find the Biblical passages cited above repugnant.

CONCLUSION

Jews need to re-examine their relationship with Judaism. I cannot overstate the significance of the Jewish rejection of Christ.

Christ represented a universal God and a universal morality. His teaching represented the natural next stage, which Jews should have embraced, while retaining their racial integrity.

By rejecting Christ's teaching, the Pharisees placed the Jewish people in perpetual opposition to the best interests of humanity, to the ultimate and inevitable path of human spiritual evolution.

They have placed Jews in a state of permanent metaphysical revolt which on a personal level leads to alienation and dysfunction.

Christ taught that God is Love. Love is the Master Plan. Love is Light. Love thy neighbor. Do unto others, as you would have them do unto you. What fault could Pharisees have with a gospel that preaches human brotherhood and putting others before yourself?

It denies their special claim to be God's "chosen people" and to administer God's will, which is really their own.

Best Picture "Chicago" Celebrates Jewish Power & Duplicity

"Don't shoot, I'm all alone," a husband pleads with his gun wielding wife after she catches him in bed with two naked women.

"But I can see two women," she objects.

"Don't believe what you see," he instructs her, echoing the principle of propaganda. "Believe what I tell you."

The wife shoots her husband in this scene from the movie musical "Chicago." But the movie is dedicated to the cynical premise that the public is not so astute.

"Chicago" is by Fred Ebb, the author of "Cabaret." Where the mantra of "Cabaret" is "money makes the world go round," the sequel proclaims power turns on deception, secret societies and control of the media.

It is significant that when many Americans suspected Zionists of finagling their country into yet another manufactured war, a movie that privately celebrates Jewish power and duplicity won the 2002 Best Picture award.

CHICAGO

"Chicago" is set on death row in Chicago's women's jail, where man-killers brazenly proclaim, "He had it coming."

"Roxie Hart," murdered her lover because he broke his promise to make her a singing star and dumped her instead.

"Irish" lawyer Billy Flynn is the only person who can save Roxie's neck. Flynn is played by half-Jewish Richard Gere who is made to look Jewish in this role. By making him "Irish" the playwright passes off Jewish experience as American experience. But Jews get the message.

Flynn's modus operandi is to invent a crowd-pleasing story about his client and create media hysteria in her favor. There is an eerie scene where Flynn is portrayed as a giant puppeteer controlling dozens of reporter-puppets below.

In another scene, he is a ventriloquist voicing Roxie Hart's words. (Imagine Dubya or McCain or Obama on his lap.) Finally, in a courtroom scene he exchanges winks and Masonic hand signals with the judge.

Flynn cynically proclaims to Roxie: "You got nothing to worry about. It's all a circus, kid. A three-ring circus. This trial, the whole world --all show business. But kid you're working with a star, the biggest!"

He breaks into a song suggestive of Jewish self-loathing, chutzpah, hype and disdain for non-Jews:

"Give 'em the old razzle dazzle...
What if your hinges are all a-rusting?
What if, in fact, you're just disgusting?
Razzle dazzle 'em.
And they'll never catch wise!
How can they hear the truth above the roar?
Throw 'em a fake and a finagle
They'll never know you're just a bagel...
They let ya get away with murder..."

To drive home the point, another inmate, a devout Hungarian Catholic woman does not have the money or the "smarts" to hire Billy Flynn. We see her praying to Jesus Christ but Jesus is no help. She goes to the gallows. We see her swing. We see them take her coffin away. The Christian is a loser.

Her death is significant only in terms of what could happen to Roxie. The Jury is out. The newspapers have printed two batches with headlines GUILTY and INNOCENT. The audience knows Roxie is guilty. She killed a man with a wife and five small children just because he had her without paying her price.

If Hollywood were doing its job, Roxie would be found guilty. The world would be portrayed as a place where Billy Flynn's chicanery cannot prevail, where eternal values rule, where you can't "get away with murder." But Roxie is found innocent, of course. This is the way the world works. Anything else would be preachy.

But, isn't this preaching too? Isn't it preaching for cynicism, corruption and decline? "Chicago" epitomizes a bogus religion where man flouts God and winning is all that matters.

According to this secular religion, sex appeal gives women legitimacy. They expect this legitimacy will spill over to art and commerce. The frenetic half-naked women dancing in "Chicago" remind me of circus bears in tutus. They thrust their pelvises in our face. There is no sex appeal without dignity, no dignity without culture, and no culture without religion.

SECULAR TYRANNY

In the Finale of "Chicago," Roxie Hart and her partner, Velma Kelly, another of Flynn's satisfied clients, take to the stage.

"Thank you for your belief in our innocence," they say. "You know, a lot of people have lost faith in America. And for what America stands for. But we are the living examples of what a wonderful country this is."

Ironic isn't it? They are guilty and we all know it. Yet they still brazenly proclaim their innocence. They project their self-delusion on America as a whole.

The show is true to its message. Believe what we tell you not what you see. America's greatness under this new Satanic dispensation is that it allows you to "get away with murder." America's greatness is pretending black is white.

Communism - A Ruse for Illuminati Jewish Theft & Murder

In 1869, Jacob Brafmann, a Jewish convert to Christianity published a book in Russian about the Jewish communal organization, "The Kahal" which suggests that - unknown to many Jews and non-Jews -- organized Jewry indeed was conspiring against the gentile population in Russia. Like most books of this kind, it is now unavailable.

Luckily, in Nov. 1881, Mme. Z.A. Ragozin published a thorough summary in "The Century Magazine" (Vol. 23 Issue I) under the title, "Russian Jews and Gentiles from a Russian Point of View." This remarkable essay is online.

Ragozin was a scholar of ancient Near Eastern history who published a half-dozen books on the Chaldeans, Persians and Assyrians in the 1880's.

"THE KAHAL"

Brafmann's book was based on a thousand internal documents of the Kahal. Its most startling revelation:

The Kahal followed the Talmudic prescription that gentile property is a "free-for-all" for Jews who, for a fee, are pre-authorized by the town council ("The Kahal") to finagle it. Obviously a source of anti-Semitism, it may also explain the true predatory nature of Communism (and the New World Order) behind the idealistic sounding window dressing.

For example, Brafmann, who Jewish historian Simon Dubnow called "an informer," explains that Jew "N" buys the rights to gentile "M"'s house.

"He has acquired 'khazaka' i.e right of ownership over the house of gentile "M," in force thereof he is given the exclusive right, guaranteed from interference or competition from other Jews, to get possession of the said house...'by any means whatever.' Until he has finally succeeded in transferring it to his official possession, he alone is entitled to rent that house from its present owner, to trade in it, to lend money to the owner or to other gentiles who may dwell in it-to make profits out of them in any way [that] his ingenuity may suggest...."

The second part may provide a model of how individuals became subjects of a Jew.

"Sometimes the Kahal sells to a Jew even the person of some particular gentile without any immovable property attached. [This is called 'meropie'.] It is in some places forbidden for Jews to enter into relations with that person with prejudice to the first; but in other places it is free to every Jew to...lend him money, give him bribes, and despoil him, for it is said that the property of a gentile is 'hefker.' [free to all] and whoever gets possession of it, to him it shall belong." (p.912)

According to Brafmann, the documents "show as clearly as possible [how] Jews, notwithstanding their limited rights, have always succeeded in driving alien elements from the towns and boroughs where they have settled, to get into their hands the capital and immovable property in those places, and to get rid of all competition in commerce and trades, as has been the case in the western provinces of Russia, in Poland, Galicia, Romania..."

Selling alcohol and money lending were ways to finagle property. The Jewish vodka dealers would show up at harvest time and sell alcohol to farmers on credit. Before long the drinking habits of the peasants and compound interest combined to transfer the property and future harvests into the vodka dealers' hands. (E. Michael Jones, "Russian Roulette" Culture Wars, May 2006, p. 24.)

A REVOLUTIONARY WAY OF STEALING

Fifty years after "The Kahal" was published, Christian Russian civilization was brutally annihilated by the Bolshevik Revolution which was a front for the Illuminati Jewish bankers. The salient aspects of this revolution, apart from the imposition of a ghastly and depraved police state, was the confiscation of untold gentile wealth and the slaughter of millions of non-Jews mostly by Jews. This holocaust gets little notice because Illuminati Jews control the mass media and education system using self-righteous and highly-paid dupes to enforce their intellectual tyranny.

The Rothschild front Kuhn Loeb & Co. got a handsome return for their $20 Million financing of the 1917 revolution. In 1921 Lenin gave them $102 million. ("New York Times" Aug. 23, 1921.) As well, they may have kept bank accounts the (Tsar) Romanovs foolishly entrusted to them.

In addition, Illuminati Jewish bankers took ownership of Russian industry. German Secret Service documents instructed the Bolsheviks to "destroy the Russian capitalists as far as you please, but it would by no means be possible to permit the destruction of Russian enterprises."

The German Imperial Bank sent the Bolsheviks in excess of 60 million roubles. In this context, A. N. Field cites Documents 10 and 11 between the bankers and the Bolsheviks: "They give a complete synopsis of the terms on which the German banks after the war were to control Russian industry." ("The Truth About the Slump," 1931, by A.N. Field. pp.62-72)

"THE RED TERROR"

Lenin and Trotsky created the infamous secret service "Cheka" (later OGPU, then NKVD and finally KGB) to steal property and crush resistance.

"The first Cheka units set up in every city or town were engaged first and foremost in the extermination of Tsarist bureaucrats, gendarmes and high ranking officers, the families of White Guards and all citizens whose property was valued at 10,000 roubles or more. There were thousands of scientists and engineers who were killed as "exploiters" and about half the country's doctors were either killed or forced to emigrate. People were murdered at home, in the streets, and in the cellars of Cheka headquarters irrespective of their age." (Slava Katamidze, "Loyal Comrades, Ruthless Killers -The Secret Services of the U.S.SR 1917-1991" p. 14)

Thousands of Christian priests and monks were sent to the Gulag and slaughtered.

"The Church became the target of Bolshevik hostility from the very beginning. Resistance to the confiscation of church properties, especially silver and gold items, was especially fierce...Now priests called on their parishes to resist confiscation, accusing the authorities of pocketing most of the proceeds." (Katamidze, p. 25)

It is estimated that the Cheka was responsible for at least 20 million deaths, according to courageous Jewish writer Steve Plocker who says the Cheka was led and staffed mainly by Jews. The Cheka was empowered by Lenin and Trotsky, who were Illuminati Jews and financed by Illuminati Jewish bankers.

"Many Jews sold their soul to the devil of the Communist revolution and have blood on their hands for eternity," Plocker writes. "We mustn't forget that some of the greatest murderers of modern times were Jews."

Not to excuse the murderers, many rank-and-file Jewish and non-Jewish Communists truly were duped into thinking Communism represented poor workers, the sharing of wealth and social justice. Much like today, Illuminati Jews had brainwashed the flock. However, some other Jews did see through the deception and heroically fought against Communism.

The Illuminati puppet-masters work arms-length in order to maintain the illusion that history is unfolding in a random fashion. Thus at various times, Stalin did rebel against his handlers and did persecute their Jewish agents. Many believe Stalin was ultimately murdered when he attempted a final crackdown.

The mirror reverse image of the "Red Terror" was the Nazi persecution of the Jews and confiscation of select Jewish property in the 1930's. I suspect the Illuminati Jewish bankers were responsible for the rise of the Nazis and benefited by expropriating the wealth of their "lesser Jewish brethren" and non Illuminati Jewish competitors. The big German bankers were very involved in the "Aryanization" of Jewish property.

CONCLUSION

A cancer is destroying Western civilization. The source is the Illuminati central bankers who control our economic, political, cultural and spiritual institutions. In other words, our "leadership" represents an occult imperial power at war with us; and we can't even recognize it because our institutions have been subverted.

America today can be compared to Russia before the Revolution. According to W. Schulgin, "the brain of the nation was in [Illuminati] Jewish hands. and it became business as usual to think in Jewish categories....In spite of all the restrictions, the

Jews controlled the mind of the Russian people." (Jones, Culture Wars, p. 42) Of course, the Illuminati control the Jewish mind.

A real Jew (and Christian and Muslim) stands for God and a universal Moral Order. Thus, world government can never be "good for the Jews" no matter what elite status they enjoy.

Secular humanism cannot replace God. It is a foil for a demented Satanic agenda and for more of the bestiality that characterizes the past.

Soviets Spared Synagogues, Razed Churches

A reader sent a penetrating question: "When Bolshevism took over Russia, they tried to eliminate religion. Their stated philosophy was atheism and they closed Christian Churches and killed or imprisoned the clergy."

"However, did they also close Jewish synagogues and kill or imprison the rabbis? The answer to this question will explain many things about the early days of Communism and I hope you can provide the truth."

Last week I stumbled across the answer in a book by American historian Edwin Schoonmaker:

"Fifteen years after the Bolshevist Revolution was launched to carry out the Marxist program, the editor of the "American Hebrew" could write: "According to such information that the writer could secure while in Russia a few weeks ago, not one Jewish synagogue has been torn down, as have hundreds—perhaps thousands of the Greek Catholic Churches...In Moscow and other large cities one can see Christian churches in the process of destruction...[whenever] the Government needs the location for a large building." (American Hebrew, Nov. 18, 1932, p. 12) Apostate Jews, leading a revolution that was to destroy religion as the "opiate of the people" had somehow spared the synagogues of Russia." ("Democracy and World Dominion," 1939, p.211)

If the Communists hated God and religion so much, why didn't they destroy synagogues too? Do Christianity and Judaism worship the same God? Or can a religion that claims an exclusive ownership of God be a religion? Could it be that Judaism is a really a secret society like Freemasonry where the members don't know the hidden agenda, which is in fact expressed by Communism? Although many religious Jews were indeed anti-Communist, Schoonmaker's information suggests there may be an affinity between Talmudic Judaism and pagan Satanic Communism.

The London-based Judeo Masonic banking cabal sponsored the Bolsheviks and is behind the NWO. Communism was part of a grand dialectical process by which "life in the United States... can be comfortably merged with the Soviet Union," in the words of Ford Foundation President Rowan Gaither to Congressional Investigator Norman Dodd in 1953.

If indeed Communism and Democracy are being "comfortably merged" under the pretext of the phoney "war on terror," then church destruction will be disturbing to Christians and all God fearing people, including ethnic Jews like myself.

The decisive presence of Jews in Communist movements is well documented. What Jews don't realize is that Satanic Communism is the source of anti-Semitism. The pentagram is the symbol both of the occult and the Soviet Union. Throughout history Christians have regarded Jews as agents of Satan. Some Jews may have deserved this reputation but all have suffered as a consequence.

Secular Jews were duped by promises of "public ownership," "equality" and "social justice." Rejecting spiritual redemption, they embraced the devil's lure of a worldly utopia. The same enticements now are used to enlist useful idiots for world government.

It is appalling that Communism, an ideology that represents Pure Evil, whose stated goal is to steal our property and destroy our love of family, God, nation, race and freedom is not only accepted but enjoys prestige in our society. How far we have fallen! Communism attacks our very humanity. Of course, Communism travels under new names today-- human rights (for some), feminism, diversity, post-modernism, communitarianism, world government-- always presenting a happy face, the better to dupe.

The banker-owned mass media mutes the story of how Communists razed civilization in Russia and murdered over 25 million people. We must revive this knowledge before they do it again. Remember, the Illuminati-Communist credo is "the end justifies the means."

The Nazis did not invent cattle cars for human transport. Schoonmaker cites Eugene Lyons, a Communist dupe himself, who wrote about the expulsion of peasants: "Millions of peasant homes were destroyed, the occupants packed into cattle cars and dumped in the frozen north or parched Central Asia...I saw batches of the wretched men, women and children peering out of air holes in cattle cars like caged animals." (239)

Like the Nazis, the Bolsheviks had difficulty killing large numbers and disposing of the bodies. Schoonmaker reports that French Navy divers found fields of corpses anchored at the bottom of Odessa harbor: "The seabed [was] peopled with human bodies standing upright, which the swaying of the water...softly rocked as though they were monstrous algae, their hair on end bristling vertically and their arms raised to the surface...[these] submarine cemeteries [were the] last resting places of some of Russia's most high-minded sons and daughters." (235)

These atrocities took place in 1920, two years after Grigory Zinoviev, (i.e. Hirsch Apfelbaum) head of the Third International called for the extermination of the Russian bourgeoisie, i.e. ten million people!

Clearly the focus on Jew as innocent victim is designed to distract us from the image of Bolshevik Jew as murderer. "History ..has recorded nothing so profoundly revolting as the nameless cruelties in which these human fiends often revelled," wrote E.J. Dillon.

According to Estonian journalist, Juri Lina, Karl Marx, Lenin and Trotsky, all Jewish Freemasons, were essentially dysfunctional losers who were employed by the Illuminist bankers to hoodwink the masses. Lenin for example had been an unsuccessful lawyer who had only six cases in which he defended shoplifters. He lost them all. A week later he gave up the law to become a highly paid revolutionary.

Lenin declared: "Peace means quite simply the domination of Communism over the entire world." His reign of terror caused nine million deaths but you never see him compared to Hitler. The secret police, the Cheka, dominated by Jews, published the names of 1.7 million people they murdered in 1918-1919, including 300,000 priests.

"A river of blood flowed through Russia," Lina writes. "According to official Soviet Reports, 1,695,904 people were executed from January 1921 to April 1922. Among these victims were bishops, professors, doctors, officers, policemen, lawyers, civil servants, writers...Their crime was 'anti social thinking.' " ("The Sign of the Scorpion," p. 90)

FROM BOURGEOISIE TO CHRISTIANS

With the same zeal that the Communists slaughtered the Bourgeoisie, Schoonmaker writes they "hunted down the clergy. Christian holidays were abolished... parents were forbidden from giving religious instruction to children...a League of the Godless was organized to mock out of existence every vestige of faith and reverence."

Law courts were reorganized. Justice was now defined by Bolshevik orthodoxy. Anti-Semitism became a state crime. Science, art and education were all put to the Marxist standard and often ruthlessly suppressed. The Classics and even fairy tales disappeared from libraries and schools.

The institution of marriage was changed. You could obtain a divorce by merely sending your partner a card. They even considered the "public ownership of women" but demurred. In 1936, "emancipation" resulted in women making up: "26 percent of all workers in the metal and machine trades, 40% of woodworking and 24% of all Soviet coal miners..." (201)

Today in America, we can witness the steady decline of culture, education, religion, marriage, free speech, free press and objective truth. We can see attempts to increasingly control every aspect of our lives as the two systems are "comfortably merged."

CONCLUSION

Jewish commentators wring their hands trying to understand the "irrational" gentile disease, "anti-Semitism." They need look no further than to Communism and the bankers' attempt to hijack the human race from its natural course: family, nation, race and religion (God).

If Jews refused to be agents and dupes of the megalomanical banking cabal, if they had fought Communism alongside their Christian neighbours, there would have been no anti-Semitism. (Although many Jews were never Communists, there would never have been Communism without Jews.)

Jewish commentators need to ask where the diabolical spirit threatening humanity originates. They need to denounce it as both evil and alien to them.

The "God" That Serves Elite Jews

Recently, I noted that the Soviets razed thousands of churches but spared synagogues. If Communists considered religion "the opium of the masses," why didn't they include Judaism? Do Christians and Jews worship the same God? Is there an affinity between Communism and Judaism?

Perhaps the Jewish elite has a different God. A reader, "George," knew the heiress of a rich Jewish banking family "not the Rothschilds, although her family dwelled in a palace neighbouring the Rothschilds."

"Leah was one of my classmates in the Geneva University (Switzerland) where I was studying psychology ...She was an attractive blue-eyed blonde lady. ...As she was wearing a Star of David, I asked if she was a believer. She answered "yes and no" and added that she believed in a god of the Jews who was serving the Jews rather than served by them. I immediately asked whether she was speaking of an egregore ...Her only response was "yes" and she broke that conversation. Never again did we mention the subject."

According to Wikipedia, "egregore" is an occult concept representing a "thought form" or "collective group mind", an autonomous psychic entity made up of, and influencing, the thoughts of a group of people. The symbiotic relationship between an egregore and its group has been compared to the more recent, non-occult concepts of the corporation (as a legal entity) and the meme."

George speculates that elite Jews created the Jewish God as their "egregore," i.e. an instrument of their collective will, i.e. their desire to vanquish the heathens and rule supreme:

"Could it be possible that the ancient Levite priests found a way to create a supernatural entity from the collective mind of the tribe of Judah? An entity born from a collective mind the Levites were shaping into self-isolationism and segregationist a.k.a, extreme ethno-centrism? ...An entity designed to help the "chosen people" destroy the "alien" nations and provide it with material rewards? An entity resulting from the black magic of the Levite priests who, as the first indoctrinated atheists, were denying the universal God of Moses because they didn't want to submit to a "Lord and Master" but rather become themselves "Lords and Masters" through their slavish "egregorious" god?"

This "egregore" is Lucifer. Elite Jews have made him the master meme of the New World Order. The elite Jews are the "Communist Capitalist International", the intermarried German Jewish banking families who, according to Christian Rakovsky include the Rothschilds, Warburgs, Schiffs and many others.

They have also intermarried with the corrupt gentile elites of Europe and America, many of whom think they are Jews.

THE DEPRAVED SPIRIT OF OUR AGE

Since the Jewish egregore is also behind the New World Order, we should recall that according to this mindset, only the subscribers ("believers") are human; everyone else is an animal to be exploited and/or slaughtered.

Nicholas Lysson, in his brilliant essay on the Ukrainian Holocaust, ("Holocaust and Holodomor") provides examples of this "us-vs-them" thinking in the Talmud and the Old Testament. For example: Isaiah 60:12 ("...The nation and kingdom that will not serve [Israel] shall perish; yea, those nations shall be utterly wasted"); Isaiah 61:5-6 ("...Strangers shall stand and feed your flocks...: Ye shall eat the riches of the Gentiles...")

Nicholas Lysson says the most damning passages of the Talmud are toned down or not translated. Information about the dreaded "Arendar" system is suppressed. (See-"The Real Cause of Anti-Semitism" below.)

Lysson discusses how the Jewish leadership actively provoke anti-Semitism because it is indispensable for Jewish cohesion and survival. Jews acknowledge this. Are they saying that, without its "egregore" i.e. its predatory agenda, Jews would have no corporate raison d'être? Of course this secret is kept from the rank-and-file, as in Freemasonry which Rakovsky said is designed to bring about "the triumph of Communism."

THE COMMUNIST EGREGORE

The greatest mass slaughter in history was not the Jewish holocaust but the Ukrainian holodomor i.e. the "hunger". By Stalin's own estimate, ten million Ukrainians died, mostly at the hands of Bolshevik Jews.

The holodomor took place because the Bolsheviks confiscated all the grain. Lysson writes: "A quarter of the rural population, men, women and children, lay dead or dying in a great stretch of territory with some forty million inhabitants, like one vast Belsen. The rest, in various stages of debilitation, had no strength to bury their families or neighbours. [As at Belsen] well-fed squads of police or party officials supervised the victims."

The extermination of the Ukrainian Kulaks was directed from the Kremlin where the Bolshevik leadership lived in family apartments and maintained a fraternal atmosphere suffused by collectivist idealism i.e. their egregore. This is how historian Simon Sebag Montefiore, the scion of an elite British Jewish family, describes the scene during the holomodor. Of course he doesn't mention that most of the main players were Jews.

"The Party was almost a family business. Whole clans were members of the leadership... This pitiless fraternity lived in a sleepless frenzy of excitement and activity, driven by adrenalin and conviction. Regarding themselves like God on the first day, they were creating a new world in a red-hot frenzy..." ("Stalin: The Court of the Red Tsar," p. 40, 45)

CONCLUSION

The Soviets didn't raze synagogues because Communism expressed the Jewish "egregore." Christians and Jews apparently do not worship the same God. The Christian God represented by Jesus is universal love and brotherhood. The Jewish God has been supplanted by a Cabalistic egregore that "serves" elite Jews only. It represents their ruthless sociopathic urge for world dominion. The same egregore-- the desire to supplant God-- animates the New World Order.

The average Communist Jew or non-Jew was an idealistic dupe. Marxism, equality etc. were just window dressing to hide the real agenda: the destruction of race, religion, family and nation; the accumulation of all wealth and the enslavement of mankind. The methods have changed but the agenda has not.

The same ersatz idealism infuses the world government movement, which is full of pious opportunists who have sold their heritage for a seat at the globalist table.

Let's not kid ourselves. We are facing a diabolical evil, ruthless, vicious and cunning, with unlimited resources. In spite of this, Jews and non-Jews must join to banish Lucifer and declare that only God is God, He is moral and we serve only Him.

The Real Cause of Anti-Semitism

Born in Poland in 1919, my Jewish mother remembered visiting her grandfather's "estate" as a child and riding in a big horse drawn carriage.

This memory contradicted my impression that Jews in Poland were persecuted and poor. Most, like my father's family, indeed were very poor. But my mother's memory reveals that other Jews were part of the ruling class.

Israel Shahak's book "Jewish History, Jewish Religion; The Weight of 3000 Years" (1994) suggests that this social pattern developed over centuries may continue to the present day.

According to Shahak, historically the Jewish elite often had a symbiotic relationship with the governing class. The Jews would "administer the oppression" to the masses. In return, the governing class would force Jews to obey their "leaders." Sometimes a pogrom would do the trick.

Today, specific Jews (in finance, government, education and especially the media) play a prominent role in the elite's preparation for "globalization," which many see as a modern form of feudalism.

THE TRUTH IS BITTER

History is propaganda about the past. Most historians don't tell the truth because they would be fired. Israel Shahak, who died in 2001, was not an historian. He was a Professor of Organic Chemistry at Hebrew University. He had a scientist's respect for objective truth. He was also a concentration camp survivor, an Israeli army veteran and a campaigner for Arab human rights.

Shahak believes that Jews need to re-educate themselves about their history and religion. Jews are "a closed society" that uses "anti-Semitism" to quash criticism which is considered "hatred" or "self hatred." (In fact, to expose folly is love not hate.)

Shahak says Judaism is largely a primitive, materialistic, authoritarian credo. The Talmud is devoted to Jewish supremacy and contempt for Christ, Christianity and non-Jews in general. The Cabala embraces many gods including Satan. (Shahak, p. 33)

The following is a brief summary of Shahak's argument in the chapter, "The Weight of History."

In spite of persecution, Jews throughout history always formed an integral part of the privileged classes. The poorest Jew was immeasurably better off than the serfs. Until roughly 1880, their most important social function "was to mediate the oppression of the peasants on behalf of the nobility and the Crown."

Classical Judaism (1000-1880 AD) developed hatred and contempt for agriculture as an occupation and for peasants as a class. "The supposed superiority of Jewish morality and intellect...is bound up with a lack of sensitivity for the suffering of that major part of humanity who were especially oppressed during the last 1000 years, the peasants." (53) Shahak traces Jewish "hatred and contempt" for peasants— "a hatred of which I know no parallel in other societies"—back to the great Ukrainian uprising of 1648-54, in which Ukrainian Cossack leader Bohdan Khmelnytsky killed tens of thousands of "the accursed Jews."

At the time, Jews were serving the Polish szlachta (nobility) and Roman Catholic clergy on their Ukrainian latifundia as "arendars"—toll-, rent- and tax-farmers, enforcers of corvee obligations, licensees of feudal monopolies (e.g., on banking, milling, storekeeping, and distillation and sale of alcohol). They also served as anti-Christian scourges who collected tithes at the doors of the peasants' Greek Orthodox churches and exacted fees to open those doors for weddings, christenings and funerals.

They had life-and-death powers over the local population (the typical form of execution being impalement) and no law above them to which that population had recourse. The arendars leased estates for terms of only two or three years and had every incentive to wring the peasants mercilessly, without regard to long-term consequences.

Shahak points out that, in traditional Judaism, a non-Jew was never "thy neighbor" for purposes of Leviticus 19:18—which was doubtless an advantage in such taxing work as an arendar.

While gentiles in general were reviled, Jewish laws made an exception for the elite. Jewish physicians, tax collectors and bailiffs could be relied upon by a king, nobleman, pope or bishop in a way that a Christian might not. (53)

In Shahak's words, "Israel and Zionism are a throw-back to the role of classical Judaism, writ large on a global scale..."

"The state of Israel now fulfills towards the oppressed peasants of many countries, not only in the Middle East, but far beyond it, a role not unlike the Jews of pre-1795 Poland: that of a bailiff to the imperial oppressor. " He refers to Israel's role as a linchpin in the imperial system. It helps keep neighboring Arab regimes in power (11) and arms Third World dictators. He wonders why religious Jews are major participants in the arms trade and rabbis are silent.

Shahak believes the Jewish people need to overcome the "tyranny" of their religion. Only by an "unrelenting critique" of the past will they achieve a "genuine revolution." (74)

CONCLUSION

A Jewish reader wrote to me: "It is the Jewish mission to be a light or spiritual guide to the nations...We [uphold] an ethical and moral God, without which we would descend into barbarism in an instant. And it is THIS which has caused Christianity to murder Jews throughout the centuries."

I beg to differ. Far from being a "light unto humanity" many Jews "mediate the oppression" for the governing class. This and a general tendency to monopolize money, power and culture toward socially destructive ends is the real cause of anti-Semitism.

BOOK TWO

Illuminati, Sabbateans and Protocols

The Conspiracy is Against God

Have you noticed?

Every year, there is a little less Christ in Christmas, a little less Christian spirit.

The spirit of giving now is confined to gifts. Scarcely is there mention of Christian love. That might offend some people, Satanists perhaps.

God is Love. Satanists aren't big fans of Love. They have a lot of clout these days.

Incredible and bizarre as this sounds, a Satanic cult, the Illuminati, rules the world. Barack Obama is a member, as are many of the world's political and economic elite.

The Illuminati consist of many of the world's richest families including the Rothschilds, the Rockefellers and the Windsors. While they pay lip service to religion, they worship Lucifer. Their agents control the world's media, education, business and politics. These agents may think they are pursuing success, but success often literally means serving the devil.

Prisoners of their wealth, the Illuminati prefer hatred and destruction to Love. Understandably, they can't go public with this. They pretend to be moral while working behind the scenes to enslave humanity in a New World Order.

Hiroshima, Dresden, Auschwitz, Cambodia and Rwanda were sacrifices to their Satanic god. They are responsible for the two World Wars, the Depression and the Cold War. Sept. 11, the "War on Terror" and the Iraq War are their latest achievements.

We imagine they want unlimited power and wealth but these are by-products. The Illuminati is motivated by hatred of God and humanity.

OUR LUCIFER LOVING ELITE

The purpose of the New World Order is the same as Communism. The Illuminati created Communism as a means to flout God's will and enslave mankind. Karl Marx was hired to sell totalitarian rule ("the dictatorship of the proletariat") by pretending to espouse equality. He was a Satanist as were Trotsky, Lenin and Stalin.

In his book, "Marx and Satan" (1986) Richard Wurmbrand illustrates Marx`s true hatred of God and humanity. As early as 1848, Marx wrote about a "coming world war" that will eliminate "riffraff" like Russians, Czechs and Croats.

"The coming world war will cause not only reactionary classes and dynasties, but also entire reactionary peoples, to disappear from the face of the earth. And that will be progress...the revolution...cares as little about the human lives it destroys...as an earthquake cares about the houses it ravages. Classes and races that are too weak to dominate the new conditions...will be defeated...their very name will vanish." (42)

In his poem "Human Pride" Marx writes that he will "wander Godlike and victorious through the ruins of the world... I will feel equal to the Creator."(31)

Far from champion of the working class, Marx was a police spy. In 1960, the Austrian Chancellor Raabe gave Khrushchev an original letter by Marx proving the "founder of Communism" informed on other revolutionaries. (33)

The reason only 13 of the 100 Volumes of Marx's writings have been published is to hide the true character of Communism. (32)

THEY HATE THE GOD IN YOU

Wurmbrand, a pastor who was imprisoned in Romania, says Communism is in essence Satanism empowered. Christians weren't just brutally persecuted and murdered, they were made to blaspheme. Communism's goal, the goal of the New World Order, is to mock God and to praise Lucifer. A Communist newspaper confessed,"We fight against God: To snatch believers from him."(77)

In "German Ideology" Marx referred to God in Hegelian terms as the Absolute Spirit. Marx opined, "we are concerned with a highly interesting question: the decomposition of the Absolute Spirit."(77)

According to Wurmbrand, the Russian Revolution was a time when "love, goodwill, and healthy feeling were considered mean and retrograde. A girl hid her innocence, and husbands their faithfulness. Destruction was praised as good taste, neurasthenia as the sign of a fine mind. This was the theme of new writers who burst on the scene out of obscurity. Men invented vices and perversion, and were fastidious in their avoidance of being thought moral." (85)

The Luciferians portray their rebellion against God and nature as progress and freedom. This permissiveness refers only to tearing down the Divine order. In the initiation into the Seventh degree of Satanism, the adept swears, "Nothing is true and everything is permitted." In the Communist Manifesto, Marx said all religion and morals will be abolished and everything permitted.

The religion of modern western society, secular humanism, is a front for Illuminism (Lucifer worship). The purpose of Illuminism is to divorce humanity from the Divine Purpose and enshrine Lucifer (i.e. the Illuminati) in God`s place. Under the guise of a humanist utopia, they are constructing an Orwellian hell -- the New World Order, a.k.a. globalism.

The goal of globalism is the same as Communism. The world's elite masks its Luciferianism in new age paganism and Gaia worship. The Lucifer Trust runs the only chapel at the United Nations and the only statue in the UN building is the pagan god Zeus.

CHRIST WOULD BE CRUCIFIED TODAY

Christ represented the rule of God. The Pharisees worshipped Lucifer. The question facing mankind hasn't changed. Are we going to serve God or Lucifer?

The Satanists have conditioned us to short circuit at the mention of religion. They have made God seem mysterious, unknowable or non-existent.

Christ said, "God is a Spirit, obey Him in spirit and in truth." (John 4:23,24). God is Absolute Love, Truth, Justice, Goodness and Beauty. If you believe these things are real, whether you accomplish them or not, you believe in God.

Love is the principle of human evolution. God wants to be manifested by His creation. This requires that we obey Him. We were made in God's image. "Be ye therefore perfect, even as your father which is in heaven is perfect," (Matthew 5:48). The more we embody spiritual ideals, the more God-like and Real we become. The opposite is also true.

We sacrifice ourselves for what we love. If we love God, we sacrifice ourselves to Him. People ask how to fight the New World Order. Nothing would disturb the Illuminati more than a revival of belief in God. Millions willing to fight and die for God would scare the hell out of them. That's why they are uprooting Islam.

CONCLUSION

We are being prepared in consciousness for slavery or destruction. They are laying the groundwork now with the "war on terror." Once they get Islam under control, they will turn to the West in earnest.

In the meantime, the mass media (movies, music and video games, TV) accustoms us to brutality and violence. There is a repetitive and reductive obsession with sex, nudity, bodily functions and homosexuality.

If our leaders weren't Luciferians, the media and the arts would be preoccupied with issues of truth and falsehood, good and evil, beauty and ugliness. We would be uplifted and inspired.

Instead, our souls are fed sawdust. We are degraded, distracted and deceived, like people with a terminal illness, like squatters on someone else's planet.

If the Illuminati's real purpose is to eliminate God, it follows we should make God the centre of our consciousness. People ask, "What should we do?" Don't look for direction from others. Look for direction from God. The best way to fight the darkness is to shine the light.

This is what the Illuminati fears. In the Protocols of the Elders of Zion (5) the author writes: "There is nothing more dangerous to us than personal initiative; if it has genius behind it, such initiative can do more than can be done by millions of people among whom we have sown discord."

Don't feel oppressed by the world. It hasn't changed just because we are now aware of its true nature. Devote each new day to fulfilling God's purpose for you.

The Root Problem:
Illuminati or Jews?

"Henry, the only solution to all these problems is to kill all the Jews."

I got this email last week from Bob in response to my article about bionic women.

"Kill all the Jews and overnight these things will change. I know you'll never make that suggestion, but it's the only solution. The Protocols have come to fruition. Just tell the people to kill the Jews and our problems will be solved. You Henry could become a Marrano and lie like a bastard."

As economic and political conditions worsen, resentment against Jews will grow.

"There is coming a time soon in which we shall have to fight Jews because they are Jews and because we are not," J.B. Campbell proclaimed in "Jewish Rule" posted on Rense.com. " They will leave us with no other choice, just as they left the Russians and the Palestinians and the Hungarians and now the Lebanese with no other choice but fight or die a nasty death after captivity and thirst and starvation and torture."

John Kaminski writes, "The Illuminati is wholly Jewish, started by a Jew turned Catholic, operated by the Jews who control the money. Now used, as a convenient myth by Jewish writers to say the problem is not really Jewish."

Kaminski is referring to me. He has called me a "Zionist mole." The Satanic Jewish cult, the Sabbateans, might be at the the heart of the problem but it has gone way beyond them to embrace the occult world in general.

The epithet "Illuminati mole" could be hurled back. People like Kaminski unwittingly serve the Illuminati agenda by making ordinary Jews the scapegoat. They divert attention from the real source of the problem.

As we shall see, the Illuminati is not "wholly Jewish" by a long shot. Kill every Jew and the problem would remain. (Of course this does not absolve of guilt Jewish Illuminati and their many Jewish dupes/agents i.e. Zionists, Communists, Feminists, Liberals, Socialists, Neo Cohns etc. Nor does it absolve those Jews who refuse to disassociate from organized Jewry.)

I refer Kaminski and his ilk to Fritz Springmeier, an unsung hero of humanity, now an American political prisoner, who has debriefed dozens of Illuminati defectors. The pioneer authority on the Illuminati, he says the problem is a lot bigger than "the Jews". It is anti-religious (as in Satanic) not racial.

"To call the conspiracy Jewish is misleading. The father of it all is Satan. It is Satanic and it will use anyone it can." ("Bloodlines of the Illuminati", p.126)

FRITZ SPRINGMEIER

Humanity owes a debt of gratitude to Fritz Springmeier for exposing the Illuminati and its methods in a half dozen major works.

His definitive works are "Be Wise as Serpents" (1991) and "Bloodlines of the Illuminati" (1999). At the back, he lists hundreds of names of members of the Illuminati organizations like the Pilgrim Society, Bohemia Grove and the Skull and Bones and related fraternities. The names reflect the American establishment yesterday and today. They are not exclusively Jewish.

I'll just list a few: Astor;Ball, Bennett; Bundy; Grace; Hammer; Kennedy; Brady; Acheson; Rockefeller; Dulles; Bedell Smith; Carnegie; Cowles; Dupont; Harriman; Schiff; Roosa; Brzezinski; Kissinger; Forbes; Donovan; Javits; Mellon; Turner; Coffin; Heinz; MacLeish; Stanley; Pinchot; Whitney; Walker; Steadman; Taft...etc.

A similar membership analysis could be made of other Illuminati fronts such as the Bilderbergers, the Council on Foreign Relations, the Trilateral Commission and the Club of Rome.

Yes it is probable that Jewish Sabbateans like the Rothschilds are the mainspring behind the Illuminati but there is no shortage of non-Jews who want a piece of the Satanic action.

Did you know Doonesbury's Gary Trudeau is Skull and Bones? Ned Lamont who tried to upset Joe Lieberman is the great grandson of Thomas Lamont, the Chairman of J.P Morgan, who financed the American Communists. These guys pretend to oppose each other. We get to choose which Satanist we want.

It's frustrating that people like Kaminski can only see the Jews and never the non-Jews. Then they blame all Jews regardless of their guilt and let all the guilty non-Jews off the hook. They seem to need a simple black-and-white solution to the world's problems. They can't face the treason of their own ethnic, national and religious leaders. Easier to despise ordinary Jews than confront the powerful rich. I invite Kaminski et al to read Fritz Springmeier and focus on the guilty, whether Jew or not.

MOVERS AND SHAKERS

For exposing the Illuminati, Fritz Springmeier was framed for a 1997 bank robbery and sentenced to nine years in jail in 2003. They tried to make Springmeier out to be a Ted Kaczynski Unabomber. Read excerpts from this interview with Springmeier to see how intelligent he is and how evil they are.

Who are the Illuminati?

"The Illuminati are the movers and shakers of the world. They are an elite group of bloodlines - I call these tribes or families - there are 13 major bloodlines. They are what are called "generational Satanists." That means that they have practised their secret witchcraft for many centuries and they have passed their religion down from one generation to the next. They lead double lives. They have one life that the world sees and then they have a hidden life that the world doesn't see. There have been very few people that have been able to break through the secrecy."

"The top 13 bloodlines are the Astor, Bundy, Collins, Dupont, Freeman, Kennedy, Li, Onassis, Rockefellers, Rothschild, Reynolds, Krupp, Russell ... then there is a 13th bloodline which is the Merovingian bloodline. I just simple call it the 13th and then there is the Van Duyn Illuminati bloodline. The 13th bloodline, the Merovingian, is extremely important. It includes the royal families of Europe."

What is their goal?

"Ultimately [their goal is] to bring in what people have termed the New World Order with a man who will hold the world's attention and carry the title 'The Antichrist.' That's the ultimate goal and I am not trying to wax religious on people but that's just the simple fact. When you get into deprogramming people you will see that a lot of the things they have been programmed to do tie in with a very sophisticated plan to unify the world under the reign of the Antichrist."

"[Princeton historian] James Billington ("Fire in the Minds of Men") traces how all the revolutions were started by this occult elite. The term revolution came from the occult idea that we were going to revolve ourselves back to the Golden Age. There is this great quest for the Golden Age, this millennialism. That's what communism is about. If you look at the early founders of communism - they were trying to revolve us back through revolution to the Golden Age that had been lost. ...it's always for a socialistic, communistic type utopia, [a cross between] "1984" and "Animal Farm."

Why do they use trauma-based mind control on their own family members?

"It's really essential. If you are going to participate in the Illuminati secret life, being a programmed multiple [personality] is basic. There are a few in the Illuminati who aren't programmed multiples.... You've got a number of standard rituals involved - St. Weinbald, St. Agnes, Grand Climax, Walpurgis, Beltane, all your solstices and equinoxes, Lamas, All Hallow's Eve, High Grand Climax -- all of these standard rituals. These rituals are very horrific. They involved human sacrifice. Sacrifices of babies on the High Grand Climax. On various Sabbats you've got a young female or a male being sacrificed.

This is not something that the normal mind is going to be able to handle. The mind control and the creation of multiple personalities where you get a Dr. Jekyll and Mr. Hyde effect - is very crucial to this thing continuing from generation to generation. They will be trained in alchemy, in Indian sorcery, Druidism, Enochian magik, Gnosticism, Hermetic magik, cabbalism, Plato, Sufism - they will know all the different branches of occult systems."

What is the function of trauma?

"The Illuminati take a small child about two years old, and they begin traumatizing it with the worst traumas that are imaginable so that they can create these amnesia walls. They find these dissociated pieces of the mind that are just like ...floppy disks, often they put in their programming to the dissociated parts of the mind as to what they want that part to become... [Elsewhere he says mind control was behind Josef Mengele's experiments; that Mengele was Illuminati and continued his work in the U.S. after the war.]

The Illuminati can take a particular child and manipulate things from behind the scenes and open all the right doors for this person, and they can get them the grants and the schooling and everything they need and adding impetus to this person's career is the mind control that is steering them in that direction too. The end product is you end up with somebody who is an engineer or a lawyer or a politician who is very highly qualified for what they are doing. Barack Obama fits this description.

A very conservative estimate - I shouldn't even say estimate because I have computed it from about seven different angles - a conservative figure is 2 million Americans have been programmed with trauma based total mind control."

The Ultimate Goal?

"The whole long-range goal of this, and when I say long-range, it's not going to take them long to get us there at the rate they are going - the end goal of all of this is to eventually create an entire planet of mind controlled slaves that can be controlled by one super computer. They are manipulating our thoughts and our attitudes, and steering us, herding us (they consider us animals - the Illuminati consider themselves god, god men and us to be the animals) they are herding us in the direction they want to us to go."

CONCLUSION

Let's not fall into the Illuminati's divide-and-conquer trap. Springmeier says this is "a war against evil not race." He says that, as a virtuoso with an old violin, a "Master's hand can turn anyone into a beautiful thing." He says that many members of Illuminati families have found Christ and broken free. Similarly many Illuminati dupes, whether Jewish or not, can be reached by a message of Truth and Love. We can all be deprogrammed.

Highest Illuminati Defector: "Rothschilds Rule with Druid Witches"

Halloween is an appropriate time to learn that a "Grand Druid Council" of 13 "Witches" control the Illuminati, and meets eight times annually on the "Witches' Sabbaths" (incl. Halloween) when millions of occult practitioners engage in orgies, which sometimes involve human sacrifice.

My source is the highest Illuminati defector in history, a Witch High Priest, a member of the Council of Thirteen, and part of the Collins Illuminati bloodline that brought Witchcraft to the U.S. in the 17th Century.

He casts the Illuminati as a vast, highly organized and powerful occult conspiracy that holds mankind in a Satanic vice.

The Illuminati are "thousands of conspiracies operating in parallel," he says. For example, the vows and initiation rites of witchcraft closely mirror Freemasonry.

His name is John Todd (also Cristopher Kollyns). In 1972, when Todd was "saved," and exposed the Illuminati, he ruled a 13-state U.S. region consisting of 5000 covens, i.e. totalling 65,000 priests and priestesses. That's just the ministers, not the congregation.

This champion of humanity would be unknown today but for a website maintained by "James", an American living in Japan, and another belonging to the redoubtable Wes Penre.

Skeptics say that if the Illuminati were real, there would be defectors. There are plenty of defectors; clinics that deal with CIA mind control and Satanic ritual abuse are full of them.

But the vocal ones get put away. In 1987, Todd was framed for rape and sentenced to 30 years. According to Fritz Springmeier, when Todd was freed in 1994, he was "picked up by a helicopter" and murdered. ("Bloodlines of the Illuminati" p.93)

But James' website has a record of Todd being released from prison in South Carolina in April 2004 and then being re-incarcerated in the "Behavioral Disorder Treatment Unit" of the South Carolina Dept. of Mental Health. Calls to the Director Chad Lominick were not returned. (Could someone find out if Todd is there and still alive? We owe him that at the very least.)

Todd has provided many shocking revelations, which Fritz Springmeier confirms could only come from a man who was in fact a member of the Council of Thirteen.

ILLUMINATI USE JEWS

Speaking in about 1978, Todd said the Illuminati use the Jews as a front.

"The Illuminati knows the people are going to find out about them ...the best thing they can do is call your attention towards something else & say that's that. So they have reflected the attention on Zionism ...The only problem is that most of the people in the Illuminati aren't Jews. Their founders were Jews by birth, but not by religion. But most of its leaders, except for the Rothschilds, are Gaelic: Scotch or French Gaelic. It's got nothing to do with Jews. My family & most of the people serving on the Grand Druid, their family trees go back to the pagan temples in Rome & Greece & England, to the original priesthood. Some go back as far as Egypt & Babylon. It's got nothing to do with the Jews."

[David Livingstone writes: "Elizabeth Hirschmann and Donald Yates in their study, "When Scotland was Jewish", documents the Jewish origin of many of Scotland's leading families, beginning with the Sinclairs and Stuarts, but also the families of Forbes, Bruce, Campbell, Gordon, Caldwell, Fraser, Leslie, Christie, Kennedy, and Cowan (Cohen).]

Todd makes clear the Rothschilds, a family of Sabbatean Jewish Cabalists, top the Illuminati hierarchy:

"The Rothschilds lead the Illuminati and in every country they have a family ...being the head of the Illuminati. In the United States, we have the Rockefellers. David Rockefeller is both the head of the Council of Foreign Relations and the Trilateral [Commission] which is the name of the Illuminati within the United States."

"On the top of each pyramid you will see a capstone with an eye in it. The capstone is the Rothschild Family or Tribunal that rules the Illuminati; they were the creators of it. The eye is Lucifer, their god and their voice. The first 3 top blocks are on every pyramid. The top block is what I was initiated into, the council of 13 called the Grand Druid Council. They only take orders from the Rothschilds and nobody else. They're their private priesthood. The Council of 33 is directly under them, that is the 33 highest Masons in the World. Next is the Council of 500, some of the richest people and conglomerates in the World—[including the Bilderbergs and the families like the Duponts and Kennedys.]

"The Golden Dawn is the organization of witchcraft, the 4th block up there, and it's the Rothschild's private coven. They choose every member personally." He says C.S. Lewis and J.R.R. Tolkein were both members of Golden Dawn. Grand Druid Isaac Bonewitz and the ACLU started an organization to sue Christians who defame the Occult. He includes Scientology and The National Council of Churches in the Illuminati structure.

TODD'S DEFECTION

Todd traces his defection to a meeting that took place around Labour Day 1972. They had received eight letters by diplomatic pouch from London.

"Dr. [Raymond] Buckland cut the seal on it and took out six letters that were sealed with this Illuminati crest. The first four were just business, money that we were to pay here and there and so on. Actually, the Grand Druid Council is nothing but glorified bankers. They write millions of dollars worth of checks to people in political and religious fields every month. But the last two letters led me to want to get out.

"Now even though I was a part of setting up a world government, I always kind of snickered that [this] was ever going to happen, that we were serious, that it was kind of a little game we were playing. As long as the Rothschilds had all of the money to spend on our plans, we went ahead and spent the money. So I never took it seriously until we opened the last two letters.

"Now in the first letter that we opened of those last two, was a chart, and in that chart it listed an eight-year plan for world take-over ending in the December month of 1980. ...Next, the last letter we opened ...said:

"We have found a man whom we believe to be the son of Lucifer. We believe that through his works and our backing he can become ruler of this world, stop all wars, and bring peace, finally, to this war-stricken World." Now that literally meant that we had found a person so fantastically-powered that he could convince people he was their only salvation. Now that literally meant in Christian terms, he was demon-possessed like nobody had ever seen!"

Todd said the take-over plan involved economic breakdown where even Illuminati companies went broke. They have the means to survive such a catastrophe. He says Phillip de Rothschild gave the plan to his mistress Ayn Rand for her novel "Atlas Shrugged." (Interestingly, a movie of this novel starring CFR member Angelina Jolie is in the works.)

Todd says that in the face of economic breakdown, the Illuminati have trained a military force (including prison inmates) to take over the U.S.. This echoes Svali, another Illuminati defector, who has gone into hiding.

He says that, as in the Bolshevik Revolution, millions will be killed in a "helter skelter" rule of terror. Todd says the only thing deterring this plan is widespread gun ownership among the U.S. population.

In the 1980's, he spoke of a plan to reduce the world to rubble in World War Three, to spare only Jerusalem, and rule from there.

FINAL POINTS

As suggested above, Todd says the Illuminati spend a lot of money bribing people, especially Christian evangelists and preachers.

"Much that you see in churches that you just think is liberalism is pay-offism. ...It's kind of hard for a minister ...to turn down half-a-million dollars if it's laid down as a bribe, and they can get even higher. In fact, one church I know of got eight million dollars in two years, and another one got ten million dollars in one year! So, they can receive some money."

Todd says rock and roll music is designed to cast a demonic spell on the listener. I know this sounds farfetched but I urge you to listen to Todd's presentation "Witchcraft of Rock and Roll" on the net. He says the Illuminati started Jesus Rock to control the message. The group, "KISS" stands for "Kings in Satanic Service."

CONCLUSION

Anyone reading Todd's lectures can see he was raised in Satanism as he claimed, and had a profound understanding. Fritz Springmeier said Todd knew things that had taken him (Springmeier) years to grasp.

Todd's message seems too bizarre to be believed. But in the context of the phoney 9-11 attacks, the phoney war on terror, the suspension of Constitutional protections, the erection of a police state, the failure of Congress and the media, the dumbing down and homosexualization of society, the sexualization of children, the explicit Satanism, depravity and pornography in the "entertainment" industry, Todd makes a lot of sense.

Humanity is the victim of a monstrous conspiracy of unspeakable proportions. Our leaders, whom we pay to defend us from this sort of thing, are either dupes or traitors.

Mankind has the intelligence and the means to evolve as intended, but we are being dragged back into an abyss by Evil incarnate. What can we do? You tell me. They need to deceive the masses. Help spread the truth while we still can.

Illuminati Sex Slaves
Paint Horrifying Picture

Two women tortured, brainwashed and prostituted by the Illuminati paint a disturbing picture of how the world is really run. Both say they were prostituted to world leaders as children.

They are Brice Taylor, author of "Thanks for the Memories" (1999) and Cathy O'Brien (with Mark Phillips) author of "Trance-Formation of America" (1995).

These books are consistent and confirm the revelations of Illuminati programmer "Svali" ("Illuminati Defector Details Pervasive Conspiracy" on my website.) If you want to understand the world, you must read these three women.

Essentially every country is run by a shadow government, which owes its loyalty to the New World Order controlled by a 13-member Illuminati Council.

According to Svali, "each ruler represents an area of Europe held under its sway; and each one represents an ancient dynastic bloodline." American leaders are often direct descendants, whether legitimate or illegitimate.

According to Taylor, Henry Kissinger is the CEO for the Illuminati who naturally prefer to remain in the shadows. Our political leaders are chosen for their moral frailties, blackmail-ability, and willingness to advance the Illuminati plan. Strings are pulled and they mysteriously rise to prominence. It doesn't matter which party they belong to. They secretly serve the "Cause."

Many are products of a life that may include pedophilia, drug trafficking and consumption, child pornography, bestiality, mind control, rape, torture, Satanic rituals and human sacrifices. They are given many opportunities to indulge their vices, which ensures continued obedience and solidarity.

Drug trafficking, white slavery, prostitution and pornography finance secret New World Order programs. Elements of the CIA, FBI, Coast Guard, Military, and police are all involved, as is the Mafia.

This information may upset or enrage some people. I could not bring myself to read these books for over two years. The torture and depravity they describe is excruciating. My mental filters would not accept it. Writing about it is difficult.

The public has a child-like trust in its leaders, especially Presidents. The charge that they really belong to a sadistic, criminal, traitorous syndicate is a betrayal beyond belief.

We respond with denial and anger. We don't want to admit that we are dupes and our perception of reality is false. Dumbed down, we are incapable of common sense and concerted action. We refuse to contemplate what they may have in store. Better to ridicule the messenger and change the channel.

These women could have remained silent and found some deserved peace and happiness. Instead they are taking great risks to warn humanity of our danger. Are we going to listen?

SEX ROBOTS

Both Cathy O'Brien and Brice Taylor were victims of the CIA's MK-Ultra mind control program, which is designed to create human robots to serve functions ranging from prostitutes to couriers to killers.

Their families belong to secret Satanic sects that sexually abuse their children generation after generation to produce the trauma which causes multiple personality disorder. In this traumatized condition the mind splinters into many compartments. Victims exhibit extraordinary powers of recollection and endurance and can be easily programmed to do anything.

These cults operate within many organizations including charities, churches, boys/girls clubs, Masonic lodges, daycares and private schools.

Society is being subjected to the same type of trauma-based programming using constant war and atrocities that include Auschwitz, Hiroshima, the Kennedy assassinations, Sept. 11, Abu Ghraib and financial turmoil. We are being collectively desensitized on the one hand, and programmed to focus on sex, violence, trivia and empty social rituals on the other.

Both women were sexually abused as babies. Cathy O'Brien was often given her father's penis instead of a baby bottle. Congressman Gerald Ford, who was involved in drug trafficking and child pornography with the Michigan mob, initiated her into the MK Ultra Program. (No wonder Betty Ford drank.)

O'Brien's father prostituted her as a child to friends, business associates and politicians as a favor, or for money. She also appeared in numerous child pornography and bestiality films. When you read this book you will understand who Jon Benet Ramsay was and why there was no resolution to her murder.

DEPRAVITY

O'Brien (born in 1957) says she serviced an array of politicians including the cocaine snorting Clintons (A Three-Way), Ronald Reagan, George H.W. Bush, Dick Cheney, Pierre Trudeau, Brian Mulroney, Governors Lamar Alexander and Richard Thornburgh, Bill Bennett (author of "The Book of Virtues"), Senators Patrick Leahy, Robert Byrd (her handler) and Arlen Spector. Notable by their absence were Jimmy Carter and Richard Nixon. Taylor (born in 1951) slept with JFK and LBJ as a preteen and teenager.

When O'Brien's daughter Kelly was born in 1980, they often worked as a mother-daughter team. George H.W. Bush particularly liked Kelly. Cheney is not a pederast because his large genitals horrify children. (195)

Referring to George Bush, Dick Cheney told her: "A 'Vice' President is just that, an undercover agent taking control of the drug industry for the President." (158)

George Bush Jr. was present on one occasion but is not accused. (196) O'Brien was rescued by Mark Philips in 1988. It is likely that Bush Jr. is involved in this mind control, drug and sex scene. Rumors swirl around him and his behavior is erratic. Remember the pretzel incident? In 2003, Margie Schroedinger, a Black Texas woman who was suing the President for rape, "committed suicide."

Sen. Robert Byrd, who controls the nation's purse strings, justified to Cathy his involvement in drug distribution, pornography and white slavery as a means of "gaining control of all illegal activity world wide" to fund Black Budget covert activity that would "bring about world peace through world dominance and total control."

He said, "95% of the people want to be led by the 5%." Proof is that "the 95% do not want to know what really goes on in government." Byrd believed that mankind must take a "giant step in evolution through creating a superior race."

Byrd believed in "the annihilation of underprivileged nations and cultures" through genocide and genetic engineering to breed "the more gifted, the blonds of the world." (118)

O'Brien visited a series of secret paramilitary compounds throughout the U.S. like one at Mount Shasta in California. "I learned that this not-so-secret military build-up consisted of special forces trained robotic soldiers, black unmarked helicopters, and top secret weaponry including electromagnetic mind control equipment."

At these compounds O'Brien and her daughter were often hunted like wild animals, tortured and raped for the amusement of CIA, military and politicians.

O'Brien worked as a sex slave at Bohemian Grove, the elite's perversion playground on the Russian River in California. She says the place is wired for video in order to capture world leaders in compromising acts.

"Slaves of advancing age or with failing programming were ritualistically murdered at random in the wooded grounds of Bohemian Grove...There was a room of shackles and tortures, an opium den, ritualistic sex altars, group orgy rooms...I was used as a "rag doll" in the toy store and as a urinal in the "golden arches" room." (169-170)

Strangely, mind controlled sex slaves are used as diplomats and lobbyists as well. At a Governor's Conference, Secretary of Education Bill Bennett advised O'Brien to "persuade these Governors at their weakest moment, bring them to their knees while you are on yours, and convince them that global education [the Education 2000 initiative] is the way to the future if there is to be any future at all." (173)

CONCLUDING REMARKS

Why did the Illuminati let these women live? I don't know. I don't know how many they have killed. Perhaps they want the truth to be known gradually. Perhaps they have a shred of decency left. Perhaps they are confident of their power, and think these women won't be believed.

As the Kennedy assassination and 9-11 prove, the United States (and most countries) have been totally subverted by a Luciferian international criminal elite. The role of politicians, media and education is to keep the sheep deluded and distracted while the elite stealthily advances its goal of world tyranny. Western society today is a massive fraud.

It is tragic that brave young American soldiers have been brainwashed to believe they are advancing freedom when the opposite is the case. A reader tells me that this article is treason. Is it patriotic to obey traitors?

The populations of the West are spoiled, self centred and complacent. How can things be so bad when we have so much? We don't realize that the goodies can be taken away in a second by tightening credit.

We don't realize that we are being distracted while our political and social institutions, our bulwarks against tyranny, are being infiltrated and dismantled. Our children are being brainwashed.

Don't ask, "What can we do?" That is conditioned helplessness. Figure it out yourself. Take responsibility. There is no quick fix to this mess. But we must stand up for truth. They may have the weapons of mass deception, but, as Cathy O'Brien says, "the truth doesn't go away."

An Illuminati Primer

Politics has banished Religion from public discourse but Religion still offers the best description of political reality.

The essence of political struggle is actually spiritual, a cosmic battle between God (Good) and Satan (Evil) for the soul of man.

The struggle is between an international financial elite dedicated to Satan led by the Illuminati, and the remnants of humanity that still uphold God's Plan. The unsuspecting masses inhabit a fool's paradise like children.

This struggle is not between nations, religions or between ideologies of Left or Right. This occult elite creates and controls both sides of every conflict in order to obscure and at the same time advance its long-term agenda.

The elite plan is to remake the planet as its private neo feudal preserve. This involves the reduction of the world's population through plague, catastrophe or war; mind control/breeding of the survivors as serfs; and the elevation of Lucifer as god.

A cataclysm could happen within the next 10-20 years. We're living on borrowed time, duped by the media and distracted by sex while the elite tests and imposes various methods of manipulation and control.

Thousands of organizations like the UN promote the elite's "world government" agenda with practically no public scrutiny. More recently, the elite instigated the Sept. 11 attacks in order to justify their "war on terror" the repressive "Patriot Act", and Iraq War. The flooding of New Orleans, vaccinations and the bird flu epidemic, power black-outs are other tests or possible harbingers. They established a seed bank on a remote Norwegian island in case of nuclear war.

Sophisticated and dedicated people roll their eyes when told about this conspiracy. They are hypnotized by their "education" and the mass media.

The "Illuminati" sounds fantastic but it is NOT a chimera. Hidden within Freemasonry, it is the Church of Satan. Its membership was known; its premises were raided. Plans and correspondence were seized and published. At formal inquiries, defectors testified to the grave danger. It was suppressed but went underground. It has since grown so powerful that it has literally defined the modern age (under the guise of "progress," "reform" and "revolution") and now threatens the future of humanity.

THE ORIGIN OF MODERN DYSFUNCTION

The term "Illuminati" means "enlightened ones" and refers to Lucifer, the "light bringer." Its essential philosophy is to substitute "reason" (i.e. expedience) for what was called "right reason" (i.e. universal morality.)

"Do as thou wilt" (i.e. "tolerance") was the Freemason-Illuminati motto. The Illuminati will define reality, not God or nature. Illuminism or "humanism" is a secular religion and a transition to Satanism. The decline of public decency makes this increasingly apparent. Look for the world to increasingly resemble the game "Grand Theft Auto" or a Hollywood horror or disaster movie.

Whether it's a plant, a dog or a child, given a little nourishment and love, each will flourish according to an innate design. The Illuminati wishes to unplug us from this inherent design by promoting dysfunction in such guises as "sexual liberation' and "equality."

In 1770, Mayer Rothschild hired the 22-year-old Adam Weishaupt, a university instructor (son of a rabbi raised as a Catholic) to attract the cream of European society to a secret cult designed to reverse the course of Western (i.e. Christian) civilization.

I am referencing "Final Warning" an online book by David Allen Rivera and James Wardner's excellent book "Unholy Alliances." (pp.34-51)

The Illuminati was founded May 1, 1776. Weishaupt wrote: "The great strength of our Order lies in its concealment, let it never appear, in any place in its own name, but always covered by another name, and another occupation. None is fitter than the three lower degrees of Freemasonry; the public is accustomed to it, expects little from it, and therefore takes little notice of it."

An understanding was reached with the Masons at the Congress of Wilhelmsbad on December 20, 1781 to add the Illuminati hierarchy to the first three degrees of Masonry. On returning home, Comte de Virieu, a Mason from the Martiniste lodge at Lyons, reported: "I can only tell you that all this is very much more serious than you think. The conspiracy which is being woven is so well thought out that it will be impossible for the Monarchy and the Church to escape it."

Nesta Webster in her book "World Revolution" describes the modus operandi of the Illuminati. It applies to Adolph Hitler as well as Timothy Leary: "The art of Illuminism lay in enlisting dupes as well as adepts, and by encouraging the dreams of honest visionaries or the schemes of fanatics, by flattering the vanity of ambitious egotists, by working on unbalanced brains, or by playing on such passions as greed and power, to make men of totally divergent aims serve the secret purpose of the sect."

The Illuminati also used bribes of money and sex to gain control of men in high places, and then blackmailed them with the threat of financial ruin, public exposure or assassination. This continues to the present day.

Weishaupt wrote: "One must speak sometimes in one way, sometimes in another, so that our real purpose should remain impenetrable to our inferiors." And what was that purpose? It was "nothing less than to win power and riches, to undermine secular or religious government, and to obtain the mastery of the world."

The first priority was to enlist writers, publishers and educators. The modern pantheon of great thinkers, from Darwin to Nietzsche to Marx, were Illuminati pawns or agents. Of one university, Weishaupt wrote: "All the professors are members of the Illuminati...so will all the pupils become disciples of Illuminism." (Wardner, 45)

As the Order spread throughout Germany, money was contributed from such leading Jewish families as the Oppenheimers, Wertheimers, Schusters, Speyers, Sterns and of course, the Rothschilds. Gerald B. Winrod wrote in his book "Adam Weishaupt: A Human Devil "of the thirty-nine chief sub-leaders of Weishaupt, seventeen were Jews."

From Bavaria, the Order of the Illuminati spread like wildfire... Soon they had over 300 members from all walks of life, including students, merchants, doctors, lawyers, judges, professors, civil officers, bankers, and even church ministers. Some of their more notable members were: the Duke of Orleans, Duke Ernst Augustus of Saxe-Weimar-Coburg-Gotha, Prince Charles of Hesse-Cassel, Johann Gottfried von Herder (a philosopher), Count Klemens von Metternich, Catherine II of Russia, Count Gabriel de Mirabeau, Marquis of Constanza ("Diomedes"), Duke Ferdinand of Brunswick ("Aaron"), Duke Karl August of Saxe-Weimar, Johann Wolfgang von Goethe (a poet), Joseph II of Russia, Christian VII of Denmark, Gustave III of Sweden, and King Poniatowski of Poland.

By the time of the 3rd Masonic Congress in Frankfurt in 1786, the Illuminati virtually controlled all the Masonic lodges, which represented three million secret society members across the various German provinces, Austria, Hungary, England, Scotland, Poland, France, Belgium, Switzerland, Italy, Holland, Spain, Sweden, Russia, Ireland, Africa, and America. (Wardner, p. 39)

In the 1790's there was an Illuminati scare in the United States. At Charlestown, in 1798, the Reverend Jedediah Morse preached: "Practically all the civil and ecclesiastical establishments of Europe have already been shaken to their foundations by this terrible organization, the French Revolution itself is doubtless to be traced to its machinations..." (Wardner 48)

In 1832 William Russell established a chapter of the Illuminati at Yale called the "Skull and Bones." President G.W. Bush, his father and John Kerry are members.

On Sept. 9, 1785, Joseph Utzschneider, a lawyer, and two other defectors revealed the Illuminati goals before a Court of Inquiry in Bavaria: Abolition of the Monarchy and all ordered government; Abolition of private property (which the Illuminati will assume); Abolition of Patriotism (nations); Family, (through the abolition of Marriage, Morality, and by government providing "Education" for children) and finally, Abolition of all Religion, particularly Christianity.

These are exactly the goals of Communism, enunciated by Marx in 1848. The Illuminati and Communism go hand-in-glove. The term "Reds" originates with "Red Shield" the Rothschild name.

In 1794 the Duke of Brunswick, issued a Manifesto based on confiscated Illuminati documents. He said, "The ferment that reigns among the people is their work....They began by casting odium on religion..They invented the rights of man ...and urged the people to wrest from their princes the recognition of these supposed rights. The plan they formed for breaking all social ties and destroying all order was revealed in their speeches and acts. They deluged the world with a multitude of publications; they recruited apprenticeships of every rank and every position; they deluded the most perspicacious men by falsely alleging different intentions." ("Light-bearers of Darkness," p.10)

CONCLUSION

Mankind has taken a wrong turn and appears doomed. The political, cultural and economic elite are either dupes or willing agents of a Satanic conspiracy of cosmic proportions.

If we and our children are to suffer and die prematurely, at least we will know the real reason. That is a privilege not granted to millions of our ancestors.

God and Satan made a wager for the soul of man. If God wins, man revels in the glory of his Divine Birthright. If Satan wins, man is destroyed. In a nutshell, this is the religious nature of politics.

Humanity is Under Occult Attack

As you know, the financial elite attaches great importance to providing us with an external enemy: Huns, Nazis, Communists, Muslim Terrorists etc. It also creates internal enemies by dividing us on race, sex and class. Then it dreams up economic, social and natural enemies like the war on poverty, drugs and global warming.

Thus, it diverts attention from itself, the real enemy, the Illuminati organized in Freemasonry, an international Satanic cult which controls our political, cultural and economic life with magical acumen.

Their smug victory symbols are everywhere: on the U.S. Great Seal and the logos of countless corporations, the UN and even the city where I live, Winnipeg. Look for dots in circles, pyramids without capstones, eyes of horuses and swooshes denoting sunrises.

All politicians who stand a chance are Masons including Bush, Obama, Clinton and McCain. They don't pose serious opposition. Bush has doubled the national debt and cut the value of the U.S. dollar in half but did you hear him criticized for this? On his watch we had, 9-11, the Iraq War, Hurricane Katrina (levees blown) and the mortgage meltdown. No one was held responsible.

On the international front, Obama and Ahmadinejad, Sarkozy, Merkel and Putin, Bush and McCain are all members of this club despite pretend disputes. They work for the international banking cartel, aided by a small army of dupes and opportunists. None of this would be possible if they didn't also own the mass media.

Our political life essentially is theatre. The author of the "Protocols of Zion" chortles: "Who will ever suspect then that all these peoples were stage-managed by us according to a political plan which no one has so much as guessed at in the course of many centuries?" (Protocol 13)

As early as 1823, Hoene Wronski wrote: "Secret societies are detached into groups distinct and apparently opposed, professing ... the most contrary opinions of the day, so as to direct, apart and with confidence, all parties, political, religious, economic, and literary. They, in order to receive common direction, are again united to an unknown centre...an Unknown Supreme Committee who governs the world." ("Light-bearers of Darkness," p.2)

World government, "the New World Order" is the goal of Freemasonry. Order is created out of chaos. It will be achieved by a "dialectical process" of phoney wars caused by false flag operations, brainwashing ("sensitivity training") propaganda, slander and coercion.

According to Jyri Lina's book "Architects of Deception," Freemasonry is Judaism for gentiles. It is based on the Cabala and is "the executive political organ of the Jewish financial elite." (See "Freemasonry: Mankind's Deathwish" on my site.)

Masonic Jews run it. Apparently, Jews belong to all lodges but non-Jews can't belong to Jewish ones like the B'nai Brith. These comprise the Executive Branch.

We are witnessing the culmination of a millennium-long crusade by certain Pharisaic Jews and their allies to overthrow Christian civilization and establish a primitive tyranny outlined in detail in "The Protocols of Zion."

EXTENSION OF FINANCIAL MONOPOLY

Juri Lina cites Professor Valeri Yemelyanov who told a Soviet Communist Party Congress in 1979: "the Jewish Freemason pyramid controls 80% of the economy of the capitalist countries and 90-95 per cent of the information media." (163)

In 1938, an insider Christian Rakovsky (Chaim Rakover) described the situation as follows:

"In Moscow there is Communism: in New York capitalism. It is all the same as thesis and antithesis. Analyze both. Moscow is subjective Communism but [objectively] State capitalism. New York: Capitalism subjective, but Communism objective. A personal synthesis, truth: the Financial International, the Capitalist Communist one. 'They.' " "They" refers to the "Illuminati" the highest rung of Freemasonry.

On 19th Nov. 1937 the influential Fabian Nicholas Murray Butler addressed a banquet in London with the words, "Communism is the instrument with which the financial world can topple national governments and then erect a world government with a world police and world money."

Rakovsky says the real aim of Freemasonry is to bring about Communism. Communism (i.e. the NWO) involves the destruction of the four pillars of our human identity: race, religion, nation and family. This is the real meaning of "diversity," "multiculturalism," "feminism," porn, "sexual liberation" and "gay rights." (See "Rothschilds Conduct Red Symphony" on my web site or in "Cruel Hoax.")

The pagan Masonic spell is cast with an amazing consistency and conformity through the mass media and education systems. For example, lately you cannot escape images of powerful women in male roles and exhortations to women in traditional societies to seek independence.

In 1909, Paul Copin Albancelli wrote: "Masons repeat what they have heard from the preachers of the Occult Powers: the journalist ..the publisher..the pornographer...the professor...The state of mind created and filled in the lodges.. is the profane medium met everywhere and the mind is altered by it. And as Freemasons perform this duty as propagandists without revealing themselves as Masons, the activity which they exert is not recognized as Masonic." ("The Jewish Conspiracy Against the Christian World" pp.173-174)

DISCERNMENT

Freemasonry shows a false face to the world. Lina writes that Freemasonry "is closely associated with socialism and communism, as well as with organized crime. The primary task of Freemasonry is to combat knowledge of the real world and to ignore the facts from true history." (281)

Exoteric Freemasonry is for the rubes. It is about charity and "making good men better," etc. The real Freemasonry, the esoteric (or occult) known only to adepts, is about conquering the world for Lucifer.

Thus, we always must discern between the formal and the informal, the subjective and the objective.

Formally, we live in a free society. Informally our "leaders" are dupes or traitors dedicated to our ultimate enslavement.

Formally, we have a free press and education system. Informally, only those views that correspond to the occult (Masonic, "enlightenment") agenda get a hearing.

Formally, art and entertainment are free expressions. Informally, with a few exceptions, only entertainment that advances the occult program will be encouraged. Countless movies fall under the category of predictive programming - teaching people to expect Satanic scenarios and horrifying catastrophes.

Formally, Muslim terrorists flew planes into the symbols of American freedom and prosperity on Sept. 11, causing them to collapse killing over 3000 people. Informally the instruments of the Masonic financial elite—intelligence agencies, secret societies-- detonated the buildings to justify gutting civil rights and starting gratuitous wars and a $5 trillion boondoggle.

Formally, elections express the peoples' will and desire for change. Informally, elections are required to maintain the illusion of freedom and secure the taxes and bodies needed for endless wars.

Formally, they believe in our country. Informally, they are doing everything to undermine it so the population will accept world government.

Formally, they are Christians. Barack Obama is a Christian. Informally, Luciferianism (Freemasonry, Cabalist Judaism, secularism) is the religion of the post-Enlightenment West. George Bush and Barack Obama are Satanists who proudly uses the horned goat symbol. By professing Christianity, they discredit it.

CONCLUSION

Right now, I'd say the most revealing book on our predicament is Jyri Lina's "Architects of Deception." I reviewed it once but I commend it to you again. Here's another example of the revelations it contains: "Most of George Washington's generals and the signatories of the Declaration of Independence were Masons. The values of the Declaration are valid but they fall under the category of the "formal."

Informally, Lina says: "The freemasons created the United States of America as an effective base for their world-encompassing activities and to attain their utmost aim - world supremacy."

Our lives are built on a monstrous fraud. Our political and cultural leaders are chosen by their willingness to betray us for fame and fortune. Humanity has passed into a Twilight Zone between reality and an occult spell. Our only hope is for the "formal" to trump the "informal," and for the dupes to wake up before it is too late.

The Satanic Cult
that Rules the World

"How can one chase a thousand, and two put ten thousand to flight unless...God had delivered them into enemy hands?" Deuteronomy 32:30

"Either convert to Islam or die." This was the choice the Turkish Sultan put to Sabbatai Zvi, self-proclaimed Jewish "Messiah" in 1666.

By pretending to convert, Zvi resorted to a common practice among Jews. But Zvi was not an ordinary Jew. He led a popular heresy, based on a Satanic strain of the Cabala. The rabbis had denounced him and his followers.

After his "conversion," over a million followers, who later included financiers like the Rothschilds, imitated his example. But they didn't just pretend to be Muslims or Christians. They pretended to be Jews as well. They were the forebears of the Illuminati and Communism.

Communist defector Bella Dodd revealed that during the 1930's the Communist Party had 1100 members join the Catholic Priesthood. They became Bishops, Cardinals and Popes.

By adopting this chameleon strategy, this Satanic cult infiltrated and subverted most governments and religions, and established an invisible tyranny without drawing much attention. In the words of the gifted Jewish researcher Clifford Shack:

"Through infiltration, stealth and cunning, this invisible network has come to rule us all. Forty-one years after Shabbatai Zevi's death, in 1717, they would infiltrate Masonry guilds in England and establish Freemasonry.... [Zevi's successor] Jacob Frank would have a great impact on the inner core of Freemasonry known as the Illuminati, formed in 1776. Freemasonry would become the hidden force behind events like the [American, French and Russian] revolutions, the creations of the U.N. & Israel, both World Wars (including the Holocaust!), and the assassinations of the Kennedy brothers who, together with their father, tried to thwart the efforts of the network on American soil.

Sabbatean/Frankists, also referred to as the "Cult of the All-Seeing Eye" (look at your one dollar bill to begin to understand their influence in YOUR life) are political and religious chameleons. They are everywhere...there is power. They are the good guys AND the bad guys. The World War Two era is a prime example. The following leaders were members of the "Cult of the All-Seeing Eye" (Sabbatean/Frankists): Franklin D. Roosevelt; Winston Churchill; Adolph Hitler; Eugenio Pacelli (Pope Pius XII); Francisco Franco; Benito Mussolini; Hirohito and Mao Tse-Tung."

IMPLICATIONS

If Mr. Shack is correct, historians, educators and journalists collaborate by upholding a false reality and distracting us from the truth. Our world, our perception of the human experience, are shaped by an occult secret society. Our culture is an elaborate psy-op.

Obviously, the Sabbateans and their descendants should consume our attention. Instead, they are hidden from view. They were decisive in the so-called "Enlightenment," "secularism" and "modernism," which are but baby steps to their Satanism.

According to Rabbi Marvin Antelman, they believe sin is holy and should be practised for its own sake. Since the Messiah will come when people either become righteous or totally corrupt, the Sabbateans opted for debauchery: "Since we cannot all be saints, let us all be sinners."

Their blasphemous benediction "who permits the forbidden" later became the Illuminist "do as thou wilt" the expression of their "religious" feeling. Totally amoral, they believe the "end justifies the means." ("To Eliminate the Opiate,"Vol. 2 p. 87)

In 1756, Jacob Frank and his followers were excommunicated by the rabbis. Antelman says the Sabbateans were behind the Liberal and Revolutionary movements of the Nineteenth century. They were also behind the Reform and Conservative movements in Judaism, including the "Haskalah" i.e. Jewish assimilation. In other words, Jews have been influenced by the Sabbateans "to blend in" and don't even know it.

That is their tactic. They don't advocate a Satanic kingdom on earth. They gently steer you that way by questioning the existence of God, by demanding "sexual liberation," "independence" for women, "internationalism," "diversity" and "religious tolerance." These all have a hidden agenda: to corrupt and to undermine "all collective forces except our own" (i.e race, religion, nation and family.)

SEXUAL EXCESS AS A RELIGION

We are told "free sex" is "progressive and modern." In fact, the Sabbatean sect has indulged in wife sharing, sex orgies, adultery and incest for more than 350 years. They also promoted interracial sex. They have inducted many of us into their cult.

Antelman cites the proceedings of a rabbinical court where Shmuel, son of Shlomo tearfully confessed he had rejected the Torah and had encouraged his wife to have sex several times with Hershel. "I am guilty. She did not want to." (111)

Sexual abandon is characteristic of Communism, a direct outgrowth of Sabbateanism. Jacob Frank pimped his beautiful wife to recruit influential men. Female members of the Communist Party were used in the same way. Adam Weiskaupt, the founder of the Illuminati, got his sister-in-law pregnant.

A pertinent anecdote: In his book, "The Other Side of Deception," Mossad defector Victor Ostrovsky described how the Mossad relax. At a party, the staff, including many unmarried young females, congregated around a pool, totally naked.

THE "HOLOCAUST"

The influence of the Sabbatean conspiracy is hidden in plain sight. For example, the term "holocaust" is used without regard to its true meaning. Rabbi Antelman states that well before World War Two, the term meant "burnt offering" as in sacrifice. (p.199)

He quotes Bruno Bettelheim who says "calling the most callous, most brutal, most horrid, most heinous mass murder a 'burnt offering' is a sacrilege, a profanation of God and man." (205)

Whose sacrifice was it? For what purpose? Obviously, it has something to do with the Sabbateans' occult practice. Every time we use that word, we unwittingly join in their sacrilege.

According to Antelman, the Sabbateans hated Jews and sought their extinction. He cites rabbis who warned as far back as 1750 that if the Jews didn't stop the Sabbateans, they would be destroyed by them. (209)

And indeed when some Jews tried to save European Jewry from genocide, Antelman says "the conservative and reform communities [in the U.S.] went their merry way ignoring these activities. So called establishment organizations like the American Jewish Congress, American Jewish Committee, and B'nai Brith did virtually nothing." (217)

Sabbateans only marry within their demonic sect. They often marry rich, influential gentiles. Thus, the current Fourth Baron Rothschild (Jacob's) mother was not Jewish nor is his wife.

Another example is Al Gore's daughter Karenna's 1997 marriage to Andrew Schiff, the great, grandson of Jacob Schiff. Gore's father was a Senator sponsored by Armand Hammer (Occidental Petroleum) whose own father was the founder of the American Communist party. Like the Clintons, Dubya and Obama, Al Gore is another Illuminati agent.

CONCLUSION

Mankind is in the grip of a vicious Satanic cult whose guile and power are so great, they can make their war against humanity seem normal and inevitable. Even when their plot is exposed, they can convince everyone that it is racist and in bad taste to believe it. They have men fixated on porn while they erect a police state.

Western society is morally bankrupt. This elaborate cult network controls politics, information and culture. Most leaders are dupes or traitors. The "Intelligentsia" has been bribed while the public is distracted and lives in ignorance.

Like most nations and religions, Jews have been subverted from within. Zionists are pawns of the Sabbateans who used the "holocaust" to engineer the creation of Israel. Millions of Jews been "sacrificed" to create a capital for the Sabbatean New World Order.

Why Do the Illuminati Hate Jews?

"Where the rubber meets the road, the Illuminati have an absolutely Satanic hatred for Jews," a contact that did business with a prominent Illuminati family notified me.

"Jew-hatred spiritually energizes them," he continued. "I read too much out there that falls for the lie that the conspiracy is Jewish at its highest levels. Granted, it appears that way, and a lot of data is hard to argue with, but I have first-hand knowledge of the depth of Jew-hatred among people who are the real thing. These people (at least the ones I knew) are not Zionist Bankers, but totally gentile."

To all appearances Jews have a disproportionate role in the Illuminati New World Order. How do we account for this apparent contradiction?

Following the research of Rabbi Marvin Antelman, Barry Chamish has exposed the heresies of Sabbatai Zvi and Jacob Frank that created a schism in European Jewry in 17th and 18th century respectively. This was essentially a Satanic movement that turned Jewish teaching on its ear. Everything that was forbidden by God was now permitted. Sin and not righteousness was the way to salvation. Sexual depravity (especially wife swapping orgies) was encouraged as a means to destroy the family and the social fabric. They wanted a clean slate on which to redesign society. These are the roots of Freudianism and sexual liberation.

A fierce hatred developed between Satanic Jews and the rabbis who tried to expel the heretics from the community. This schism was partially reflected in the divide between western Jews who shed their religion for "secular humanism and reason" and eastern Jews ("Ostjuden") who largely remained Orthodox. Many secular Jews became radicals as they tried to replace religion with belief in a worldly utopia. The Illuminati duped them with their fraudulent Communist/Socialist dream. "Change the world" was and is their deceptive motto. It survives in Barrack Obama's "Change."

Sabbatai Zvi's successor Jacob Frank (1726-91) formed an alliance with the Rothschilds, the power behind the Illuminati. They started the Reform and Conservative schools of Judaism, which posed as "liberation from the confines of Jewish inner law and ghetto." They encouraged Jews to assimilate, inter-marry, change their names and even convert to Christianity. They tapped selected followers to advance their Satanic agenda by subverting Christian civilization from within.

Sen. John Kerry's background fits this profile perfectly. His grandfather was a Frankest Jew "Kohn" who adopted an Irish name and converted to Catholicism. His father worked for the CIA. His mother was part of the Forbes family, which made its fortune in the drug trade (opium), like many of America's "first families." Kerry himself is a member of the Illuminati "Skull and Bones."

During the last election, Wesley Clark discovered he was half-Jewish. Madeleine Albright admitted she was Jewish. Her father Josef Korbel was Condoleezza Rice's mentor at Denver University. Before that he was accused of stealing art treasures from a prominent Czech family when he was a Communist official in the post-war period.

The picture that emerges is a conspiracy of Jews, gentiles, part Jews and hidden Jews united by allegiance to a Satanic world dictatorship. Winston Churchill, whose mother was Jewish and the current Baron Jacob Rothschild, whose mother was not Jewish, fit this description.

There is a surprising list of American Presidents who are suspected of being part-Jewish including Abraham Lincoln, Teddy Roosevelt, FDR, Eisenhower, and Lyndon Johnson.

It is possible that members of the Nazi hierarchy were also part-Jewish. Hitler's grandmother left the Rothschild's employment in Vienna when she became pregnant with Hitler's father. In his 1964 book "Before Hitler Came" author Dietrich Bronder, a Jew himself, claims the following personages all had Jewish blood: Hesse, Goering, Strasser, Goebbels, Rosenberg, Frank, Himmler, von Ribbentrop, Heydrich and many more. (Kardel, Hitler Founder of Israel p.4) In the 1930's the Jewish German intermarriage rate was 60% and this must have gone on for some time. There were far more mixed Jews than 'pure' ones and 150,000 "mischlings" served in the Nazi army.

Svali suggests a reason why the Illuminati hate religious Jews: "The Jews historically fought against the occult. See Deuteronomy and the Old Testament for how God through the Jewish people tried to cleanse the land of the occult groups that were operating there, such as those who worshipped Baal, Ashtarte, and other Canaanite and Babylonian gods."

It's time Jews rediscovered this heritage and took up this mandate again.

In conclusion, a Satanic heresy has corrupted Judaism. These Satanists are part of the Illuminati and hate other Jews, possibly because Jews were supposed to represent a moral God. Or maybe just because they are rubes.

The long-term goal of the Illuminati is to divert mankind from its Divine purpose and subjugate it using sophisticated means of mind control (ie. mass media, "education," "sexual liberation," migration, diversity etc..) Humanity is being remade in the Illuminati laboratory.

What Every Jew (and Non-Jew) Should Know

A Chicago-area scholar, Christopher Jon Bjerknes, 42, thinks he knows what plagues mankind and believes this knowledge is necessary to stop Armageddon.

He says a heretical cult, the "Sabbatean Frankists," controls organized Jewry, including Zionism and Freemasonry. They began as followers of Shabatai Zvi (1626-1676) and later Jacob Frank (1726-1791.) They believe Shabatai was the Messiah (God) and his soul has transmigrated down to the Rothschild dynasty, who are now "king of the Jews."

According to their messianic system, Redemption requires that the Rothschilds become God, i.e. king of the world. This will see the sacrifice of 2/3 of all Jews and the destruction and enslavement of the rest of mankind. Bjerknes believes this demented creed actually is the motive force behind history, including all wars, and "world government."

Bjerknes (B-YERK-NES) is proud of his Norwegian Jewish heritage, (maternal grandfather, a famous musician, was Jewish.) He has written two massive books-- one about Albert Einstein as a plagiarist, and another about the Sabbatean inspired Armenian Genocide -- that include hundreds of pages of suppressed Jewish history. They can be found as PDFs at his web site http://www.jewishracism.com/

Bjerknes' message is compelling and consistent with the "Protocols of Zion" where the author talks about coming into his "kingdom."

The Sabbateans believe their king is duty bound to restore the Jews to Israel and exterminate the gentiles. They believe the Messiah won't appear until the world succumbs to evil and are determined to make this prophecy self-fulfilling. Thus evil is good in their Satanic view. In Bjerknes' view, this constitutes a "Jewish war against humanity." When Bjerknes refers to Jewish, he means "Sabbatean."

The Sabbateans are often sexual degenerates who engage in wife swapping, orgies and incest. They often pretend to be Christians or Moslems to worm their way into gentile society in order to destroy it. ("The Jewish Genocide of Armenian Christians," pp.64-65.)

Bjerknes cites Deuteronomy as an example of this Jewish supremacism: "the LORD thy God hath chosen thee to be a special people unto himself, above all people that are upon the face of the earth. " (7-16) "And all people of the earth shall see that thou art called by the name of the LORD; and they shall be afraid of you." (28:10)

He points to Zachariah [13;8-9] as evidence that Jews will be slaughtered: "And it shall come to pass, that in all the land, saith the LORD, two parts therein shall be cut off and die; but the third shall be left therein."

"And I will bring the third part through the fire, and will refine them as silver is refined, and will try them as gold is tried: they shall call on my name, and I will hear them: I will say, It is my people: and they shall say, The LORD is my God." (He also cites Ezekiel 5:12-13 to this effect.)

On pp. 43-46 of "Jewish Genocide", Bjerknes cites references from the Talmud and the Old Testament to the plan to exterminate and enslave gentiles.

For example, Genesis 25;23, and 27;38-41 promises the gentiles to the Jews as their slaves and slave soldiers, and gives an incentive to exterminate the gentiles simply because they dare resent their fate.

ROTHSCHILDS FOLLOW BIBLICAL BLUEPRINT

At the beginning of the 19th century, the Rothschilds started campaigning to return the Jews to Israel, purchasing land there and scheming to breakup the Ottoman Empire. They later bought the Suez Canal to project their power into the Middle East. Bjerknes writes:

"The ruin of the Turkish Empire and the mass murder of the Armenian Christians were one step on the long and tumultuous Jewish march toward the death of mankind. The ruin of the Russian empire was another, followed by the repeated destruction of Europe, particularly Germany, in the World Wars this Jewish cult created in an attempt to artificially fulfill Messianic prophecy and force the Jews of Europe against their will to flee to Palestine." (66)

According to Bjerknes, Jewish support was the only thing lacking in the Rothschilds' plan to establish a world government in Jerusalem, with them as king:

"They could bankrupt Egypt and Turkey. They could bring Russia to ruins. They could buy Jewish ne'er-do-wells. They could even buy the Pope but the only way to force Jews in large numbers to Palestine was to put Hitler and Stalin in power and persecute Jews on a massive and unprecedented scale." (291)

CHRISTIANS ARE BEING DUPED

Bjerknes has a poignant warning to Christians:

"In the Jewish dominated media of today, we find many Jews preaching to the public that the End Times are coming and that Christians ought to view their own destruction in a positive light as if it were the divine fulfillment of Christian and Jewish prophecy. Many Christians have been duped by these charlatans...the destruction of the world and its nations is occurring as the result of the deliberate intervention of immensely wealthy Jews and not as the result of God's will. These Jewish leaders view the Hebrew Bible as a plan, which they are deliberately fulfilling.... (327)

As my readers know, I see the New World Order as an elite conspiracy driven primarily by the central bankers' desire to consolidate their monopoly on credit and power. I believe there is a strong "Jewish" element but Illuminati Jews are as contemptuous of some of their "lesser brethren" as they are of non-Jews. Rather they have co-opted gentile elites (who are more powerful and useful) using intermarriage, Freemasonry, and Aryanism. Look at the gentile membership of the Illuminati Skull and Bones for example. Bjerknes doesn't think the Illuminati is still in business and downplays the gentile role. In my view, this is a blind spot.

In an e-mail, Bjerknes replies that intermarriage is part of the "Jewish" strategy:

"I believe that powerful Jewish interests have been deliberately attempting to fulfill Jewish messianic prophecy for 2,500 years and have duped many gentiles into helping them obtain their objectives. They have also recruited many gentiles through intermarriage, friendship and selfish interests, who are not dupes, but commit inhuman acts out of greed, vanity, or for other immoral reasons. Do they believe that what they are doing is evil? I suspect some do.

I am not opposed to identifying secret societies and the ties among the elite. I simply do not see any justification for calling them Illuminati. As for the overall path of politics and the faces of those who are pushing the cart toward WW III, I think I and countless others have proven that it is a Jewish movement, and that the Illuminati were nothing but a small part of this Jewish movement to gin up an apocalypse, which dates back at least 2,500 years. Of course not everything happening today has a Jewish hand steering its course. But I do believe that powerful Jewish interests ...have the ability to exert more influence than all other groups combined, for the very reason that they have infiltrated so many organizations, religions and governments, and have such disproportionate influence in the media."

CONCLUSION

I wouldn't be presenting this material if I didn't think it important to examine Jewish messianism. If world events indeed are driven by the Rothschilds' megalomania propped up by Sabbatean, Cabalistic, Old Testament and Talmudic fanaticism, I think Jews and non-Jews alike would want to know, and take exception.

Independent Historian Unveils Cabala Conspiracy

David Livingstone, 41, author of "Terrorism and the Illuminati- A Three Thousand Year History" (2007) says Cabalists determined to be God have hijacked mankind.

"The Cabala states that God created man to know Himself," says Livingstone. "Cabalists take this to mean they can usurp the role of God. They don't have to meet an absolute moral standard first."

Livingstone says that all occult movements originate in the Cabala (which dates to 6th century B.C. Babylon.) Cabalism does not uphold the universal moral standards enunciated by Moses. (This is the Judaism I identify with.)

Livingstone maintains that most Illuminati bloodlines, including European royalty, are heretical Jews, crypto Jews and wannabe Jews. ("Crypto Jews" are Jews who pretend they are Christians, Muslims or from other religious or ethnic backgrounds.)

In his book, Livingstone traces the genealogies of these Khazar bloodlines, which include the Rothschilds, the Hapsburgs, the Sinclairs, the Stuarts, the Merovingians, the Lusignans, and the Windsors.

"The great secret of history is this story of the ascent of heretical Cabalists to world power," says Livingstone. "Ordinary Jews and people in general have no idea how they are being manipulated."

"These Cabalists believe Lucifer is the true God. They care nothing for their own nations. Their whole aim in life is to humiliate and degrade mankind, and prove to God that the human experiment is a failure. They are gradually achieving this goal through their control of the economy, education, media and government."

PERSONAL

David Livingstone was born in Montreal in 1966 of a Jamaican-Canadian father (a school teacher) and French Canadian mother. At age seven, he asked his parents who Plato and Socrates were. Told they were truth seekers, he was shocked. "You mean people don't know what the truth is?" He resolved to find it out.

Livingstone studied history as an undergraduate but dropped out in 1992 when he realized he was being indoctrinated."When I read that the Indo European [Aryan] race emerged from the Caucuses, out of nowhere, I got suspicious, and began the 13 years of research that led to my first book, "The Dying God – The Hidden History of Western Civilization."

In this book, Livingstone deconstructed the myth of Western Civilization, which tries to portray progress in terms of the rejection of religion and the adoption of the secular, which is really a mask for the occult, i.e. the Cabala. (See my site for "Lucifer is Secret God of Secular Society.")

While writing this book, Livingstone paid his bills by planting trees in British Columbia and upholstering furniture in Montreal. Raised as an agnostic, he converted to Islam in 1992 after making a study of the major world religions. He married in 2000 and has three children, all under the age of six.

TERRORISM AND THE ILLUMINATI

Livingstone's latest book, which traces the 2500-year Cabala Conspiracy from ancient times to the present day, is packed with interesting new information.

For example, the Illuminati Order was preceded in the 1500's in Spain by the "Alumbrados," a Christian heresy started by crypto Jews called "Marranos." The founder of the Jesuit Order, Ignatius of Loyola, was a Marrano/Alumbrado. (114) Thus when people today argue whether it is the Jesuits or Zionists who are responsible for our troubles, they are really talking about the same beast.

Cabbalist Rabbi Isaac Luria, a follower of Loyola's, enunciated the principle that they must work actively to bring about prophesy, i.e. redemption through the coming of the Messiah and the rule of the Illuminati. This meant "manipulating the course of fate through the use of magic, and finally, of preparing the necessary political and moral circumstances to receive [the Messiah i.e. Antichrist's] coming, that is a New World Order." (115)

With the mass media and the education system in the hands of these Cabalists it is easy to work this "magic." It is easy to convince millions that passenger jets hit the Pentagon and Shanksville PA (even though there was no passenger jet wreckage) and the World Trade Centre fell due to "fire."

The Sabbatean and Frankist heresies of the 1600's succeeded the Alumbrados and led directly to the Illuminati in the 1700's. Livingstone writes:

"The Frankists were bent not only on the eradication and humiliation of the majority of the Jewish community, who refused to accept their deviations...but of all religions, and they exploited the Zionist ideals to disguise their quest for world domination. The Frankists believed that...all that had been prohibited [by the Torah] was now permitted, or even mandatory. This included prohibited sexual unions, orgies and incest...."

"Despite the fact that they were outwardly religious, the Frankists sought the annihilation of every religion and positive system of belief, and they dreamed of a general revolution that would sweep away the past [social order] in a single stroke ...for Jacob Frank, anarchic destruction represented all the Luciferian radiance, all the tones and overtones, of the word Life." (125)

[Citing Frank's book "The Words of the Lord," Juri Lina writes: "He believed God was evil. Frank proclaimed himself as the true Messiah. He vowed not to tell the truth, rejected every moral law, and declared the only way to a new society was the total destruction of the present civilization,. Murder, rape, incest and the drinking of blood were perfectly acceptable actions and rituals." ("Under the Sign of the Scorpion" p.22)]

It is easy to recognize the origin of Communism and Anarchism in this demented philosophy. It is easy to recognize the terror of the French and Bolshevik revolutions, the Soviet Gulags and Nazis Concentration Camps, the killing fields of Cambodia and China, the "Shock and Awe" of Iraq, and the dust of the World Trade Centre.

It is easy to recognize that this degenerate Jewish sect is the reason why all Jews have been tainted with suspicion of immorality and subversion. Many Jews were tricked by the (Frankist) Communist promise of economic justice and public ownership. (This is what the Cabalist means by "magic"—deception and lies.) Yet ordinary Jews have been slow to distance themselves from this pernicious movement, and its Zionist, Neo Conservative and Masonic manifestations (which are not what they pretend.)

The Rothschilds and most of the Jewish banking establishment were Frankists. Intermarrying with indigenous elites, they were responsible for the Bolshevik Revolution and the First and Second World Wars. Unfortunately they may be planning a Third World War that will pit Islam against Zionism.

Livingstone goes into detail about how the Cabalists, operating through their control of Saudi Arabia, the Bank of England and British/American Imperialism, conspired to break up the Ottoman Empire and keep the Middle East backward. He also explains how they continue to use a variety of cults like Wahhabism (1700's) and Salafi (1900's), and Masonic secret societies like the Muslim Brotherhood (1930's) to divide Islam, create fanatical fundamentalism and foster terror in preparation for the coming "War of Civilizations."

"The lowest [terrorist] ranks may sincerely believe they are defending Islam and confronting "Western Imperialism." However [they] serve the same Illuminati cause...their channels penetrate to the upper reaches of power in the British and American governments, and outward into the nether regions of the criminal and occult undergrounds." (241)

Livingstone does not believe the current Iranian regime is independent of the Illuminati. They created it when they deposed the Shah and installed Ayatollah Khomeni. In every war, the Illuminati controlled both sides of the conflict, and the Third World War will not be an exception.

CONCLUSION

One of the rewards of my work is knowing people like David Livingstone. I urge students of the Cabalist Conspiracy to read "The Illuminati and Terrorism: A Three Thousand Year History." Few works offer as much insight into the true character of the world we inhabit. Livingstone's website is www.thedyinggod.com

The Cabalist Plot
to Enslave Humanity

God's Creative Force enters humanity through a man's love for his wife and desire to raise his family in a secure and wholesome environment. It is reciprocated by a woman receiving her husband's seed (which symbolizes his spirit) and nurturing it.

Thus, the Cabalist central bankers are keen to neutralize the male-female (active-passive) dynamo by making women usurp the male role. The bankers ultimately assume the initiating male or "God" role themselves.

According to the book, "Lightbearers of Darkness" the Jewish Cabala is a powerful system for gaining control over people by harnessing and perverting sexual energies. (20)

In Studies in Occultism, (Quoted in "Lightbearers of Darkness") Henri de Guilbert says the Cabalist Jew "looks upon himself as the sun of humanity, the male, opposed to which other peoples are but the female, manifesting and assuring the coming of the Messianic era. In order to realize this sociological manifestation, the Jew organically extends his influence by means of secret societies, created by him in order to spread everywhere his initiating force...[hoping to realize] the universal republic controlled by the god of humanity, the Jew of the Cabala." (21)

ERASING GENDER

Thus everywhere, the Cabalist bankers have used education and media to neuter the populations of the West and undermine the institution of marriage and family.

"We have castrated society through fear and intimidation," Harold Rosenthal boasted in 1976. "Its manhood exists only in combination with a feminine outward appearance. Being so neutered, the populace has become docile and easily ruled. As all geldings...their thoughts are not involved with the concerns of the future and their posterity, but only with the present and with the next meal." ("The Protocols of Zion Updated by a Jewish Zealot," within.)

In a recent article, "Man-Child in the Promised Land", researcher Kay Hymowitz says American males have extended their adolescence into middle age.

"In 1970, 69 percent of 25-year-old and 85 percent of 30-year-old white men were married; in 2000, only 33 percent and 58 percent were, respectively. "

Playboy Magazine used to promote itself with an ad, "What Kind of Man Reads Playboy?" The description best fits a homosexual. (See my "Playboy and the (Homo) Sexual Revolution.")

Meanwhile women have postponed marriage and usurped the male role as protector and provider. "In 1960, 70% of American 25-year-old women were married with children; in 2000, only 25% of them were. In 1970, just 7.4% of all American 30-to-34-year-olds were unmarried; today, the number is 22%. That change took about a generation to unfold, but in Asia and Eastern Europe the transformation has been more abrupt. In today's Hungary, 30% of women in their early thirties are single, compared with 6% of their mothers' generation at the same age." (Hymowitz, "The New Girl Power")

Unmarried women had 40% of all U.S. babies born in 2007. (*U.S. News and World Report*, March 19, 2009)

Meanwhile an estimated one million U.S. children were conceived using sperm donors, with 30,000 added every year. Many are born to lesbians who are determined to change the "hetero-normative" model of society. California is on the vanguard of the Cabalist banker plan to replace heterosexual norms with homosexual ones.

A new law requires schools "to positively portray sex changes, cross-dressing, homosexual marriages, and all aspects of bisexuality and homosexuality." This mandate affects children from kindergarten through 12th grade in California public schools.

Bruce Shortt, author of "The Harsh Truth About Public Schools" notes, "No longer will children raised in these schools understand that God made us male and female. Children will be told that because there are many sexual orientations and gender identities, they simply have to reach their own conclusions about which sexual orientation and gender 'possibilities' are 'right for them.' Along with this will come the message that you really can't tell whether you like something unless you have tried it. The likely consequences of this for children, the institution of the family, our churches, and our culture are horrendous."

The Christian European majority is subjected to a relentless program of social engineering by the Cabalist bankers. Brainwashed ("guilted") to think that only minorities have human rights, the majority is being undermined and transformed into "slaves who love their slavery."

THE LONG TERM PLAN

The video "The History of Political Correctness" shows that much of this social engineering was devised by intellectuals of "The Frankfurt School" to subvert Western civilization. Some of these "cultural Marxists" literally were Soviet NKVD agents. Almost all were Marxist Jews. The video shows how Americans were gulled to think revolution was trendy and to welcome the destruction of their society. These dupes now occupy all the positions of power in U.S. culture.

Basically mankind is the victim of a "cruel hoax" of cosmic proportions. When you create money out of thin air, you can buy a lot of "change agents." Our elite actually thinks it is creating a better world. Thus they can haul in giant salaries and feel saintly too. In fact, they are building a world police state, the "New World Order" secretly dedicated to Satan. They are complicit in the cover-up of 9-11; and the "war on terror" is a ruse to deprive us of our rights.

The "Jew of the Cabala" is the central banker, his allies and minions. The average Jew doesn't know anything about this plan. However, he is wrong to assume that because he is unaware, it doesn't exist. He is wrong to assume he won't some day be blamed for it. All groups and religions have been subverted. Whether Communist or Zionist, many Jews have been duped and manipulated by organized Jewry.

The average Jew is as much responsible for the NWO as the average American is responsible for the war in Iraq. However we all must take exception when our religion or nation is appropriated for evil.

Is Plan for Racial Strife Also a Hoax?

Wikipedia will tell you that the book "A Racial Program for the 20th Century" (1912) is another anti-Semitic hoax. It says the book and author Israel Cohen didn't exist.

The reason for this lie? This book contains a famous passage that reveals the Illuminati-Communist race strategy, later applied to women and other minorities in the guise of "feminism" and "diversity":

"We must realize that our party's most powerful weapon is racial tensions. By propounding into the consciousness of the dark races that for centuries they have been oppressed by whites, we can mould them to the program of the Communist Party. In America we will aim for subtle victory. While inflaming the Negro minority against the whites, we will endeavour to instil in the whites a guilt complex for their exploitation of the Negroes. We will aid the Negroes to rise in prominence in every walk of life, in the professions and in the world of sports and entertainment. With this prestige, the Negro will be able to intermarry with the whites and begin a process which will deliver America to our cause."

Rep. Thomas Abernathy read this passage into the Congressional Record on June 7, 1957 (Vol. 103, p. 8559, top of page.) Wikipedia tells you Abernathy read the quotation in a Letter to the Editor of *The Washington Star*, and the newspaper subsequently determined it was a hoax and apologized. "The quotation has retained some popularity among racists and anti-Semites to this day," Wikipedia chortles.

I have subsequently added this line to the Wiki entry: "However, the author fits the description of Israel Cohen (1879-1961) a prolific Zionist author who wrote the Foreword to Israel Zangwill's "The Schnorrers" as well as 30 other books. Like many purported "hoaxes," the quotation does describe events as they subsequently unfolded and the operations of the U.S. Communist Party." The line has subsequently been eliminated.

Cohen was the General Secretary of the World Zionist Organization. If this is the same Cohen, it means Zionism and Communism were identical.

MYRON FAGAN

"International" Jews, like other globalists, serve the Rothschilds' sick megalomaniac program of world government dictatorship. "National" Jews, like other patriots, owe their first loyalty to their country and fellow citizens. Like Benjamin Freedman, Myron Fagan (1887-1972) was one of the latter, a courageous American who fought the bankers' Communist agenda for the greater part of his life.

Myron Fagan, a successful Broadway playwright and director, met Israel Cohen, Israel Zangwill and George Bernard Shaw at a party to celebrate the opening of Zangwill's play "The Melting Pot" in 1910. He knew the three men to be founders of the Fabian Society.

Cohen told Fagan he was planning to write "A Racial Program for the 20th Century" as a "humanitarian" follow up to "The Melting Pot." At the time, Fagan didn't realize that the play, which described how Jews and Blacks triumph against White prejudice, was pure propaganda, part of the Communist campaign of fostering "guilt" in white Liberals described above.

It all fell into place in 1957 when Fagan read *The Washington Star* quotation in the context of the debate over school desegregation. In 1966, he recalled:

"That book was published in 1913 ... the NAACP and the ADL were created [by the bankers] almost simultaneously to carry out those directives. That was more than a half-century ago. Can there be any doubt that that was intended to launch our present Negro upheaval for a Black Revolution?

"If that isn't enough evidence, in 1935, the Communist Party's 'Workers Library Publishers' issued a pamphlet entitled 'THE NEGROES IN A SOVIET AMERICA.' It urged the Negroes to rise up, especially in the South, and form a Soviet State in the South, and apply for admission into the Soviet Union ... it contained implicit assurance that the 'revolt' would be supported by all American Reds, and on page 38 it promised that a Soviet government would confer greater benefits on Negroes than on Whites and that 'Any act of discrimination or prejudice against a Negro will become a crime under the Revolutionary law ...

" ... When Abernathy published that Israel Cohen excerpt in the Congressional Record, we (Cinema Educational Guild, Inc.) promptly issued a 'News-Bulletin' in which we published the entire story -- and warned of the coming Negro uprisings...

"Two years went by and nobody even tried to deny the matter, but, suddenly, after two years, during which the ADL and similar groups had ferreted out ALL copies of the book and destroyed them, they announced that the whole thing was a fraud, that there never had been such a book, or an 'Israel Cohen' ... Why did they wait two years? And how could they deny the existence of a writer named Israel Cohen in the face of all the books he had written? Copies of which I have. More important, bear in mind that Israel Cohen had been a prime mover in all 'Fabian Socialist' and Communist movements in England -- also that I had met him in person when he actually discussed the book at that banquet."

(Fagan, "UN is Spawn of the Illuminati," 1966)

IMPLICATIONS

Communism and Zionism are Rothschild proxies: two pincers in the banker's plan for world government dictatorship, currently masquerading as "globalization."

The promotion of women and minorities is part of an agenda to undermine the European heterosexual Christian character of Western society. So is mass immigration and interracial marriage. Most of what passes for modern culture (TV, movies, literature, punditry etc.) and politics are propaganda and social engineering. For example, opprobrium for "sexism" and "racism" are actually designed to undermine gender and race.

"Guilt" is a huge weapon for them. Women were taught they were "oppressed "for centuries by virtue of having to raise their children while men performed hard labor and died in battle.

Another "hoax" --the "Protocols of Zion" states "We shall erase from the memory of men all facts of previous centuries which are undesirable to us, and leave only those which depict all the errors of the government of the goyim." (16-4)

We'll never know how many other books the bankers suppressed like "A Racial Program for the Twentieth Century."

Historian Demands Action
On Powerful Doomsday Cults

A Munich-based historian Wolfgang Eggert, 46, has launched an Internet petition to demand action on powerful Jewish and Christian cults that want to instigate a nuclear holocaust to fulfill Biblical prophesy.

He thinks cult members must be exposed and removed. He points to the Jewish Chabad Lubavitcher sect who want to hasten Armageddon in order to facilitate the Messiah's return. Eggert quotes a Lubavitcher rabbi who says:"the world is waiting for us to fulfill our role in preparing the world to greet Moshiah" (i.e. Messiah.)

Their members include Paul Wolfowitz, the architect of the Iraq War which began with an attack named after a Cabalist diety, "Shekinah" ("Shock and Awe"). Especially worrisome now is Chabadnik Joe Lieberman who visited Israel in March 2008 with his buddy John McCain. There is concern over Sen. Carl Levin who is Chair of the Senate Armed Services Committee. Other prominent Orthodox Jews who might be part of this cult include Bush Attorney General Michael Mukasey, Homeland Security Director Michael Chertoff and former Pentagon Controller Dov Zakheim, implicated in the disappearance of "trillions" of dollars.

While the Chabad Lubavitchers are his focus, Eggert is also concerned about Christian Evangelists like Jack Van Impe and Timothy LaHaye who are close to the Bush administration. Their desired scenario includes the destruction of the al-Aqsa mosque, the restoration of the Third Temple on its site; the rising to heaven of the 144,000 Chosen Ones; the battle of Armageddon; mass death among Israeli Jews and the Final Coming of Jesus Christ.

The power of the Lubovitchers seems uncanny. Apparently they are very rich. On March 26 1991, the U.S. Senate commemorated the birthday of founder Rebbe Menachem Schneerson as "National Education Day." It also acknowledged the validity of the Talmudic "Seven Noahide Laws." This at a time when all Christian symbolism is being assiduously removed from society.

When Schneerson died in 1994, he was awarded the Congressional Gold Medal for his contribution to "global morals." According to Eggert, Schneerson taught that Jewish and gentile souls are fundamentally different. "All Jews are good by nature... Jews are the pride of creation, the Goyim (gentiles) are the scum."

According to Schneerson, the Goyim still have a role in serving the Chosen ones. The Jews are the Priests while the Noahide Laws provide "a religion for the rank and file." Eggert quotes another Lubavitcher rabbi: "When examining the chain of frightening events [since 9-11] with a Chassidic eye, we see that the U.S. is being pushed toward fulfilling its historic role of teaching the Sheva Mitzvos [i.e. Noahide laws] to the world."

According to Eggert, Freemasons have always called themselves "Noachids" and incorporated the statutes into their Constitution as early as 1723.

If you look, you can find pictures of many major politicians in the West posing with this sect. This website features more than a dozen of them: http://amalekite. blogspot.com/. In a You Tube, the current Chief Rabbi of the Chabad boasts of his rapport with Vladimir Putin. Eggert says Putin's mother is Jewish, which makes him Jewish, and that President Medvedev is Jewish on both sides. It's hard to say if they are beholden to the Chabadniks.

Eggert, who studied History and Politics at universities in Berlin and Munich, is the author of eight books on hidden history. He believes that all of modern history is influenced by Cabalistic plot to fulfill Biblical Prophesy. However, he is careful to distinguish between the Lubavitchers and other Hasidim who think it a crime to "force God's hand" and "hasten the redemption."

Nevertheless, as Eggert surveys modern history, the Lubavitchers seem to be in control.

"Every part of modern history is linked to another and in itself to Zionism, state intelligence, lodges and alike. Without the Balfour declaration, there would have been no democratic revolution in Russia and no America into World War One ... We may start at any historical point (even with the American revolution or more far back Oliver Cromwell) [and] we´ll see, that the maker (or profiteer) of all this is Cabalistic Judaism. All serves their plan, to implement biblical prophecy."

Eggert cites World Zionist VP Max Nordau's speech at the 1903 Zionist Convention predicting "a future World War [and] peace conference where with the help of England a free and Jewish Palestine will be created." (Eggert, "Israel's Geheimvatikan" Vol.2, pp.21-22)

He says Germany was sabotaged (strikes, revolts) in WW1 by the Zionists because it wouldn't play ball on Israel. He cites a book in Hebrew, "The Historical Moment" by M. Gonzer: "We even find nations who are slow on the uptake and who find it difficult to understand certain relations unless the rebbe--that is world history--gives them some sensible bashes which makes them open their eyes." (Israels Geheimvatikan, vol. 1, p.47.)

Protocols "Forgery" Claim is Flawed

Next to the Bible, "The Protocols of the Elders of Zion" is perhaps the mostly widely read book in the world. Published in Russia in 1903, it purports to be the leaked master plan for "Jewish world domination." It is the kind of thing that would be studied at secret workshops of an occult society.

In different ways, both Zionists and Nazis have made it synonymous with virulent anti-Semitism and genocide. But surely Jews should not be blamed for the machinations of a tiny secret society they have never heard of. The vast majority of Jews would disavow this master plan if they believed it existed.

Surely one can condemn all racism and genocide in the strongest possible terms and still believe the Protocols are authentic. In my opinion, the equation with anti-Semitism is really a ploy to divert attention away from this Master Plan.

The plagiarism claim is part of a propaganda campaign waged by conscious and unconscious collaborators in academia and the media.

THE FORGERY CLAIM

We are told that "The Protocols of Zion" is a hoax, a "proven forgery" concocted by the Tsarist political police (the Okhrana) to incite anti-Semitism and discredit revolutionaries.

But the "proof" is far from convincing. It consists of three articles published in "The London Times" (August 16-18, 1921) by Philip Graves. According to Graves, Protocols is a crude, chapter-by-chapter plagiarism of Maurice Joly's "Dialogue in Hell Between Machiavelli and Montesquieu." (1864)

It was easy to make this claim while Joly's book was unavailable. Napoleon III's police confiscated it as soon as it was published.

But it is available now and I invite you to compare the two texts. In my opinion, they are entirely different in tone, content and purpose. At 140 pages, Dialogues is twice as long as Protocols. Most of it finds no echo in the Protocols.

The crux of Graves' argument is that certain references and passages in Protocols were lifted from Dialogues. He claims there are 50 of these and produces about a dozen.

Their striking resemblance to Protocols leaves little doubt that borrowing did take place. Indeed Philip Graves is "struck by the absence of any effort on the part of the plagiarist to conceal his plagiarism." I believe that's because Joly was plagiarizing from Protocols and not vice-versa.

The plot in the Protocols is described as "centuries-old." It most likely predates the 1864 "Dialogue." Joly was well versed in the Protocols and borrowed from it to flesh out the unpopular authoritarian position of Machiavelli, which he ascribed to Napoleon III.

Joly, a Jew whose real name was Joseph Levy, was a lifelong Mason and member of the "Lodge of Mizraim" where the Protocols document originated. He was the protégé of Adolph Cremieux (Isaac Moise Cremieux 1796-1880) the head of the lodge and a Minister in the Jewish-backed government of Leon Gambetta. (See Kerry Bolton, "The Protocols in Context," Renaissance Press, 2003)

Joly, who committed suicide in 1879, was in the habit of "borrowing." He is accused of plagiarizing a popular novel by Eugene Sue, namely "Les Mystères du Paris." (1845) Also, his work is predated by one by another of Cremieux's protégés, Jacob Venedy, entitled, "Machiavelli, Montesquieu, Rousseau." (1850)

In 1884 Mme. Justine Glinka, the daughter of a Russian General living in Paris, hired Joseph Schorst, a member of Joly's Mizraim Lodge, to obtain sensitive information. For the sum of 2500 francs, Schorst provided Glinka with "The Protocols of the Elders of Zion." He was subsequently tracked down and murdered in Egypt.

The Tsarist government, already heavily infiltrated, sat on the document. Glinka subsequently gave it to a friend who passed it on to Professor Sergius A. Nilus who published it for the first time in 1901.

After the Bolshevik Revolution, Nilus was arrested in Kiev in 1924, imprisoned and tortured. The President of the Court said he had "done them incalculable harm in publishing the Protocols." ("Waters Flowing Eastward" by Paquita de Shishmareff, 1999, pp.74-76.)

However, there are internal references which suggest the published document dates from 1894 and not 1884. In Protocol 10, there is a reference to the Panama Scandal of 1892. The author says their politician puppets must have some "undiscoverable stain, some Panama."

At the end of Protocol 16, there is a reference to "one of our best agents, Bourgeois" who has already subverted the teaching of the young. Leon Victor August Bourgeois (1851-1925) became the Minister of Instruction in 1890. This leads me to believe that Glinka got the document about 1894, not 1884.

But I believe that given this was a "centuries-old plan," Joly had access to an earlier version, and hence the similarities.

POLITICAL CONTEXT

Philip Graves' article smacks of a Zionist propaganda operation. Graves "exposé" of Protocols appeared in August 1921 when Zionists were pressing the League of Nations to turn Palestine into a Jewish homeland under British Mandate.

Philip Grave tells the unlikely story that a "Mr. X" brought Dialogues to him in

Constantinople. where he was the Times' correspondent. Mr. X presented it as "irrefutable proof" that the Protocols are a plagiarism.

Mr. X was a White Russian. Given the Jewish role in the Bolshevik Revolution, it seems incredible that a White Russian would help to discredit the Protocols. Grave claims Mr. X bought the book from, get this, "a former member of the Okhrana" who had fled to Constantinople. Are we supposed to believe the Okhrana used this very copy to "plagiarize" the Protocols?

In "The Controversy of Zion," (Chapter 34) Douglas Reed, a Times' staffer at the time, provides additional background. In May 1920, Lord Northcliffe, a part owner of "The Times," printed an article about the Protocols entitled "The Jewish Peril, A Disturbing Pamphlet, A Call for an Enquiry. " It concluded:

"An impartial investigation of these would-be documents and their history is most desirable...are we to dismiss the whole matter without inquiry and to let the influence of such a book as this work go unchecked?"

This was part of a short-lived public realization, after the Bolshevik revolution, that Communism was Jewish in nature, and posed a genuine danger to Western civilization. Even Winston Churchill waded in with his famous article "Zionism Vs. Bolshevism: A Struggle for the Soul of the Jewish People."

Then in May 1922 Northcliffe visited Palestine and wrote that Britain had been too hasty to promise it to the Jews when in fact it belonged to 700,000 Muslim Arab residents.

Mr. Wickham Steed, the editor of "The Times" in 1921 refused to print the article and Northcliffe tried to get him fired. Somehow, while Northcliffe was on vacation in Europe, Steed was able to have Northcliffe declared "insane" and forcibly committed. Later Northcliffe complained he was being poisoned and died suddenly in 1922.

Douglas Reed was Northcliffe's secretary but didn't learn of these events until they appeared in the Official History of "The Times" in the 1950's. Clearly Northcliffe had offended some "big boys" when he championed the Protocols and opposed the British Mandate in Palestine.

THE FORGERY CLAIM IS EXAGGERATED

Philip Graves and other apologists are making exaggerated claims. They are incorrect to claim the Protocols plagiarize the Dialogues chapter by chapter.

Graves writes that "the Seventh Dialogue...corresponds with the fifth, sixth, seventh and part of the eighth Protocol. "

At eight pages, these Protocols are twice as long as the Seventh Dialogue. They mostly contain material not found in the Seventh Dialogue, or anywhere else. I will list a few examples from Protocol Five alone.

Protocol Five says "our kingdom will be distinguished by a despotism of such magnificent proportions" that it will "wipe out any goyim who oppose us by deed or word."

In contrast Seventh Dialogue says, "Death, expropriation and torture should only play a minor role in the internal politics of modern states."

Protocols Five says we "robbed [the goyim] of their faith in God" and "insinuated into their minds the conception of their own rights," thereby undermining the authority of Kings. There is nothing comparable in Dialogue Seven.

Protocol Five says, "we shall so wear down the goyim that they will be compelled to offer us international power [allowing us] gradually to absorb all State forces of the world and to form a Super-Government." There is nothing comparable in Dialogue Seven.

Protocol Five says the "engine" of all states is "in our hands" and that engine is "Gold." "We were chosen by God Himself to rule over the whole earth." There is nothing comparable in Dialogue Seven.

ON THE OTHER HAND

The author of Dialogues does select a few passages or references from Protocols that appear unaltered or in slightly different form.

For example, the Dialogues' say: "Everywhere might precedes right. Political liberty is merely a relative idea. The need to live is what dominates states as it does individuals."

In Protocols this is, "From the law of nature right lies in might. Political freedom is an idea but not a fact, and one must know how to use it [political freedom] as a bait whenever it appears necessary to attract the masses ... to one's party for the purpose of crushing another who is in authority." (Protocols 1)

Graves leaves out the last part to make the resemblance seem greater than it is.

Dialogues (7) say, "Revolutionary ferment which is suppressed in one's own country should be incited throughout Europe." In Protocols (7) "Throughout all Europe ... we must create ferments, discords, hostilities." There is no reference to suppressing these in one's own country.

These similarities can be explained by the fact that the Protocols predated Joly and he was familiar with it.

CONCLUSION

The two books are different in tone and relevance. The Dialogue today seems academic and esoteric and requires an exegesis. It was a veiled attack on Napoleon III whose views Joly ascribes to Machiavelli. Ironically this is where he dips into the Protocols. Napoleon wasn't fooled and Joly was arrested.

In contrast, the authenticity of the Protocols is self-evident to any informed individual with an open mind. They describe the world we live in.

If your plan for World Domination leaked out, what would you do? Would you admit it? No, you'd employ an army of ciphers to stigmatize the document as a hoax motivated by "prejudice" and "anti-Semitism." They have executed this "damage control" perfectly, a measure of their power to deceive even in the presence of the truth.

This is the only Conspiracy that has prevailed in spite of the blueprint being freely available. It demonstrates the credulity (or venality) of the intelligentsia and the masses.

The Illuminati (top-rung Masonic Jews and their non-Jewish allies) have distributed some wealth and power to the masses (liberalism, socialism) as a way of securing ultimate power for themselves. According to the Protocols, they will eventually withdraw these benefits once their "invisible government" is invincible. The "war on terror" should be seen in this context.

In my view, "Protocols Deniers" are complicit in this Conspiracy, which is responsible for most human suffering and will lead to a great deal more. As a Jew, I don't want this responsibility on my head, or on other innocent Jews or Masons.

The Protocols of Zion: Introduction and Synopsis

Many people think "The Protocols of the Elders of Zion" is anti-Semitic "hate literature" and a fraud.

Nobel Prize winner Alexander Solzhenitsyn wrote that the book exhibits "the mind of genius." Pretty good for a hoax, wouldn't you say?

Solzhenitsyn said it exhibits "great strength of thought and insight...Its design... (increasing freedom and liberalism, which is terminated in social cataclysm)...is well above the abilities of an ordinary mind...It is more complicated than a nuclear bomb."

I believe the Protocols are genuine. They are lectures addressed to Jewish Luciferians (Illuminati, Freemasons) detailing an incredible plan to overthrow Western Civilization, subjugate mankind, and concentrate "all the wealth of the world...in our hands." They were given as a regular series of workshops to these Jewish Masons in Paris. The author describes them as an "exposition of our programme" and often begins by saying, "Today we will discuss..."

Rabbi Ehrenpries, (1869-1951) the Chief Rabbi of Sweden from 1910, reportedly wrote in 1924: "Long have I been well acquainted with the contents of the Protocols, indeed for many years before they were ever published in the Christian press. The Protocols of the Elders of Zion were in point of fact not the original Protocols at all, but a compressed extract of the same. Of the 70 Elders of Zion, in the matter of origin and of the existence of the original Protocols, there are only ten men in the entire world who know." (Quoted without source online in "1001 Quotations About Jews.")

This "compressed extract" is confirmed by the widespread use of ellipsis—indicating words have been left out.

Researchers have speculated that Adam Weishaupt, Theodore Herzl or Asher Ginzberg penned the Protocols. At first I thought it was Meyer Amschel Rothschild (1744-1844) himself. Later I thought it might be Lionel Nathan Rothschild (1809-1879) or James de Rothschild (1792-1868) or Adolphe Cremieux (1796-1880.) It's hard to pinpoint because I think this document was constantly revised by different hands.

Protocols 20-23, the "financial programme... the crowning and the decisive point of our plans" is the reason I think the author was a banker and probably a Rothschild. These lectures require a detailed knowledge of finance and profound psychological insight. Moreover the author states that all power ultimately will reside in the "King of the Jews," which is how the Rothschilds were known.

SYNOPSIS OF THE PROTOCOLS OF THE ELDERS OF ZION

As you read this, it will be evident that much of this programme has taken effect. This is required reading for anyone who wishes to understand the world in which we live. The Protocols exhibit a pathological hatred for non-Jews, and a desire to undermine and enslave them. It refers to them as "goyim" or cattle.

Protocol One

Refers to the plan as "our system." Says men are governed "by force": "By the law of nature, right lies in might." Most men are willing to betray their fellow man for profit. (The "end justifies the means" is the Communist motto.)

The promise of "freedom" (i.e. liberalism, reform, revolution) is used to take power from the Old Order (monarch, landed aristocracy, church, army) and transfer it to our hands, the power of "Gold" and the despotism of Capital which is entirely in our hands." The State is dependent on us, or it "goes to the bottom."

If the state can be ruthless in subjecting an external foe, surely an "internal foe" i.e. Masonic Jews, who are "the destroyer of society and the commonweal" are justified in using any form of subterfuge.

Morality is an obstacle to successful conquest and a liability to any political leadership. The goal is to "scatter to the winds all existing forces for order and regulation" and to become the "sovereign lord" of those so stupid as to lay down their powers and fall for liberal entreaties.

Their power is "more invincible" by virtue of "remaining invisible" until insurmountable. This is a "strategic plan from which we cannot deviate" or risk "seeing the labour of many centuries brought to naught."

"Our countersign is—Force and Make-believe" i.e. deception. The writer emphasizes that the goal is to "seize the property of others" and "bring all governments into subjection to our super government."

The words "Liberty, Fraternity, Equality" were "baits" the Masonic Jews used "from ancient times" to overthrow "the genealogical aristocracy of the goyim" which was the peoples' only defence. It will be replaced by the "aristocracy of money."

Throughout history they have played upon the greed, lust and vanity of men to ensnare their agents.

In other words, "democracy" is a perfect instrument for their covert control. Monarchs were much harder to subvert. Democracy, the "replacing of representatives of the people" has "placed them at our disposal" and "given us the power of appointment."

Protocol Two

"Wars as far as possible should not result in any territorial gains," but should demonstrate to both sides their dependence on "our international agentur" [i.e. agents] which "possess millions of eyes ever on the watch and unhampered by any limitations whatsoever."

This implies they control the outcome of wars and have millions of spies (Masons, Jews?)

"Our international right will then wipe out national rights..." as the civil law of states rule their subjects.

Gentile leaders ("administrators") will be chosen for their strict obedience and will be run by "advisors." The goyim "can amuse themselves until the hour strikes..." We have implanted the false doctrines "by means of our press arousing blind confidence in these theories."

"Think carefully of the successes we arranged for Darwinism, Marxism, Nietzcheism. To us Jews, at any rate, it should be plain to see what a disintegrating effect these directives have had upon the minds of the goyim."

The Press has fallen into our hands. It fashions the thought of the people. Its role is to express and create discontent. Thanks to the Press, we have the Gold in our hands though we sacrificed many of our people. Each...in the sight of God is worth "a thousand goyim."

Protocol Three

"There remains a small space to cross before all states of Europe will be locked in the coils of the symbolic snake, by which we symbolize our people, as in a powerful vice."

"We have made a gulf between the far-seeing Sovereign Power and the blind force of the people so that both have lost all meaning, for like the blind man and his stick, both are powerless apart."

"Of States we have made gladiatorial arenas where a host of confused issues contend...."

"We appear on the scene as the alleged saviours of the worker...and we suggest that he should enter the ranks of our fighting forces—Socialists, Anarchists, Communists— to which we always give support in accordance with an alleged brotherly rule (of the solidarity of all humanity) of our social masonry. The aristocracy...was interested in seeing the workers were well fed, healthy and strong. We are interested in just the opposite—in the diminution, the killing out of the goyim."

Protocol Four

"Who and what is in a position to overthrow an invisible force? And this is precisely what our force is.

Gentile masonry blindly serves as a screen for us and our objects but the plan of action of our force, even its abiding place, remains for the whole people an unknown mystery."

Freedom would be possible if it rested "upon the foundation of faith in God, upon the brotherhood of humanity, unconnected with the conception of equality, which is negated by the the very laws of creation..."

"This is the reason why it is indispensable for us to undermine all faith, to tear out of the minds of the goyim the very principle of Godhead and the spirit, and to put in its place ...material needs."

Goyim must have no time to think but rather must be diverted to industry and trade. "All nations will be swallowed up in the pursuit of gain and in the race for it, will not take note of their common foe."

We must put industry on a "speculative basis" so wealth will pass to our classes.

The rat race will create, no has already created "disenchanted, cold and heartless communities."

This materialism will allow us to direct the lower classes of the goyim against our rivals for power "the privileged and...the intellectuals of the goyim."

Protocols Five

The author states that despotism is necessary for the world he is creating, one "where the feelings toward faith and community are obliterated by cosmopolitan convictions."

The following is the rationale behind "communitarianism" and the war on terror.

"We shall create an intensified centralization of government in order to grip in our hands all the forces of the community. We shall regulate mechanically all the actions of the political life of our subjects with new laws. These laws will withdraw one by one all the indulgences and liberties which have been permitted by the goyim, and our kingdom will be distinguished by a despotism of such magnificent proportions as to be at any moment and in every place in a position to wipe out any goyim who oppose us by word or deed."

The union of the goyim might have thwarted the Illuminati but "We have set one against another the personal and national reckonings of the goyim, religious and race hatreds, which we have fostered into a huge growth in the course of the past twenty centuries....We are too strong. There is no evading our power. The nations cannot come to even an inconsiderable private agreement without our secretly having a hand in it."

"It is through me that nations reign. And it was said by the prophets that we were chosen by God Himself to rule over the whole earth...The wheels of the machinery of all States are moved by the force of the engine which is in our hands, and that engine is ...Gold. ...Capital ..must be free to establish a monopoly of industry and trade: this is already being put in execution by an unseen hand in all quarters of the world."

"The principal object of our directorate is..to debase the public mind...lead it away from serious reflection calculated to arouse resistance; to distract the forces of the mind towards a sham fight of empty eloquence."

"We shall assume the liberal physiognomy of all parties, of all directions, and we shall give that physiognomy a voice in orators who will speak so much they will exhaust the patience of their hearers..."

"In order to put public opinion in our hands, we must bring it into a state of bewilderment by giving expression from all sides to so many contradictory opinions ...to make the goyim lose their heads in the labyrinth and come to see that the best thing is to have no opinion at all in matters political...[The second secret requisite for our success] is to sow discord in all parties, to dislocate all collective forces which are still unwilling to submit to us...By all these means we shall wear down the goyim that they will be compelled to offer us international power of a nature that will enable us without any violence to absorb all the State forces of the world and to form a Super Government."

Protocols 6

We are creating "huge monopolies" upon which even the large fortunes of the goyim are dependent so that "they will go to the bottom together with the credit of the states on the day after the political smash..."

"In every possible way we must develop the significance of our Super Government by representing it as the Protector and Benefactor of all those who voluntarily submit to us."

"We want industry to drain off from the land both labour and capital and by means of speculation transfer into our hands all of the money of the world, and thereby throw all the goyim into the ranks of the proletariat. Then the goyim will bow down before us, if for no other reason but to get the right to exist."

Communism. "In order that the true meaning of things may not strike the goyim before the proper time, we shall mask it under an alleged ardent desire to serve the working classes..."

Protocol 7

"The increase in police forces [is] essential...besides ourselves there should only be "the masses of the proletariat, a few millionaires devoted to our interests, police and soldiers..."

"We must compel the government of the goyim" to fall in with our plan "already approaching desired consummation" by requiring them to obey "public opinion" which we control through that great power already in our hands, the Press.

"In a word, to sum up our system of keeping the government of the goyim in Europe in check, we shall show our strength to one of them by terrorist attempts and to all, if we allow the possibility of a general rising against us, we shall respond with the guns of America or China or Japan."

Protocol 8

"For a time until there will no longer be a risk of entrusting responsible posts in our States to our brother-Jews, we shall put them in the hands of persons whose past and reputation are such that...if they disobey our instructions, must face criminal charges or disappear—this in order to make them defend our interests to their last gasp."

Protocol 9

A "general identical application" of our principles can change the "most stubborn [national] character" and we "shall add a new people to the ranks of those already subdued by us."

"De facto we have already wiped out every kind of rule except our own...Nowadays if any States raise a protest against us it is only pro forma at our discretion, and by our direction, for their anti-Semitism is indispensable to us in the management of our lesser brethren."

"It is from us that the all-engulfing terror proceeds. We have in our service people of all opinions, of all doctrines, restoring monarchists, demagogues, socialists, communists and utopian dreamers of all kinds. Each one of them is boring away at the last remnants of authority, is striving to overthrow the all established forms of order...we will not give them peace until [all states] openly acknowledge our international Super-Government, and with submissiveness."

"In order to carry on a contested [political] struggle, one must have money, and all the money is in our hands."

We have taken control of the "institutions of the goyim" using the "chaotic licence of liberalism. We have got our hands into the administration of the law, into the conduct of elections, into the press, into the liberty of the person, but principally into education and training as being the corner-stones of a free existence."

"We have fooled, bemused and corrupted the youth of the goyim by rearing them in principles and theories which are known to us to be false although it is by us that they have been inculcated."

Protocol 10

"How indeed are the goyim to perceive the underlying meaning of things when their representatives give the best of their energies to enjoying themselves?"

"By inculcating in all a sense of self importance, we shall destroy among the goyim the importance of the family and its educational value and remove the possibility of individual minds splitting off, for the mob, handled by us, will not let them come to the front nor even give them a hearing; it is accustomed to listen to us only who pay it for obedience and attention. In this way, we shall create a blind mighty force which will never be in a position to move in any direction without the guidance of our agents...The people will submit to this regime because it will know that upon these leaders will depend its earnings, gratification and the receipt of all kinds of benefits."

"When we introduced into the State organism the poison of Liberalism its whole political complexion underwent a change. States have been seized with a mortal illness—blood poisoning. All that remains is to await the end of their death agony. Liberalism produced Constitutional States which took the place of what was the only safeguard of the goyim, namely Despotism....Then it was that the era of republics became a possibility that could be realized; and then it was that we replaced the ruler by a caricature of a government –by a president, taken from the mob, from the midst of our puppet creatures, our slaves. This is the foundation of the mine we have laid under the goy peoples."

"The recognition of our despot ...will come when the peoples, utterly wearied by the irregularities and incompetence ---a matter which we shall arrange for—of their rulers will clamour, "Away with them and give us one king over all the earth who will unite us and annihilate the causes of discords—frontiers, nationalities, religions, State debts—who will give us peace and quiet which we cannot find under our rulers and representatives."

Thus we must utterly "exhaust humanity with dissension, hatred, struggle, envy and even to use torture, starvation, the inoculation of disease and want, so that the goyim see no other course open to them than to take refuge in our complete sovereignty in money and in all else. But if we give the nations of the world a breathing space the moment we long for is hardly likely ever to arrive."

Protocol 11

"By these combinations, I mean the freedom of the Press, the right of association, freedom of science, the voting principle, and many another that must disappear forever from the memory of man..."

"The goyim are a flock of sheep, and we are their wolves. And you know what happens when the wolves get hold of the flock?"

"...we shall keep promising them to give back all the liberties we have taken away as soon as we have quelled the enemies of peace and tamed all parties...It is not worth while discussing how long they will be kept waiting for the return of their liberties..."

This program is designed to gain for the Jews in an indirect way what isn't possible otherwise. This has been the basis of our organization of "secret Masonry" a motive unsuspected by the "goy cattle" attracted to the lodges.

"God has granted to us, His Chosen People, the gift of the dispersion,' which has "now brought us to the threshold of sovereignty over all the world."

Protocol 12

"The majority of the public have not the slightest idea what ends the press really serves. [After our revolution] no one shall with impunity [question] the infallibility of our government...among those making attacks upon us will also be organs established by us, but they will attack...points that we have pre-determined to alter. Not a single announcement will reach the public without our control."

"...we shall set up our own opposition [press] which...will present what looks like the very antipothesis to us. Our real opponents at heart will accept this simulated opposition as their own and will show us their cards."

"We shall have a sure triumph over our opponents since they will not have at their disposition organs of the press in which they can give full and final expression of their views."

Protocol 13

"The need for daily bread forces the goyim to keep silence and be our humble servants."

"We further distract [the masses] with amusements, games...art, sport ...from questions in which we should find ourselves compelled to oppose them. Growing more and more unaccustomed to reflect and form any opinions of their own, people will begin to talk in the same tones as we, because we alone shall be offering them new directions for thought...of course through such persons as will not be suspected of solidarity with us."

"Who will ever suspect then that all these peoples were stage-managed by us according to a political plan which no one has so much as guessed at in the course of many centuries?"

Protocol 14

"When we come into our kingdom it will be undesirable for us that there be any other religion than ours...We must therefore sweep away all other forms of belief."

We will also expose the folly of the goy governments' chase after "the fantastic schemes of social blessings, [i.e. socialism, communism] never noticing that these schemes kept on producing a worse and never a better state..."

"Our philosophers will discuss all the shortcomings of the various beliefs of the goyim. But no one will ever bring under discussion our faith from its true point of view since this will be fully learned by none save ours, who will never dare to betray its secrets."

"Our wise men trained to become leaders of the goyim, will compose [materials] which will be used to influence the minds of the goyim, directing them towards such understanding and forms of knowledge as have been determined by us."

Protocol 15

In order to restore order in the goy societies where we have implanted "deeply rooted discord and Protestantism" we must employ "merciless measures" to quash resistance. We must establish an aura of invulnerability such as the Russian aristocracy had. Apart from the Papacy, the Russian aristocracy "until recent times the one and only serious foe we had in the world." [Curious they could say this in 1894?]

After the revolution they will disband all secret societies but until then we will "create and multiply free Masonic lodges" for there "we shall find our principal intelligence office and means of influence...and tie together ...all revolutionary and liberal elements."

Thanks to Freemasonry: "The most secret political plots will be known to us and will fall under our guiding hands on the very day of their conception. Among the members...will be almost all the agents of international and national police, ...in a position to use their own particular measures with the insubordinate but also to screen our activities [i.e. act on our behalf without blame attaching to us] and provide pretexts for discontents etc. [i.e. provocations]" Hence the role of police and intelligence agencies in our society.

If there is a plot against us "at the end will be no other than one of our most trusted servants."

The goy Masons are totally manipulated. "The goyim enter the lodges in the hope of getting a nibble from the public pie." He disparages the goy Masons, "These tigers in appearance have the souls of sheep and the wind blows freely through their heads." We have given them the "hobbyhorse" of "collectivism" even though it violates the laws of nature. "Isn't this proof the mind of goyim is undeveloped compared to our own? This it is, mainly, which guarantees our success."

The author talks about stopping at nothing no matter the sacrifice. He cares nothing about the "seed of the goy cattle" but the sacrifice of Jews has resulted in the betterment of the rest.

We hasten the death of those who "hinder our affairs." "We execute masons in such wise that none save the brotherhood can ever have a suspicion of it, not even the victims themselves...they all die when required as if from a normal kind of illness. Knowing this, even the brotherhood in its turn does not protest. By such methods we have plucked out of the midst of masonry the very root of protest against our disposition." (See "Illuminati Murdered at Least Two Other Presidents," within.)

The superior intelligence of the Chosen People confirms that "nature herself has intended us to guide and rule the world."

Describes a paternalistic despotism based on the submission of humanity to what is stronger. In relation to this power, the peoples of the world and even their governments are "only children under age."

Protocol 16

"We must introduce into their education all those principles which have so brilliantly broken up their order. But when we are in power we shall remove every kind of disturbing subject from the course of education and shall make out of the youth obedient children of authority, loving him who rules as the support and hope of peace and quiet."

"We shall erase from the memory of men all facts of previous centuries which are undesirable to us, and leave only those which depict all the errors of the government of the goyim."

"We shall abolish every kind of freedom of instruction...teachers will read what will pass as free lectures...These theories will be raised by us to the stage of a dogma of faith as a transitional stage towards our faith."

"We shall swallow up and confiscate to our own use the last scintilla of independence of thought...[we will] turn the goyim into unthinking submissive brutes waiting for things to be presented before their eyes in order to form an idea of them."

(This suggests much social and political criticism is not constructive but genuinely subversive in intent.)

Protocols 17

"We have long past taken care to discredit the priesthood of the goyim, and thereby to ruin their mission on earth, which in these days might still be a great hindrance to us...As to other religions, we shall still less difficulty in dealing with them..." (Thinking sexual abuse by Catholic priests?)

"The king of the Jews will be the real Pope of the Universe, the Patriarch of an international Church."

"...we shall fight against [existing churches] by criticism designed to cause schism..." (Thinking gay marriage?)

"In our programme, one third of our subjects will keep the rest under observation from a sense of duty, on the principle of volunteer service to the state."

"Just as nowadays our brethren [i.e. Jews] are obliged at their own risk to denounce to the kahal [Jewish council] apostates of their own family...so in our kingdom over all the world it will be obligatory for all our subjects to observe the duty of service to the State..." (Thinking KGB, Stazi or Gestapo?)

Protocol 18

"...we have broken the prestige of the goy kings by frequent attempts upon their lives through our agents, blind sheep of our flock, who are easily moved by a few liberal phrases to crimes provided only they be painted in political colors. We have compelled the rulers to acknowledge their weakness in advertising overt measures of secret defence and therefore we shall bring authority to destruction."

[For example, Czar Alexander II was assassinated by a bomb in 1881. The Minister of Internal Affairs von Plehve was assassinated in July 1904. Peter Stolypin, the Prime Minister was assassinated in September 1911.]

Protocol 19

I hope we have succeeded in preventing the goyim from adopting this means of contending with sedition. [This "means" is 1) to taint it with some larceny or sexual abuse, and 2) to make a severe example of one offender.] It is for this reason that through the Press and in speeches indirectly—in cleverly compiled schoolbooks on history, we have advertised the martyrdom ...accepted by sedition mongers for the idea of the commonweal. This advertisement has increased the contingent of liberals and brought thousands of goyim into the ranks of our livestock cattle."

Protocol 20

This deals with the "financial programme" the "crowning and decisive point of our plans." The author's expertise in these matters suggest he is a banker.

"When we come into our kingdom our autocratic kingdom will avoid...burdening the masses with taxes remembering that it plays the part of father and protector."

A progressive capital tax will be introduced. "A tax increasing in the percentage of ratio to capital will give a much larger revenue than the present individual or property tax, which is useful to us now for the sole reason that it excites trouble and discontent among the goyim."

"Economic crises have been produced by us for the goyim by no other means than the withdrawal of money from circulation."

"The issue of money ought to correspond with the growth of population..."

"The gold standard has been the ruin of the States which adopted it, for it has not been able to satisfy the demands for money, the more so that we have removed gold from circulation as far as possible."

"How clear is the undeveloped power of thought of the purely brute brains of the goyim as expressed in the fact that they have been borrowing from us...without ever thinking that these very moneys, plus an addition for payment of interest, must be got by them from their own state pockets in order to settle up with us. What could have been more simple than to take the money they wanted from their own people?"

Protocol 22

"In our hands is the greatest power of our day—gold...Surely there is no need to seek further proof that our rule is predestined by God? Surely we shall not fail with such wealth to prove that all that evil which for so many centuries we have had to commit has served at the end of ends the cause of true well-being—the bringing of everything into order?"

"Our Order will be the crown of order, and in that is included the whole happiness of man. The aureole of this authority will inspire a mystical bowing of the knee and a reverent fear before it of all peoples. True force makes no terms with any right, not even with that of God: none dare come near to it so as to take so much as a span away from it."

Protocols 23-24

The "King of the Jews" dynastic heir of King David will be King of the world. He will replace all existing rulers. Otherwise, the Protocols end on a curiously benign note, promising a benevolent government that ensures peace and order in exchange for total submission. There are many nostrums like:

"Unemployment is a most perilous thing for a government. For us its part will have been played out the moment authority is transferred into our hands. Drunkenness will also be prohibited by law..."

"The king of the Jews must not be at the mercy of his passions...the holy seed of David must sacrifice to his people all personal inclinations. Our supreme lord must be of exemplary irreproachability."

"Signed by the representatives of Zion, of the 33rd degree."

Protocols of Zion:
Updated by a Jewish Zealot

In 1976, the plan for "Jewish world domination" outlined in "The Protocols of the Elders of Zion" had been largely realized. Harold Wallace Rosenthal, 29, a personal assistant to New York Senator Jacob Javits felt that Jewish power was unassailable. He could make some extra cash by telling the story to Walter White, Jr. the editor of the Conservative monthly "Western Front."

"Too many Jews do not have the guts to tell you how we live and plan, but I am not intimated by anything or anyone," Rosenthal told White.

"It is too late for your Christian followers to put up a defence. That time is long past. Long, long ago we had to become the aggressors! That is undoubtedly one of our great purposes in life. We are aggressors!"

This shocking 17-page interview, which contradicts the Jewish self-image as victims, has been online for some time. It ranks with the revelations of Benjamin Freedman, and C.G. Rakovsky as a description of the real forces directing the world.

Rosenthal needed gambling money but his candor cost him his life. On Aug. 12, 1976, he was killed in a foiled "PLO attack" in Istanbul. Walter White concluded that the incident was a cover for Rosenthal's murder.

A commemorative Rosenthal "Fellowship in International Relations" discreetly furthers the work he indiscreetly exposed. Oddly, there is no picture of Rosenthal on their web site.

According to Wikipedia, he graduated from Cambridge University and Harvard Graduate School, both on scholarships. After working for Congressman Hugh Carey (D-NY) he moved to the office of Senator Walter Mondale (D-MN) where he directed his legislative agenda. After a stint at the Rockefeller Brothers Foundation, Harold returned to the Senate to work for Sen. Jacob Javits. He was definitely an "insider."

Rosenthal says, "Most Jews do not like to admit it, but our god is Lucifer...and we are his chosen people. Lucifer is very much alive."

This statement applies to modern culture as a whole. We do not like to admit that our "secular" society is based on a cosmic rebellion against God. Its true Satanic character is becoming more evident every day.

INSIGHTS

Rosenthal says the "Jews" have built an earthly empire partly by rejecting Christ's vision of a spiritual kingdom based on brotherly love. They wanted a warrior king not a Prince of Peace.

"During Christ's time, the Jews were seeking a material and earthly kingdom but Christ offered the Jews a spiritual kingdom. This, they couldn't buy, so they rejected Jesus Christ and had him crucified."

Jewish bankers plan to govern the world from Jerusalem according to their own interests. He says the Jewish religion is essentially a disguise for a racial imperative. "We can live among other people and states [by] persuading them that the Jews are not a distinct people but the representatives of a religious faith..."

"Jewish" power was achieved by gaining control of the monetary system.

"We have been successful in dividing society against itself by pitting labor against management. This perhaps has been one of our greatest feats, since in reality it is a triangle, though only two points ever seem to occur. In modern industry ... capital, which force we represent, is the apex. Both management and labor are on the base of this triangle. They continually stand opposed to each other and their attention is never directed to the head of their problem. "

"Through our national bank, the Federal Reserve, we extend book credit, which we create from nothing, to all local banks who are member banks. They in turn extend book credit to industry. Thus, we do more than God, for all of our wealth is created from nothing. You look shocked! Don't be! It's true, we actually do more than God."

"With this supposed capital we bring industry, management and labor into our debt, which debt only increases and is never liquidated. Through this continual increase, we are able to pit management against labor so they will never unite and attack us and usher in a debt-free industrial utopia."

Through control of banking, the "Jews" acquired a total monopoly of "the movie industry, the radio networks and the newly developing television media...we took over the publication of all school materials... Even your music! We censor the songs released for publication long before they reach the publishers...pretty soon we will have complete control of your thinking."

He says TV programs are carefully designed "to appeal to the sensuous emotions, never to the logical thinking mind. Because of this, the people are programmed to respond according to our dictates, not according to reason. "

He says the "Jews" control Christian churches and use them to introduce ideas like racial equality.

"No law is ever passed except its merits have previously been taught from the pulpits. An example of this is race equality which led to integration and ultimately to mongrelization. The gullible clergy in one breath instruct their parishioners that we are a special, chosen people while in another breath proclaim all races are the same. Their inconsistency is never discovered. So we Jews enjoy a special place in society while all other races are reduced to racial equality. It is for this reason that we authored the equality hoax, thereby reducing all to a lower level."

He boasts that they control Americans using guilt. "Your people don't have guts. We establish your thinking -- we even place within you a 'guilt complex' making you afraid to criticize Jewry openly."

"We Jews have put issue upon issue to the American people. Then we promote both sides of the issue as confusion reigns. With their eyes fixed on the issues, they fail to see who is behind every scene. We Jews toy with the American public as a cat toys with a mouse."

Rosenthal avers that society can only escape this death clutch by violent action not education.

"History has been written in blood, not with ink. No letter, editorial or book has ever rallied the people or stopped tyranny. We understand this principle and are forever propagandizing the people to write letters to the President, to Congress...Woe be unto us if they ever see the futility of it, lay down the pen and employ the sword."

Rosenthal talks about how a "Jewish" invisible government also controls the U.S.SR.

"In Russia, there are two distinct governments one visible and the other invisible. The visible is made up of different nationalities, whereas the invisible is composed of ALL JEWS. The powerful Soviet Secret Police takes its orders from the invisible government. There are about six to seven million Communist in Soviet Russia, 50% are Jews and 50% are gentiles, but the gentiles are not trusted. The Communist Jews are united and trust each other, while the others spy on one another. About every five to six years the secret Jewish Board calls for the purge of the party and many are liquidated. When asked "why"? he said: "Because they begin to understand too much about the Jewish secret government. Russian Communists have a Secret Group Order which consists of Jews only. They rule over everything pertaining to the visible government. It was this powerful organization that was responsible for the secret removal of the centre of Communism to Tel Aviv from where all instructions now originate."

He says Jews control the UN which is "nothing but a trap door to the Red World's immense concentration camp." He says this invisible power is responsible for the wars and revolutions of the last 200 years.

AUTHENTICITY

At times the interview seems almost too damning, and we wonder if it is authentic. Why would someone who says he aspires to national prominence allow such an interview to be taped? Couldn't he be blackmailed? He makes many unflattering and untrue generalizations about Jews, which also seems implausible. At times he veers widely from arrogance to panic. At one point, he says Jews have made plans to pack up and flee.

In 2005, I had a telephone conversation with Des Griffin, author of the classic "Fourth Reich of the Rich." Des told me that he was invited to Walter White's house in California and listened to the tape of the interview. The Rosenthal character in the interview sounded like a bad actor reading from a script. Certain words were repeated. He says the information is totally credible but the conspiracy is real and does not need to be embellished by fraud.

Indeed, the first part of the interview does sound stilted and unnatural. "We are presently making plans for a rapid exodus. We know that when the light begins to dawn, there will be no stopping it. All efforts on our part will only intensify that light and draw focus upon it."

It does seem strange that he would call Jews "parasites" and say they aren't idealistic. In fact, many Jews like myself are extremely idealistic. The bankers have used idealism to manipulate their "lesser brethren" for centuries.

On the other hand, the second part of the interview sounds more credible. The two men bicker over money; the dialogue is believable; and Rosenthal uses Yiddish expressions convincingly.

Ultimately you will make up your own mind. My feeling is that there may be an explanation for what Des Griffin heard, (perhaps Rosenthal was drunk or high on drugs?) In my opinion, the interview contains information that goes further than anything an American Conservative could or would write.

The tone of racial arrogance also rings true. Rosenthal affirms that Jews are a race not a religion which I think is true. He says a Jew remains a Jew whether he converts to another religion or not. He expresses incredulity at the spinelessness and gullibility of the American people. In many places the tone is eerily like that of "The Protocols of Zion."

I doubt if a Christian Conservative like Walter White would pull off the kind of stunt he condemns "the Jews" of doing.

Illuminati Bankers Seek "Revolution" by Economic Means

The Illuminati bankers had us where they wanted Oct. 10 2008. Everyone was in a panic, dumping anything of real value -- gold, real estate, oil -- and rushing into U.S. dollars, a medium of exchange created by the Illuminati bankers out of nothing with the help of their government lackeys.

Why the sudden appeal of U.S. dollars? There is a huge shortage of them because the bankers put our money into mortgages and then they crashed the housing market. Trillions disappeared. Now their lackeys in government have to "borrow" trillions to make up the deficit. The result: the bankers are trillions richer.

Did they do this deliberately? Do you think Rich Fuld, the CEO of Lehman Brothers, got a $250 million send-off for driving his company into bankruptcy? No, that's likely his payoff for selling out his employees and his country. Multiply that throughout the financial industry.

Throughout history the Illuminati bankers have always used war and economic turmoil to advance their goal. Since we have enjoyed prosperity, I have been focused on war. But now I must consider how they use economic hardship to advance their world government.

It's brilliant when you think about it. Depression doesn't involve bloodshed and the destruction of valuable property. On the contrary, it allows the bankers to suck up real wealth at bargain prices. And people under duress will accept anything to regain the delicious prosperity they once knew.

THE RED SYMPHONY

The key to understanding our world is the 1938 interrogation of Illuminati insider Christian Rakovsky (Chaim Rakover) by the Stalinist secret police, the NKVD. Rakowsky was an associate of Trotsky, and a former Russian ambassador to Paris. ("The Red Symphony" is available online at http://mailstar.net/red-symphony.html)

Rakovsky explains that the real goal of Communism is the same as the New World Order, essentially a dictatorship of the Masonic Jewish central banking cartel. The real meaning of "revolution" and all socialist and liberal enterprise is this dictatorship, thinly veiled as "internationalism" and "world government." The propaganda about championing the working class and equality etc. is a ruse to hide the centralization of wealth and power in the hands of this relatively small network of Satanist bankers and tycoons known as the "Illuminati."

His interrogator pressed him to name them. Rakovsky replied that he was only sure of Walter Rathenau and Lionel Walter Rothschild. But he assumed the following were members: "As an institution, the bank of Kuhn Loeb & Company of Wall Street: [and] the families of Schiff, Warburg, Loeb and Kuhn; I say families in order to point out several names since they are all connected ... by marriages; then Baruch, Frankfurter, Altschul, Cohen, Benjamin, Strauss, Steinhardt, Blom, Rosenman, Lippmann, Lehman, Dreifus, Lamont, Rothschild, Lord, Mandel, Morganthau, Ezekiel, Lasky....any one of the names I have enumerated, even of those not belonging to "Them" could always lead to "Them" with any proposition of an important type."

Rakovsky explains that war is necessary to revolution. The Illuminati bankers financed Hitler because they had lost control of Stalin. Now Rakovsky invited Stalin to return to the fold and help them destroy Hitler or else they would give Hitler free rein. Thus Hitler was set up for a war on two fronts. First, the two dictators forged an alliance in August 1939, (mere months after the Fascists defeated the Communists in Spain.) Then when Hitler and Stalin invaded Poland, the Allies declared war against Hitler only.

Rakovsky describes how the Illuminati use economic turmoil to achieve totalitarian control.

He says Oct 24, 1929, the date of the New York Stock Exchange crash ("the beginning of the so-called 'depression'") was more important than the 1918 Bolshevik revolution. It broke the "classical American" individualism and resulted in "a flourishing of parasitism, and capital is a large parasite." It began "a real revolution."

"Although the power of money is political power, before it had only been used indirectly, but now the power of money was to be transformed into direct power. The man through whom they made use of such power was Franklin Roosevelt. Have you understood? Take note of the following: In that year 1929 the first year of the American revolution, in February Trotsky leaves Russia; the crash takes place in October...the financing of Hitler is agreed in July 1929. You think that all this was by chance? The four years of the rule of Hoover was used for the preparation for the seizure of power in the United States and U.S.SR; there by means of a financial revolution, and here [Russia] with the help of war and the defeat [of Stalin] which was to follow." (Full text in Des Griffin, "Fourth Reich of the Rich," p.273)

OBAMA IS THEIR FDR

Barrack Obama is often seen giving the Illuminati sign of Baphomet. Yes, technically the thumb should be folded in, and his excuse is that it is the American Sign Language "I Love You." Just like Bush who pretended this was the Texas Longhorn sign, these Satanists need a cover story. Have you ever wondered why the ASL signal is so similar to the sign of Satan? ASL was financed by the Rockefellers and devised by Helen Keller, a theosophist, i.e. Mason.

History repeats itself because the Masonic Jewish bankers use the same old bag of tricks. If this is an indication, we are in for tough economic times. If the government controlled its own credit, we could easily re inflate the economy at no cost in debt or interest. But with the central bankers controlling credit, I wonder if they will do enough to replace the capital they have drained from the system.

ILLUMINATI PUPPET

OBAMA'08

Familiar Illuminati motif: Dot in circle (penis in vagina) & Luciferian sunrise

The fraudulent nature of our public life all stems from this fundamental fraud, private Illuminati control of public credit. Thus we have a government-sponsored depopulation program in the guise of feminism and gay rights. Thus we had the spectacle of two mind-controlled Illuminati puppets vying for the U.S. Presidency.

The case of Barack Obama was the most egregious. He could not even prove he is an American citizen. There are reports that his real father, Communist activist Frank Marshall Davis, was a rapist and pedophile who probably sexually abused his son. Bill Ayers ghost wrote Obama's 1995 autobiography "Dreams of My Father." Did a promising Harvard Law Review President warrant a six-figure advance from the Illuminati Jewish Simon & Schuster? Who ghost wrote Obama's "The Mendacity of Hope?"

Larry Sinclair claims he has had sex and smoked crack with Obama in the late 1990's. Oddly, this resume is perfect for the Illuminati. Obama can be easily controlled or the Illuminati media will stop ignoring these stories. (To see a puppet malfunctioning, check out the You Tubes of Obama without a teleprompter.)

Joe Biden prophesied that Obama will be severely tested after coming to office and will betray his supporters and plummet in the polls. An odd thing to say before the election. (Notice the Republicans ignored this- suggesting they are in collusion.)

CONCLUSION

I expect a FDR-like "New Deal" from Obama which no doubt will involve much more government control and more "internationalism." Like FDR, Obama will be venerated as some kind of savior. These trends are already evident.

The goal is always the same: total control of wealth and the human race by the Satanist megalomaniacs and their minions who command our credit. Their vehicle is world government and their tool of the hour is Barack Obama.

BOOK THREE

Zionism and the Holocaust

British Jewry Tried to Stop Zionism

When the British Cabinet issued the Balfour Declaration in 1917, it was over the strenuous objections of its only Jewish member, Edwin Montagu. But non-Jews, including many anti-Semites, tipped the scales. Zionism was a way to advance British imperialism and the Masonic "New World Order."

Montagu, who was the Secretary of State for India, told Prime Minister Lloyd George. "All my life I have been trying to get out of the ghetto. You want to force me back there."

An assimilated Jew, Montagu regarded Judaism as a religion , and viewed Zionism as a "mischievous political creed, untenable by any patriotic citizen of the United Kingdom."

His story teaches us that the New World Order is an elite conspiracy led by specific members of certain wealthy Jewish and non-Jewish dynastic families who often intermarried. It is not "Jewish" in terms of a conscious plan of the Jewish people, who historically preferred assimilation.

In May 1917, a committee representing the leading Jewish organizations published a statement in the "London Times" saying: "Emancipated Jews... have no separate political aspirations...the establishment of a Jewish nationality in Palestine founded on [the] theory of a Jewish homelessness, must have the effect of stamping the Jews as strangers in their native lands."

The Balfour Declaration promised Jews a "national home" in Palestine. Partly, it was payment to Zionists for getting the U.S.A into WWI on Britain's side. Zionist president Chaim Weismann fumed that Jewish opposition was the main stumbling block to consummating the deal.

The Jewish community was split. The Samuels and the Rothschilds favored the Balfour Declaration; Cohen, Magnus, Mountefiore and Montagu were against it.

"If it had been merely an issue between Zionist and non-Zionist factions within the community, there is little question that the latter would have won," writes Chaim Bermant in "The Cousinhood." "But there were the gentile Zionists to consider and they carried the day." (pp. 260-262)

These gentiles included Arthur Balfour, Lord Milner, Lord Lothian (Phillip Kerr) and Lord Robert Cecil. Chaim Weismann recognized that Zionism is part of a much larger game: "To [Cecil], the re-establishment of a Jewish Homeland in Palestine and the organization of the world in a great federation were complementary features in the next step in the management of human affairs..." (Reed, "The Controversy of Zion," p. 249.)

Georgetown University professor Caroll Quigley lists about 100 participants in this world government conspiracy in the Appendix of, "The Anglo American Establishment" (1981) They include the above names and Cecil Rhodes, Lionel Curtis, Wiliam T. Stead, Geoffrey Dawson and Earl Grey. I recognized only three Jews: Nathan Rothschild, Leopold Amery and Alfred Beit.

Quigley relates how a group of aristocratic families centred on the Cecils has dominated British politics for centuries. They spawned the secret society organized by Cecil Rhodes and Nathan Rothschild in 1891, which Rhodes called "a church for the extension of the British Empire." (34) Known as "The Round Table" and the "Milner group," its goal was world domination by the British elite and the re-colonization of the U.S..

The "church" was Freemasonry. The politicians that backed Zionism were all high-ranking Masons. Some were probably Illuminati. "World government" is dedicated to enthroning Lucifer as God of this world. Zionism and Communism are Masonic organizations dedicated to this agenda.

A HERO FOR ASSIMILATED JEWS

Edwin Montagu, the second son of the silver bullion dealer Samuel Montagu, was caught between his father's Orthodox Judaism and desire to be an Englishman. He rejected Judaism but was not about to abandon his Jewish identity. "I will always be a good Jew according to my lights," he wrote his father, "my definition differing from yours."

As a youth he chafed at having to observe the rituals and marry a Jewish girl. As an adult, he embraced the lifestyle of a highborn Englishman. On his country estate, he hunted and was a naturalist and ornithologist . "There was something... alien in the very depth of his affection for England," Bermant remarks. (259)

A tall nerdy-looking man who wore a monocle, Montagu suffered the gibes of friends and enemies in silence. His "ugliness was obliterated by his charms," wrote his friend Duff Cooper."He had a huge ungainly body, a deep soft voice and dark eyes that sparkled with kindliness." (253)

An able debater at Cambridge, Montagu caught the attention of H.H. Asquith, the President of the rival Oxford Union. He followed Asquith into politics and after the Liberal landslide of 1906 became his private secretary and friend. An able administrator and persuasive speaker, Montagu seemed destined for great things.

Asquith became Prime Minister in 1908. He and Montagu were both infatuated with Venetia Stanley a friend of Asquith's daughter, and 35 years Asquith's junior. When the Prime Minister's amorous attentions became too much, Venetia married Montagu who was just eight years her senior.

Asquith was non-plused. Montague "is not a man: [he is] a bundle of moods and nerves and symptoms, intensely self-absorbed, and--but I won't go on with the dismal catalogue."

Like Montagu's love for England, his love for Venetia was unrequited. She lived to "get the maximum amount of fun out of life," had many affairs and a child-out-of-wedlock (which Montague adopted) and burned through his fortune. But he ignored all this and, on the eve of his premature death at age 45, wrote to her, "I am miserable at going. You have made me very happy and I hope you will be happy always." (267)

He also had a daughter out of wedlock. Montagu championed the rights of colonial subjects in India and Kenya and made himself unpopular with elements of the British establishment. His untimely death is very suspicious.

ON ZIONISM

In 1917, Montagu fought the Balfour Declaration in cabinet and circulated a document accusing the government of anti-Semitism for making all British Jews "aliens and foreigners." He said he would "willingly disenfranchise every Zionist [and was tempted to] proscribe the Zionist organization as illegal and against the national interest."

Of course he was right. But despite being a banker's son, he wasn't aware of the Masonic/Zionist plan for world government. They dedicated 1.2 million troops to securing Palestine, almost losing the European War as a consequence. They had to replace Asquith and the Army Chief-of-Staff Gen. William Robertson to get it done.

Montagu was one of those rare Jews who tried to understand the reasons for anti-Semitism instead of citing "irrational hate."

"I have always recognized the unpopularity...of my community. We have obtained a far greater share of this country's goods and opportunities than we are numerically entitled to. We reach on the whole maturity earlier, and therefore with people of our own age we compete unfairly. Many of us have been exclusive in our friendships and intolerant in our attitude, and I can easily understand that many a non-Jew in England wants to get rid of us.

"But just as there is no community of thought and mode of life among Christian Englishmen, so there is not among Jewish Englishmen. More and more we are educated in public schools and at the Universities, and take our part in the politics, in the Army, in the Civil Service, of our country. And I am glad to think that the prejudices against inter-marriage are breaking down. But when the Jew has a national home, surely it follows that the impetus to deprive us of the rights of British citizenship must be enormously increased. Palestine will become the world's Ghetto."

Montagu was responsible for inserting the provision in the Balfour Declaration that said: "Nothing shall be done that may prejudice the civil and religious rights of the existing non-Jewish communities in Palestine or the rights and political status enjoyed by Jews in any other country."

FINALLY

Jews are taught that they are scapegoats but they don't learn it is the world government cabal that is using them. By way of Zionist, Communist, Liberal, Feminist or Neo Con organizations, it dupes many Jews into advancing policies and propaganda that undercut the four pillars of human identity and social cohesion: race, religion, nation and family. This gives the appearance Jews in general are responsible for the New World Order.

It doesn't help that many Jews ignorantly deny this conspiracy exists and cry "anti-Semitism" every time a banker is criticized. It doesn't help that many have been conned into thinking they need Israel. In fact, Israelis are being used to secure the Middle East for the Masonic banking elite. The new Israeli Supreme Court building, funded and designed by Rothschilds, is replete with Masonic symbolism.

Some of the Rothschilds and their Jewish allies are part of this Satanic conspiracy. But most Jews put their countries first, and would want no part of world government. Edwin Montagu, a gentle, sincere civilized man, is an example of such a Jew and an inspiration to us all.

The Worst Anti-Semites are Zionists

"Oh, my people ! They who guide you lead you astray." (Isaiah 3:12)

The worst anti-Semites are Zionists who create anti-Semitism and use it to dupe and coerce Jews into advancing the Illuminati banker plan for world government dictatorship.

I will argue in subsequent essays that Zionism is a protection racket and conspiracy against Jews. Here I will suggest they have suppressed normal Jewish cultural/ spiritual expression and hijacked the Jewish people to serve their perverted cause.

Before Zionists took over the U.S. government, they took over the American Jewish community and made it their instrument.

Henry Hurwitz's "Menorah Journal" and Menorah Societies were an attempt by American Jewry to see itself culturally and spiritually as an end in itself, rather than a support system for the "Jewish homeland." Zionists suppressed this free and democratic group just as they deprived all Americans of their political and cultural freedom.

THE MENORAH SOCIETY

Henry Hurwitz started the first Menorah Society at Harvard University in 1906 and its journal "The Menorah Journal" in 1915. The Menorah movement stood "for the study and advancement of Jewish culture and ideals in America." By the end of the First World War, the movement had expanded to include the Intercollegiate Menorah Association, Summer School, Education Conference and Board of Lecturers.

Essentially the movement fostered non-dogmatic, non-political study of Jewish history, spirit and culture. It was open to different points of view and initially received support from the central bankers. But when Hurwitz insisted that Judaism had nothing to do with Zionism, and Jews ought to feel perfectly at home in America, the bankers froze the Menorah movement's funding.

In 1958, Hurwitz wrote a friend, "We have had more than one coy proposal from this and that wealthy organization to take us over. Our financial problems would then be solved. And our freedom--that is, our true life--dissolved." (Menuhin, "The Decadence of Judaism in Our Time," 1965. p. 366)

In the Autumn-Winter 1959 issue of the "Menorah Journal," Hurwitz describes the effect of "bigotry" i.e. Zionist banker control of organized Jewry.

"This bigotry strikes beyond one old established independent organization and its magazine, which have perhaps rendered some service to Judaism through more than half a century. This bigotry poisons the air of Jewish communal life in America. It tries to suppress...the basic American principles of free speech and free press. It penalizes honest analysis [of those] who control the Jewish public tax-exempt philanthropic funds, and hence have the power to enrich favorite organizations, while starving others that do not bend the knees...Thus, they actually hinder here a rational long-view consideration of the best interests of the people of Israel themselves.

"Moreover, as is well known, a very large proportion of the supposedly voluntary philanthropic donations are extracted from business and professional men on threats of punitive economic and social sanctions. This must be described as what it is--a species of terrorism. Such terrorism has become a most effective technique in large Jewish fund raising." (Menuhin, p. 367)

Unfortunately the Menorah movement died with its founder in 1961. Its work was partly continued by the American Council for Judaism, under its dynamic founder Rabbi Elmer Berger (1908-1996.) In 1965, Moshe Menuhin characterized American Jewish life in the following terms:

"Today in America, Jewish culture and even Jewish religion has degenerated into 'Jewish' nationalism, and Jewish philanthropists, Jewish schools, Jewish segregated services, have been all subverted (with a few noble exceptions) into serving...the up building of the 'Jewish homeland'...(468)

A measure of this is that Moshe Menuhin had to self-publish his book.

War and Depression are Forms of Extortion

"Woe unto those who call evil good and good evil, who put darkness for light and light for darkness"... Isaiah 5:20

"The individual is handicapped by coming face-to-face with a conspiracy so monstrous he cannot believe it exists." J. Edgar Hoover

At the end of the 19th Century, the Catholic church organized massive resistance to Illuminati Jewish domination of national life. The Illuminati instigated World War One partly to crush and punish a recalcitrant Europe.

Lenin defined "peace" as *the end of all forms of resistance to Communist* (i.e. Illuminati Jewish) *despotism.*

After WWI and WWII, the League of Nations and the UN both promised world government to prevent war. Indeed, Illuminati globalists always promise this--but we don't realize they are blackmailing us. They start the wars in the first place.

The Elders of Zion vowed to harass the nations with corruption and strife until they accepted their "Superstate" (i.e. world government tyranny.)

"The recognition of our despot may also come ...when the peoples, utterly wearied by the irregularities and incompetence - a matter which we shall arrange for - of their rulers, will clamor: "Away with them and give us one king over all the earth who will unite us and annihilate the causes of disorders - frontiers, nationalities, religions, State debts - who will give us peace and quiet which we cannot find under our rulers and representatives." (emphasis mine, Protocols of Zion, 10-18)

Of course, this also applies to the current economic depression. Right on cue, Henry Kissinger, CEO of the NWO, tells us: "the alternative to a new international order is chaos." The "E" in CEO stands for Extortion. "Please Mr. Kissinger, give back our prosperity. We'll agree to anything."

We are in the eighth inning of a long term conspiracy and must shake off our complacency. This is not another recession; it is a final life-and-death power grab. A Satanic cult, the Illuminati, has subverted all nations and religions and now is moving to consolidate its power. Our "leaders" (including Obama) belong to this cult. From their past record (in Russia & China), it is possible to predict the future: Conditions will deteriorate. There will be civil unrest. An assassination or some other contrived terror will result in war or martial law. Anyone who has expressed opposition to their agenda, -- patriots, Christians, "anti-Semites" -- will be put into concentration camps and possibly murdered. The war and suffering will be such that the masses will accept the Illuminati's sugar coated tyranny. I hope I am wrong.

THE CHURCH'S STRUGGLE WITH SATANISM

For centuries, until after World War Two, the Catholic Church was the bastion of Western civilization and main obstacle to Illuminati world control.

Recently, the Vatican opened their secret archives and revealed their centuries-long struggle to arrest the Illuminati (i.e. Masonic) Jewish stranglehold on European politics and culture. Jewish historian David Kertzer documents this struggle in his book *"Popes Against the Jews"* (2001) which of course he spins as the church's role in creating anti-Semitism. Nevertheless the book is a treasure trove of valuable information including a graphic account of the 1840 "Damascus Affair," the most famous instance of Satanic Jewish human ritual sacrifice. (pp.86 ff.)

The salient points about the Damascus Affair are 1. a prominent Italian Capuchin monk, father Tommaso was ritually slaughtered (and his blood drained) by prominent Cabalist Jews. 2. They confessed and led authorities to his identifiable remains and clothing. 3. The Rothschilds sent a delegation of prominent English Jews to Damascus and pressured all concerned to say the confessions were extracted by torture. 4. The Pope, Gregory XVI, had reliable intelligence and refused to knuckle under. Nor did any future Pope. They also had the testimony of a Moldavian priest, a former Jewish rabbi, who described and explained all the rituals, including the use of Christian blood in Passover matzoh. (92)

When a new ritual murder was reported in Hungary in 1899, the official Vatican newspaper *L'Observatore Romano* issued this warning "not to all Jews but to certain Jews in particular: Don't throw oil on the fire...Content yourself with the Christian's money, but stop shedding and sucking their blood." (163)

Obviously these instances of human ritual sacrifice are relatively rare. The masses of Jews are not Satanic and genuinely want assimilation. Only Satanists among them engage in this practice. Nonetheless, all Jews are implicated by denials and cries of "blood libel." Satanists --Jewish or not-- still engage in human ritual sacrifice today. The Illuminati do it regularly. In addition, they have been doing it to the human race for centuries by virtue of war.

While Jews are not Satanists, their leadership, the Illuminati bankers, are.

In 1913, Illuminati bankers went to great length to whitewash the rape and murder of a 14-year-old girl in Atlanta Georgia by Leo Frank, the head of the local B'nai Brith lodge. They even bribed the jury and the governor. (See the account in Michael Jones, *The Jewish Revolutionary Spirit*, p. 707-729)

For these Illuminati Jews, lying and deception are the norm, what they call "magic." They have convinced their fellow Jews that anti-Semitism is a sickness of the gentile mind, a delusion, when in fact it is resistance to the Satanic Illuminati agenda. Ordinary Jews will be sacrificed when the going gets tough unless they take a stand against their "leaders."

The naivete of Jewish intellectuals is well illustrated by Kertzer himself. He portrays Vatican opposition to Masonic Jewish control as an old reflex born of prejudice, envy and fear of modernity. Yet, he relates that both Bismark and Metternick, the

Austrian Chancellor, were in the Rothschilds' pocket. Metternick depended on them for loans to keep his government afloat as well as "when members of his own family needed financial help." (80)

Kertzer quotes voluminously from Catholic newspapers: "The Jews will be Satan's preferred nation and his preferred instrument...The Jew Freemasons govern the world...in Prussia of 642 bankers, 550 are Jews and in Germany, in Austria and in some parts of the Orient, the word invasion is no exaggeration to express their number, their audacity and their near-irresistible power." (172-3)

Wherever they live "the Jews form a state within a state," an Italian monk wrote in 1825. Unless Christians act quickly, the Jews will finally succeed in reducing the Christians to be their slaves. Woe to us if we close our eyes! The Jews' domination will be hard, inflexible, tyrannical..." (65)

In 1865 the editor of *Civilta Cattolica* warned of secular Jews joining Masonic secret societies "which threaten the ruin and extermination of all Christian society." Such sects "express that anger, that vendetta, and that Satanic hate that the Jew harbors against those who--unjustly he believes--deprive him of that absolute dominion over the entire universe that he Jewishly believes God gave him." (139)

In 1922, the Vienna correspondent for Civilta Cattolica wrote that if present trends continue, "Vienna will be nothing but a Judaic city; property and houses will all be theirs, the Jews will be the bosses and gentlemen and the Christians will be their servants." (273)

JEWISH BLINDNESS TO LEGITIMATE CAUSES OF ANTI-SEMITISM

Like most Jewish intellectuals, Kertzer is incapable of seeing the viewpoint of people his masters wish to despoil. Jews would not accept this kind of domination yet he treats non-Jewish resistance as "anti-Semitism." Catholic grievances are prejudice and Freemasonry was just a way of "providing satisfying social interaction." (p.174) His book was partly sponsored by the Rockefeller Foundation.

Americans eventually will figure out that the Rothschilds and their agents are responsible for the Depression and Obama is their creation and puppet. They will discover that the Illuminati has waged war on humanity for centuries and the U.S. media and education system are a farce. They will recognize the outsized role played by Jews in enacting this diabolical agenda. That's when Illuminati Jews may again turn ordinary Jews, loyal American citizens, into their scapegoats.

Hopefully, people will also see the huge role played by non-Jewish Satanists. For example, the Illuminati *Skull and Bones* was founded at Yale in 1832 but didn't admit Jews until the 1950's. Their members undermined American life from inception.

Now is the time for people to decide where they stand, with the Illuminati and the "peace" of slaves, or with their fellow citizens and freedom. As Leonard Cohen wrote in his song, "The Future"--"*I've seen the future baby and it is murder.*"

Communism–
Zionism's Twin Brother

Recently, I wrote that KGB generals have been given important positions in the Dept. of Homeland Security, run by Lenin look-alike, Zionist Michael Chertoff.

I described this development as the "stealth Communist takeover of the U.S.A. How better do it than when everyone is thinking Muslims, and our elected officials are too corrupt and compromised to protect us?"

We don't recognize what has taken place because we were taught that Communism was an idealistic but discredited "working class" experiment, tried mainly in Russia and China.

This misconception has duped millions of unsuspecting socialists and liberals including myself. As recently as 1999-2000, I was singing the praises of Canadian Maoist dupe Dr. Norman Bethune to my English literature class.

The Illuminati bankers created Communism to harness the working class to their program of a comprehensive world dictatorship (now known as "globalization.") The Illuminati and Communists are Masonic secret societies that celebrate the same anniversary, May 1, 1776 and share the same Satanic symbols. Coincidentally, "Chertoff" means "devil" in Russian.

The program took a giant step in 1913 when these Luciferian London-based bankers gained control over America's finances through the passage of the Federal Reserve Act. This gave them means and incentive to step up their covert war against humanity. The two world wars were the immediate result.

Communism is a Satanic movement devoted to human degradation and enslavement, not public ownership and social justice. Of course, no one would support it if they knew the truth.

AN EX-COMMUNIST SPEAKS

Many high-ranking former Communists have risked their lives to alert their fellow Americans. One is Bella Dodd whose shocking book "School of Darkness" I reviewed in my book, "Cruel Hoax."

She describes how Communists morph into liberals, feminists and socialists, and myriad front groups (identifiable by words like "human rights," "equality," "international" and "peace") to divide and subvert society.

In "Return to My Father's House"(1972), Maurice Malkin, a Jew, provides more revelations. He was a leader of the American Communist Party (CPUSA) in the 1920's and 30's, and part of the Soviet secret service (GPU). When he left the CPUSA, he testified before Congress and suffered a stabbing attack as a result.

Malkin had been involved in the Bolshevik underground in Russia. His older brother Joseph, a devoted Marxist who was later killed by Stalin, taught him that by overthrowing the Czar, workers could "eliminate all injustices and create a heaven on earth." All problems were due to the "class war." The dogma for the dupes went like this:

"The capitalist bourgeoisie owned everything yet the working class did all the work. The mission of the working class was to take through violence what rightly belonged to them...[Only Marxism] could relieve the human race of brutality, discrimination [i.e. anti-Semitism] and injustice, of hunger, poverty and the drudgery that filled the lives of ordinary working people everywhere." (27-29)

Malkin immigrated to New York with this ersatz religion of a workers' heaven on earth ringing in his ears. Lev Bronstein (Leon Trotsky), a close family friend taught him "bullets, not ballots would liberate the workers." (50)

His brother Joseph was one of the 150-175 mostly Jewish radicals who left for Russia with Trotsky in 1917 aboard the S.S. Christiansfjord, financed by banker Jacob Schiff.

The ship was stopped in Halifax and the occupants interned. Despite (or because of) Trotsky's public declaration that they "were going home to Russia to dig the grave of capitalism," Woodrow Wilson intervened on their behalf. Rothschild agent Edward House controlled Wilson.

Communism and the New World Order is basically monopoly capitalism taken to its logical outcome. Government is the ultimate monopoly. The Illuminati bankers despise capitalism because it involves competition and market forces. It allows other people the opportunity to prosper and be independent. Monopoly or state capitalism allows the bankers to own everything and everyone. Of course, this is disguised as "public ownership" but they control the government, its wealth and its security apparatus.

A quote from a 1924 edition of the American Banker's Association Digest sums up what is currently happening under the guise of the "war on terror." Keep this in mind when you vote.

"When, through the process of law, the common people lose their homes, they will become more docile and more easily governed through the strong arm of government applied by a central power of wealth under leading financiers. These truths are well known among our principal men who are now engaged in forming imperialism to govern the world. By dividing the voter through the political party system, we can get them to expend their energies in fighting for questions of no importance. "

"ELITE" SUBVERSION

Thus, for most of the last century the United States has tolerated a party openly dedicated to the violent overthrow of the U.S. government and the enslavement of its people.

This party, the CPUSA was funded and directed by a hostile foreign government. It engaged in industrial and military espionage, trained guerrilla units on American soil, forcibly took over unions, raided their treasuries and controlled whole industries. It slandered, harassed and killed opponents; bribed police and judges and infiltrated the military.

Yet all the while, our highest elected officials defended it as a harmless idealistic enterprise. "Some of my best friends are Communists," FDR famously said.

Malkin reports that Adlai Stephenson (as Assistant to Navy Secretary Knox) sabotaged efforts to curtail Communist activities. In 1956, Eisenhower "liquidated all anti-subversive sections in the Immigration Dept and halted deportation and prosecution of known alien Communists. [He] stopped prosecutions of Communists under the Smith Act, giving the Party a chance to regroup and organize new mass fronts." (191)

The Liberal media marginalized and ridiculed as "right wing fanatics" people who warned of the Communist threat. To this day, people don't accept that the Rosenbergs were indeed Russian spies. The House Un-American Activities Committee is portrayed as a "witch hunt."

Communism is nothing but a sugar-coated goon squad for the Illuminati bankers. Malkin reports that the CPUSA even had a formal alliance with the Mafia, another Masonic sect.

Moscow provided the Mafia with heroin to sell in the U.S.A. The Mafia "lent" money to the Communist Party, provided muscle for taking over the labor movement, and disposed of enemies or members who woke up. (One Communist leader, Juliet Stuart Poyntz, was kidnapped, killed at sea and thrown overboard.) The Mafia also distributed counterfeit U.S. dollars printed in Moscow.

Following Stalin's example, American Communists robbed banks, calling it "expropriation." In his book, "Left Wing Communism" (Vol. 30) Lenin counselled: "Communists are to be ready to cheat, lie, perjure and do everything possible to gain their ends." Thus, when evidence of their skulduggery surfaced, it was little matter to denounce it as a "forgery" and smear the messenger.

The Communist Party infiltrated the Negro Civil Rights movement and got Ralph Abernathy and Martin Luther King to work with their Moscow-trained Negro mercenaries. W.E.B. BuBois and Ralph Bunche were among their "Black" front men but they hardly had any Black followers. American Negroes were too patriotic.

"The Reds realized that the only way to weaken our country is by dividing it through anarchy and chaos," Malkin writes.

They had more luck with women. The Communist attitude to women is instructive since second-wave feminism is Communist in origin. Feminism is recycled "class war" adjusted for gender.

Young female members were used on the waterfront to recruit sailors and longshoremen and bring them to party functions. "Girls would always be found in the

Communist summer camps doing the party's bidding plus offering a little enjoyment on the side. The Party believes that the only laws and morals are Communist morals. .... Communists do not believe in family institutions or morals so everything is free." (239)

The Communists had a department dedicated to "the destruction of the morale of the American people by undermining their faith in their moral and social patterns." (71) You can bet that something like this is behind the promotion of homosexuality and same-sex marriage.

CONCLUSION

When Hitler and Stalin made a pact in 1939, Malkin realized there was little difference between the two and quit the Party. He devoted the rest of his life to defending American institutions, working for the U.S. Dept. of Justice from 1948-1956. He realized belatedly that his religious father's condemnations of Communism were correct. Hence "Return to My Father's House".

Although this book was published in 1972, the Communist conspiracy is more active than ever. Conscious and unconscious agents abound especially in homosexual, feminist, Socialist, Zionist, Neo-con and Liberal circles. "Human Rights" commissions, "employment equity" and diversity officers are modern political commissars. "Hate speech" is censorship applied selectively.

Once, a lesbian running for the head of the English Department at the local social engineering facility began her speech by saying she believed in "peace." What did this have to do with English literature? "Peace" is code for the end of resistance to the NWO, i.e. Communist global tyranny. She was elected Chair of the Department.

The New World Order is full of empty platitudes about "peace" "tolerance" and "human rights." But in light of the NWO's murderous Communist (and Fascist) pedigree, these platitudes are no more convincing than if they were uttered by Ted Bundy or Jeffrey Dahmer.

Western elites (including the intelligentsia) suffer from a peculiar death wish. We would be slaves already were it not for the fact that ordinary Americans own firearms. This, the Internet, and the inherent self-destructiveness of evil, are my main reasons for hope.

Zionism-
A Conspiracy Against Jews

In 1935 the steamer "Tel Aviv" made its maiden voyage from Nazi Germany to Haifa with Hebrew letters on its bow and a Nazi flag fluttering from its mast. The Captain of the Zionist-owned ship was a member of the Nazi Party. A passenger described the spectacle as a "metaphysical absurdity."

Actually it made perfect sense.

The ship transported German Jews who had taken advantage of the "Haavara" program, which allowed them to exchange their money for its value in German products in Palestine. As a result, the fledgling Jewish colony received about 70,000 highly educated German Jews and 140 million Reich marks in German industrial equipment. This laid the foundation of Israel's infrastructure.

The arrangement also boosted the Nazi economy at a time when Jews worldwide were boycotting German products. (My main source here is "The Secret Contacts" by Klaus Polkehn a prominent German journalist. It is included in Olivia O'Grady's "The Beasts of the Apocalyse," 2001, 421-447.)

Why retell this story of Zionist-Nazi co operation now?

Because "Jewish" leaders continue to exploit their innocent "lesser brethren." Ordinary Jews pay the price for their demented plot against humanity and this price could rise.

In my opinion, Zionism is a movement to deceive Jews into advancing the objectives of "British" imperialism. Zionists who have built their lives on a false premise naturally will reject this view.

Specifically, Jews helped the British-Jewish elite colonize the oil-rich Middle East under the pretext of Jews needing a national home. Despite the appearance of neutrality, the British (and Americans) financed, trained and equipped the Jews. (John Coleman, "Diplomacy by Deception," p. 107.)

The "British" are really the London-based international banking cartel associated with names like Rothschild and Rockefeller. It doesn't answer to any government. Its goal is to colonize the world and everyone in it. Jews are a means to this end.

As seen in Iraq, Zionists (a.k.a Neocons) play a major role in the colonization of the Middle East. The important thing to remember is that Israel is the creation of this cartel; both Israel and the U.S. are its tools.

Iraq is only a phase in the emerging New World Order, which represents a continuation of the goals of "British" imperialism. Any new President will take up in Iraq where George Bush left off. Democracy is a charade.

NAZIS MADE-TO-MEASURE FOR ZIONISTS

In 1925, Germany's 500,000 Jews were overwhelmingly indifferent or actively hostile to Zionism. The German Zionist movement had only 9000 members.

The "Central Union of Germans of the Jewish Faith " represented most German Jews and favored active participation in German life. Its main focus was combating anti-Semitism.

Zionists, on the other hand, welcomed the Nazis' anti-Semitic policies. Like the Nazis, they believed in a Master Race, just a different one. Like the Nazis, they believed Jews had no future in Germany.

The Zionists did not protest Nazi persecution such as the removal of 2000 Jewish scholars and scientists from German universities in 1933. The Nazis rewarded this "restraint" by allowing the Zionists to go about their work unhindered. All other Jewish and anti fascist organizations were disbanded and their leaders imprisoned.

The Nazis required all Jews to join the Zionist-led "Reich Union" whose goal was emigration. Jews were to be converted to Zionism at any cost. The Zionists were the only group allowed to publish books and newspapers critical of the Nazis so long as the audience was restricted to Jews.

The cooperation extended to political and economic spheres. Adolph Eichmann set up agricultural training camps in Austria to prepare young Jews for Kibbutz life. He visited Palestine and conferred with Zionist leaders who confessed their true expansionist goals. There was even talk of a strategic alliance between Nazi Germany and Jewish Palestine. His report is in Himmler's Archives.

[For more on Zionist-Nazi cooperation, see online Lenni Brenner "Zionism in the Age of Dictators" Also, Lenni Brenner, 51 Documents: Zionist Collaboration With the Nazis (2002)]

The cooperation may have extended to the Jewish holocaust and explain why most Jews passively accepted their fate. In his book, "The Holocaust Victims Accuse" Rabbi Moshe Shonfeld claims that Zionist-led Jewish Councils ("Judenraten") collaborated with the Nazis and deceived non-Zionist Jews.

Europe's non-Zionist Jews were worth more dead than alive to Zionists and their financial sponsors. The holocaust provided a political and moral rationale for the establishment of the Jewish state.

WHO WAS HITLER?

In 1919, Hitler was an Intelligence Officer with the German Army assigned to spy on the tiny German Labor Party. He became its leader. Max Warburg, brother

Illuminati: The Cult that Hijacked the World

of Paul Warburg, founder of the U.S. Federal Reserve, was the chief of German Intelligence. Both were Directors of the I.G. Farben conglomerate. There is no record of when Hitler stopped working for these Illuminati figures.

Hitler was sponsored by the banker oligarchy, and may have been their pawn. Certainly the Nazis received millions of dollars from New York and London.

The book "Financial Origins of National Socialism" (1933) by "Sydney Warburg" provides a glimpse of how the Illuminist clique supported Hitler. This 70-page booklet was suppressed for many years but was republished in 1983 as "Hitler's Secret Backers."

"Warburg" describes a July 1929 meeting with "Carter," the President of J.P. Morgan's Guarantee Trust, the Presidents of the Federal Reserve Banks, "the young Rockefeller" and "Glean from Royal Dutch." These are all Rothschild dominated.

It was determined that Warburg who spoke German should travel to Germany and ask Hitler how much money he needed to overthrow the state. The only stipulation was that Hitler adopts "an aggressive foreign policy."

"Warburg" details five meetings with Hitler between 1929 and 1933. The first took place in a beer cellar and Hitler calculated his needs on the back of a paper plate. About $25 million was transferred. This was extremely important in the depth of the depression because the Nazis provided jobs to their supporters.

Hitler wasn't told the reason for this support and did not ask. On two occasions, he wondered out loud if "Warburg" was himself Jewish but dismissed the idea before "Warburg" could reply.

There is no "Sydney Warburg" but the internal evidence suggests the author was James P. Warburg, son of Federal Reserve founder Paul Warburg. General Ludendorff testified at the Nuremburg trials that James P. Warburg was the conduit through which eventually $34 million was transferred from Wall Street to the Nazis.

The bottom line is that both Nazism and Zionism were sponsored by the same banking cartel and had complementary goals. The rise of anti-Semitism in Europe served to create the State of Israel, which President Assad of Syria described as a "dagger in the heart of the Arab nations."

Think about it. Hitler could have just confiscated all the Jewish wealth. Instead he used the "Haavara Program" to help establish the State of Israel. According to Polkehn, Hitler personally guaranteed this program in the face of stiff opposition. It lasted until the beginning of the war.

This cartel, which controls the world today, has no compunction about using Jews (or anyone) as a means to an end.

CONCLUSION: JEWS AS PAWNS

Consider the words of an Illuminati defector, Svali.

"The conflict in the Middle East is only to the advantage of the Illuminists. They

HATE Israel, and hope one day to see it destroyed, and are biding their time. One of the olive branches offered by the UN when it takes over is that they will prevent war in the Middle East, and this will be greeted with joy by many.

"At the same time, the Illuminati covertly supply guns and funds to BOTH sides to keep the conflict fuelled. They are very duplicitous people...These people love the game of chess, and see warfare between nations as creating an order out of chaos."

In a personal email, she added:

"I have always wondered this, though, why some of the highest ranking financial families in the group (Baron Rothschild of France is one of the 13 European lords, or "kings" that run the group in Europe, and sits on the World Council) are Jewish, yet the group espouses hatred of their own race."

Zionists Made A Deal
With the Devil

Under the 1935 Nuremberg Laws, only two flags were permitted in Nazi Germany. One was the swastika. The other was the blue and white banner of Zionism.

According to Lenni Brenner's online book "Zionism in the Age of Dictators" (Ch.7), the Zionist party was the only other political party in Nazi Germany that enjoyed a measure of freedom. Zionists and Nazis had a common interest, making Jews go to Palestine.

History is not always what you'd expect. There are more shocking examples in Brenner's book (Chapters 24 & 25). In November 1942, Rabbi Michael Dov-Ber Weismandel, a Jewish activist in Slovakia approached Adoph Eichmann's representative, Dieter Wisliceny: "How much money would be needed for all the European Jews to be saved?"

Wisliceny went to Berlin and returned with an answer. For a mere $2 million they could have all the Jews in Western Europe and the Balkans. Weismandel sent a courier to the World Zionist Organization in Switzerland. His request was refused. The official, Nathan Schwalb sent enough money to save only Weismandel and his cadre. He wrote:

"About the cries coming from your country, we should know that all the Allied nations are spilling much of their blood, and if we do not sacrifice any blood, by what right shall we merit coming before the bargaining table when they divide nations and lands at the war's end? ....for only with blood shall we get the land." (p.237)

Brenner writes that Zionism had come full turn. "Instead of Zionism being the hope of the Jews, their blood was to be the political salvation of Zionism." (p.238)

In Chapter 25, Brenner relates how Zionist leader Rezso Kastner agreed with Adolph Eichmann to save a few thousand hand-picked Zionists and wealthy Jews in return for leading more than 750,000 Hungarian Jews to their death. In 1954, when Kastner was accused of collaborating, the Israeli government sprang to his defence.

Brenner documents how the Zionist and World Jewish leadership prevaricated and obstructed all efforts to save the Jews of Europe.

I am Jewish and my family suffered from Nazi persecution. When I first heard this information, I immediately rejected it. It boggles the mind. However, as I learned more about the Illuminati's ancient plan for world domination, with its Satanic overtones and Masonic plan for rebuilding Solomon's Temple, I became more receptive.

I came to the conclusion that Jews must be sceptical of Zionist leaders who have used the Jewish holocaust to gain undeserved moral authority, and to bludgeon Jews (and others) into hysterical unthinking conformity.

It is possible that Israel was set up for purposes that have nothing to do with the Jewish people, and that Israelis and Jews in general are being duped.

Notes:

Adolph Eichmann told of his dealings with the Zionist Dr. Rudolf Kastner, which ultimately resulted in the deaths of countless assimilated Hungarian Jews, and the survival of the fittest Zionist Jews, Kastner's friends, for Israel. Eichmann stated, "As a matter of fact, there was a very strong similarity between our attitudes in the SS and the viewpoint of these immensely idealistic Zionist leaders who were fighting what might be their last battle. As I told Kastner: 'We, too, are idealists and we, too, had to sacrifice our own blood before we came to power.' I believe that Kastner would have sacrificed a thousand or a hundred thousand of his blood to achieve his political goal. He was not interested in old Jews or those who had become assimilated into Hungarian society. But he was incredibly persistent in trying to save biologically valuable Jewish blood—that is, human material that was capable of reproduction and hard work. 'You can have the others,' he would say, 'but let me have this group here.' And because Kastner rendered us a great service by helping keep the deportation camps peaceful [by not revealing their fate], I would let his groups escape. After all, I was not concerned with small groups of a thousand or so Jews."—A. Eichmann, "Eichmann Tells His Own Damning Story", Life Magazine, Volume 49, Number 22, (28 November 1960), pp. 19-25, 101-112; and "Eichmann's Own Story: Part II", Life Magazine, (5 December 1960), pp. 146-161; at 146.

The Zionist Roots
of the "War on Terror"

Until recently I accepted Israel's self-image as a beleaguered, peace-loving nation in a sea of blood thirsty Arabs. The idea that this tiny state had imperialist designs seemed ludicrous.

But what if, unknown to most people, including Israelis, the world's power elite were using Israel to advance their plan for New World Order?

What if Israel's role were to colonize the Middle East, and to become the seat of the new World Government and Religion?

"Israel's Sacred Terrorism" (1980) by Livia Rokach, a 63-page on line monograph suggests that this bizarre scenario is not so preposterous.

Rokach's monograph is based on revelations from the personal diary of Moshe Sharett, who was Israeli's first Foreign Minister from 1948-1956, and Prime Minister from 1954-1956.

According to this diary, which the Israelis tried to suppress, Israel's image of vulnerability was a ruse. Israel had always planned to become the dominant power in the region, and "invented dangers" in order to dupe its citizens and provoke wars.

In his diary, Sharett quotes a conversation with Army Chief of Staff Moshe Dayan in May 1955:

"We face no danger at all of an Arab advantage of force for the next 8-10 years... Reprisal actions which we couldn't carry out if we were tied to a security pact are our vital lymph...they make it possible for us to maintain a high level of tension in our population and in the army. Without these actions we would have ceased to be a combative people... "

Sharett concludes: "The state.... must see the sword as the main if not the only instrument with which to keep its morale high and to retain its moral tension. Toward this end it may -- no it MU.S.T -- invent dangers, and to do this it must adopt the method of provocation and revenge.... And above all, let us hope for a new war with the Arab countries so that we may finally get rid of our troubles and acquire our space." (41)

"COVERT AGGRESSION"

This policy of "reprisals" or "provocation and revenge" was also called "covert aggression." The U.S. "war on terror" is a continuation of it. Essentially it involves disguising a policy of aggression as retaliation for bogus or false flag provocations.

For example, Israeli patrols would cross the border to attack Jordanians or Egyptians, and then claim the actions took place in Israel. Once attacked, the army pursued the "aggressors" into enemy territory and wreaked havoc. Ariel Sharon was the leader of a squad ("Unit 101") that specialized in these murderous forays. His 1953 raid on the Jordanian village of Kibiyah killed dozens of civilians. (30)

In March 1954, an Israeli bus travelling between Eilat and Beersheba was attacked and 10 passengers were killed. The UN armistice Commissioner, a Col. Henderson said, "from the testimonies of the survivors, it is not proved that all the murderers were Arabs." He attributed the attack to "terrorists intent on increasing the tensions in the area." (28) Thereupon the Israelis left the Armistice Commission in protest.

In June-July 1954, an Israeli terrorist squad blew up many British and American institutions in Cairo in an attempt to sour relations between the Arabs and the West. Dubbed the "Levon Affair," this could have been the thinking behind the 2001 attack on the World Trade Centre.

From the point of view of "covert aggression," if terrorism didn't exist, Israel would have to create it. Possibly, Israel's security establishment inspired some recent attacks on Israelis. In some instances, the terrorists are described as "white." Remember the sniper who killed 10 Israeli reservists at a checkpoint Feb. 3, 2004? If he were Palestinian, wouldn't he have struck again?

Israeli commentators lament that Israel is not a democracy. They say its security establishment has hijacked the country. One pundit remarked, "Israel is not a state with an army, but an army with an affiliated state." They also lament that a culture of corruption, brutality and immorality pervades the army. (See Ran Ha-Cohen, "Israeli Elections So What?")

I believe the Illuminati (i.e. Masonic central bankers) controls Israel's security establishment and government. Many prominent Israeli politicians are Freemasons.

THE USES OF ANTI-SEMITISM

The Illuminati has always used anti-Semitism to trick Jews into advancing its nefarious goals.

In the "Protocols of the Elders of Zion" the speaker confesses the Illuminati has "wiped out every kind of rule except our own." Nevertheless it allows attacks on its plan for world domination in order to create anti-Semitism. "Anti-Semitism is indispensable to us for the management of our lesser brethren." (9-2)

From childhood, Jews are taught that they are disliked for no rational reason and Israel is insurance against another holocaust. This attitude dehumanizes their opponents and obviates the need for genuine self-criticism. Often the question asked by Jews is not, is something true or false? Right or wrong? But, "Is it good for the Jews?"

Traumatizing people and convincing them that irrational fiends threaten their survival is an effective form of mind control. Such people will throw morality and reason to the wind and, if necessary, become savage, mindless killers themselves. They are easily exploited by forces that may not be Jewish at all, that may be anti-Semitic, and plot their ultimate destruction.

Now the Illuminati is using the same tactic on Americans. The Mossad's fingerprints are all over 9/11. Apparently, Israel's Zim Container Lines moved their 200-man office out of the WTC a week before and paid a hefty penalty to break the lease. Seven of the supposed Arab "hijackers" seem to be alive.

If Osama bin Laden didn't exist, the United States and Britain would have created him. There is evidence that he has received money from the British MI-6 as recently as 1996. According to the French daily Le Figaro, Ben Laden met with the CIA station chief in Dubai in July 2001. He serves the purpose of those inciting a bogus "clash of civilizations."

In the domestic sphere, the persecution of Jews has become a cultural paradigm. Lately, women and gays are the Jews, taught they're oppressed. Millions of lives are being ruined. The Illuminati's hidden agenda is to destroy society's immune system (its ability to resist tyranny) by attacking its red blood cell, the nuclear family.

In conclusion, "covert aggression" or "false flag operations" is the primary means by which the Illuminati enacts its long-term plan. Americans have been incited to become oppressors by a phoney Muslim threat. Unaware of what's done in their name. Americans are now, like Jews, asking: "Why do they hate us?"

Zionism:
Compulsory Suicide for Jews

On Nov. 25, 1940, a boat carrying Jewish refugees from Nazi Europe, the "Patra," exploded and sank off the coast of Palestine killing 252 people.

The Zionist "Haganah" claimed the passengers committed suicide to protest British refusal to let them disembark. Years later, it admitted that rather than let the passengers go to Mauritius, it blew up the vessel.

"Sometimes it is necessary to sacrifice the few in order to save the many," Moshe Sharett, a former Israeli Prime Minister said at memorial service in 1958.

In fact, during the holocaust, Zionist policy was that Jewish life had no value unless it promoted the creation of Israel. "One goat in Israel is worth more than the whole Diaspora," Yitzhak Greenbaum, head of the Jewish Agency's "Rescue Committee" said.

Rabbi Moshe Shonfeld accuses the Zionists of collaborating in the Nazi slaughter of European Jewry directly and indirectly.

These charges are contained in his book, "Holocaust Victims Accuse" (1977) which is available on line.

Rabbi Shonfeld calls the Zionists "war criminals" for usurping the leadership of the Jewish people, betraying them to be slaughtered, and then reaping the moral capital from their own treachery.

Shonfeld states: "The Zionist approach that Jewish blood is the anointing oil needed for the wheels of the Jewish state is not a thing of the past. It remains operable to this very day."

Other books by Jews that reiterate this theme include Edwin Black, "The Transfer Agreement;" Ben Hecht, "Perfidy," M.J. Nurenberger, "The Scared and the Damned;" Joel Brand, "Satan and the Soul;" Chaim Lazar, "Destruction and Rebellion;" and Rabbi Michael Dov Ber Weismandel "From the Depth."

The implication is that at heart Zionism is not really a pro-Jewish movement. In the words of veteran Israeli politician Eliezar Livneh, "The Zionist heritage had in it something flawed to begin with."

SHOCKING "HIGHLIGHTS" OF RABBI SHONFELD'S BOOK

While European Jews were in mortal danger, Zionist leaders in America deliberately provoked and enraged Hitler. They began in 1933 by initiating a worldwide boycott of Nazi goods. Dieter von Wissliczeny, Adolph Eichmann's lieutenant, told Rabbi

Weissmandl that in 1941 Hitler flew into a rage when U.S. Zionist Rabbi Stephen Wise, in the name of the entire Jewish people, "declared war on Germany" which held six million Jews hostage in occupied Europe.

Hitler fell on the floor, bit the carpet and vowed: "Now I'll destroy them. Now I'll destroy them." In Jan. 1942, he convened the "Wannsee Conference" where the "final solution" took shape.

Rabbi Shonfeld says the Nazis chose Zionist activists to run the "Judenraten" (Jewish government) and to be Jewish police or "Kapos." "The Nazis found them to be loyal and obedient servants who because of their lust for money and power, led the masses to their destruction."

The Zionists were often intellectuals who were "more cruel than the Nazis" and kept the trains' final destination a secret. In contrast to secular Zionists, Shonfeld says Orthodox Jewish Rabbis refused to collaborate and tended their beleaguered flocks to the end.

Rabbi Shonfeld cites numerous instances where Zionists sabotaged attempts to organize resistance, ransom and relief. They undermined an effort by Vladimir Jabotinsky to arm Jews before the war. They stopped a program to send food parcels to the ghettos (where child mortality was 60%) saying it violated the boycott.

They thwarted a British parliamentary initiative to send refugees to Mauritius, demanding they go to Palestine instead. They blocked a similar initiative in the U.S. Congress. At the same time, they rescued young Zionists. Chaim Weizmann, the Zionist Chief and later first President of Israel said: "Every nation has its dead in its fight for its homeland. The suffering under Hitler are our dead." He said they "were moral and economic dust in a cruel world."

Rabbi Weismandel, who was in Slovakia, provided maps of Auschwitz and begged Jewish leaders to pressure the Allies to bomb the tracks and crematoriums. The leaders didn't press the Allies because the secret policy was to annihilate non-Zionist Jews. The Nazis came to understand that death trains and camps would be safe from attack and actually concentrated industry there. (See also, "Are Jews Being Set Up for Another Holocaust?" within.)

None of the above is intended to absolve the Nazis of responsibility. However, the holocaust could have been prevented or at least alleviated had the Zionist leadership behaved honorably. One can't help but suspect that the Zionists needed to increase the number of Jewish victims to hide their own role in bringing Hitler to power and instigating World War Two. (See "Did the Illuminati Hire Hitler to Start World War Two?")

WHAT IS "ZIONISM"?

Lord Acton said, "The truth will come out when powerful people no longer wish to suppress it." Since Sept. 11, more and more people are turning to the "conspiratorial" or "suppressed" view of history.

In 1891, Cecil Rhodes started a secret society called the "Round Table" dedicated to world hegemony for the shareholders of the Bank of England and their allies. These priggish aristocrats, including the Rothschilds, realized they must control the world to safeguard their monopoly on money creation as well as global resources. Imperialism never reflects national interests but the agenda of these bankers.

They were united also by a commitment to freemasonry, which at the top, is dedicated to the destruction of Christianity, the worship of Lucifer, and the rebuilding of a pagan temple in Jerusalem. They see humanity as "useless eaters" and pioneered eugenics and brainwashing to decrease population and turn us into their servants. The eventual annihilation of non-Zionist Jews was rooted in this movement.

In 1897, the first Zionist Congress took place in Basle. In 1904, the founder of Zionism Theodore Herzl died at age 44 under suspicious circumstances. The movement was taken over by the Round Table. Zionism and Communism were two pincers to advance their plan for world hegemony. During the same week in November 1917, the Bolshevik Revolution took place and the Balfour Declaration promised Palestine to the Jews.

The Round Table group planned three world wars to degrade, demoralize and destroy mankind, rendering it defenceless. The Third World War, now beginning, pitted the Zionists against the Muslims.

The purpose of Zionism is to help colonize the Middle East, subvert Islam, and control the oil fields. For this reason Israel continues to receive blank checks. (One analyst estimates the U.S. taxpayer has spent $1.7 trillion on Israel.) This is why the founding of Israel took precedence over the welfare of the Jewish people. People complain that Israel controls the U.S.. It is just an instrument of the central bankers who control both.

Israel has little to do with the Jewish people. Zionism, Communism, Feminism, Nazism, are all creations of the same Satanic cabal. These "isms" are all means to the final goal, a neo feudal global dictatorship. FBI Director J. Edgar Hoover referred to this when he said: "The individual is handicapped by coming face to face with a conspiracy so monstrous he cannot believe it exists".

As unwitting overseers, Israelis will continue to be victims of "compulsory suicide." Americans too are being fitted for this role. Sept. 11 was an example.

Arab terrorism is also backed by this cabal. Osama Bin Laden made more than 260 phone calls to England between 1996-1998. The aim is to contrive a "war of civilizations" as an excuse to grind down both Muslim states and the West to create the global police state.

What I have been calling "compulsory suicide" is really Satanic "culling." The constant references by Zionist and other leaders to "blood sacrifice" refers to the practice of human sacrifice. Apparently energy is released when people are slaughtered. Recently U.S. Deputy Secretary of State Richard Armitage said the Hezbollah owes the U.S. a "blood debt."

Our rulers design wars as offerings to Lucifer. They find slaughter and mayhem exhilarating, as long as it is someone else who is sacrificed.

WHERE DOES THIS LEAVE THE JEWS?

Mankind has been betrayed by its leadership. Of Jewish leadership, Israeli journalist Barry Chamish says: "The richest appoint themselves to the highest posts. Thus the greediest and most unscrupulous run the show. [They] ... will sell their souls and those of their people for power and acclaim." (Barry Chamish, "Just as Scared, Just as Doomed.")

There are a few hundred thousand orthodox Jews like Rabbi Shonfeld who have always understood Zionism. They have always rejected the state of Israel and remained faithful to the Torah. They could form a core for a genuine Jewish revival. Their websites are www.jewsagainstzionism.com, www.jewsnotzionists.org. and www.netureikarta.org.

In conclusion, a Satanic cult governs the world. These people hate God, hate mankind and want to destroy it. They believe the end justifies the means and are ruthless. They use the Jews, and everyone else, as cannon fodder. We are "children of the matrix," duped, distracted, stunted and sacrificed. Without the vision provided by God, we are lambs being led to slaughter.

The Jews' Worst Enemy - Illuminati Jews

In 1962, Christopher Story was the only 'goy' working at Jewish banker "S. Japhet & Co." in the City. The Eichmann trial was in the news and Story asked a Jewish co-worker, a "nice middle aged lady," if Adolf Eichmann wasn't himself Jewish?

She replied:" Didn't you know that a Jew's greatest enemy is another Jew?"

Story, 68, now a veteran British journalist, believes that many Nazis who planned and implemented the holocaust had Jewish blood. Jews who belonged to the (Masonic) Illuminati conspiracy "sided with the Luciferian German Nazis to exterminate millions of their own race in what amounted to an inter-Jewish civil war and ethnic cleansing operation..." ("The New Underworld Order," 532)

The motivation? Prevent Jews from disappearing as a nation and trick them into becoming Zionists and advancing the New World Order. He cites the famous article in the Jewish owned "Daily Express" headlined "Judea Declares War on Germany" (March 24, 1933). It states that Hitler "has aroused the whole Jewish people to a national consciousness." (535)

Before Hitler came to power, less than 3% of Germany's 500,000 Jews belonged to the Zionist movement. By the 1930's, 60% of all German Jewish marriages were interracial. In another generation or two, the Jews of Germany would have disappeared.

As a child, Eichmann was persecuted because he looked Jewish. Eichmann's stepmother had Jewish relations and he associated with Jews. Later, as a Gestapo officer, Eichmann learned Hebrew, visited Palestine and worked closely with Zionists preparing Jews for emigration. (David Cesarani's "Eichmann: His Life and Crimes.")

Reinhard Heydrich had a Jewish maternal grandmother and this forced Heydrich to commit heinous crimes out of gratitude for not being exposed. (Wighton, "Heydrich: Hitler's Most Evil Henchman" 1962). Himmler's grandfather was also Jewish, as Hitler's was half-Jewish.

THE HORST HOYER MEMORANDUM

SS Lieutenant General Horst Hoyer was in charge of a labor force of 250,000 Jews in the Lemburg (Lvov) region of Poland. In 1952, when Germany and Israel were negotiating holocaust reparations, Hoyer submitted a memorandum arguing that the main responsibility for the "final solution" should fall on both Nazis and certain Jews.

Hoyer writes that the "final solution" emanated from "official Jewish and German departments" in the German Military Transportation Command in Akademizca Street in Lemburg.

"There, to the best of my knowledge, is where the details of the "final solution" were clearly laid out. Sephardic Jews could hardly have been victims, for these were taken out of Galicia by the hundreds, as entire families were flown out by the German Armed Forces with their Allies, in connection with the "final solution". Thus, in October 1943, sixteen selected Jews were taken from my labor camp to Lublin and then to the old civilian airport on the Chortower Highway and flown to neutral Spain, to be handed over to the United States, including a relative of Henry Morgenthau, a member of President Roosevelt's cabinet."

"From July 1941 to march 1943, I was Chief Administrator of some 250,000 Jews, officially organized as the German Four Year War Effort. Our orders included manufacturing army clothing, processing scrap metals, captured war materials and the like. These Jews were paid volunteers. To secure smooth operations, I had to trust "my Jews" as head of departments and keepers of logs. Through them I was informed of all world happenings, even on an hourly basis. This was, for me, incomprehensible and even fantastic. Thus, I got insights which left me speechless, for "my Jews" knew full well, what World Jewry had in store for them and they were as helpless as the German people themselves."

Lieut. General Hoyer gives their names.

"Is Siegfried Langsam, the onetime Austrian officer still alive? Are Walter Sonnenschein and Dr. Wachter with their wives still alive? What about Zuckerhorn, Spitze, Loewenstein, Gregor, Fackler and many, many others? Are they anywhere in the world? If so, let them now step forward and tell their people, as well as the German people, fearlessly, what took place in the Akademizca Street! At the time, they feared World Jewry, putting me in their confidence, didn't they? They pleaded for my help, knowing full well that I was utterly helpless in the face of these underhanded activities. From that street in Lemburg emanated actions which neither the German nor the Jewish people, nor the SS, nor the front soldiers knew about, or could have known."

Hoyer describes a strange event that took place after a business meeting with leaders of the Warsaw ghetto:

"As our official deliberations were ended, an orderly announced, 'Officials! Leaders! The gentlemen have arrived.' Some sixteen or seventeen serious looking Jews were ushered in, introduced and took their seats around a large oval table. In a festive short hour, recognition was given these Jews with personalized certificates (on white hard paper, 40 by 40 cm). On the left was a large golden national insignia with letters in Gothic and a seal with the original signature of Adolf Hitler."

"These certificates assured the full protection of these Jews, their families and properties by the Greater German Reich. Included were words of thanks and blessings by Hitler in the name of the German people. Around this table with its distinguished Jews and in this festive hour, one sensed no hatred, no war and no conspiracy. "

Hoyer describes the behavior of the Warsaw Ghetto "upper crust":

"As part of my official duties, I became intimately acquainted with the Ghetto in Warsaw. There a small class of workers, artisans and professionals, did their duties faithfully and diligently. But, in this, they were forced to live miserably as the upper classes were involved in underhanded dealings in the black market. Thus by haggling, one could obtain in the Ghetto all which made life happy, pleasant and alluring. Over and above all of this, capsuled off, was a thin upper crust celebrating apocalyptical orgies, as champagne and various brands of beverages flowed freely with an abundance of exquisite foods. Meanwhile, the Jewish proletariat lay in the streets, starving, begging and dying."

"Once in our discussions, I was told, passionately, "Our race has to learn to sacrifice!" Later I was told by Jewish Fascists, "Of those here, we shall still let 60% 'bite the dust' before Madagascar."

Hoyer claims that he was offered 300,000 DM to renounce his memorandum as a hoax. He refused and was later murdered. His wife committed suicide.

Dr. Harrell Rhome helped make the Hoyer Memorandum public on his website "Gnostic Liberation Front." He writes: "the number of persons involved in the "final solution" was extremely small and they were masters of deception. In this one must be mindful of the intense inner-Jewish tensions and contrasts, above all between the goals of the nationally assimilated Jews and those of world Jewry and Zionism. These contrasts are much, much deeper than the one between believing and non-believing. As one becomes aware of this, many things otherwise incomprehensible about Jewry become clear, foremost, that one group of Jews fell victims to another, and that of those targeted, few escaped."

"...Wartime collaboration should be no surprise, and is easily verified. Did you know that some Jews lived openly in Berlin during the war, with synagogue services? When the Soviets entered Berlin, they found over 800 who had been sheltered in a special hospital that was open for them all throughout the war. If the Germans were so intent on killing them all, how could this be?"

CONCLUSION

The "Jewish Conspiracy" is really the "Half-Jewish Conspiracy." Many prominent members intermarry or are the products of intermarriage. John Kerry is an example. Many are Jewish and many are not. What they all really have in common is loyalty to the Masonic Illuminati Order, which has subjugated the planet by manufacturing war.

Obviously part of their strategy was to martyr assimilated non-Zionist Jews in order to hoodwink the rest of the world into supporting Zionism. This is why Hitler pretended to be a racial purest while being part-Jewish himself, having many part-Jewish associates, and making thousands of exceptions to his race policies. His race policy mirrored the Jewish one. He had to convince Jews and the rest of the world that Jews are hated on the basis of race alone, and must have a "national home."

The Holocaust as Mind Control

Israel's most potent psychological weapon is the holocaust. The Zionist battle cry is "Never again!"

In a previous article, I suggested that the real motivation behind traumatic events like Hiroshima and Sept. 11 might be to impose a new mental paradigm upon humanity. Zionists and their globalist sponsors may have contributed to the severity of the holocaust for the same reason.

Because of the holocaust, Jews became convinced that they needed their own country and the world agreed. The Palestinians were identified (in many minds) with the Nazis, and the Israelis were given moral sanction to drive them from their homes and land and subjugate them. Criticism of Israel is often equated with Nazi anti-Semitism.

As a psychological weapon, the holocaust also serves an array of New World Order causes.

The world is divided into heroic victims (Jews) and haters (Nazis). The "victims", who are championed by Rockefeller liberals, include oppressed women, homosexuals, and the minority flavor-of-the-day. The "haters" are the intolerant people who defend the things the globalists want to destroy: nuclear family, religion, democracy, individualism and nationhood. The haters are "right-wingers" for whom the tolerant liberals have "zero tolerance."

It is not my intention to mitigate Nazi responsibility for the Jewish holocaust but to scrutinize its use by Zionists and globalists as a psychological weapon. Before I continue, I had better declare myself.

I am a non-observant, non-self-hating Canadian Jew who believes in God and Christ's gospel of love. My grandparents all died in the holocaust; my parents narrowly survived by passing as non-Jews. I lived in Israel in 1972-3 but left because Israelis seemed as materialistic as Canadians. Israel also struck me as a country that devoured its own people.

Nevertheless I remained a Zionist until I discovered its true character. I still support Israel's existence within the 1967 boundaries, with restitution to the Palestinians. I believe most Israelis and Jews have been hoodwinked as I was.

DEFENDING A PSYCHIC MONOPOLY

The definitive history of the holocaust is "The Destruction of the European Jews" by the late Rolf Hilberg, a Jewish professor of Political Science at the University of Vermont. Hilberg's three-volume work is largely based on meticulous Nazis documentation.

Hilberg could barely get his book published because he documented the extent to which the Nazis depended on the Jewish Councils ("Judenrat") to administer the final solution, and the lack of any real Jewish resistance. He estimated that fewer than 200 Nazis died due to Jewish resistance.

Why the negative reaction? Hilberg concluded that the mythology of the holocaust requires that the victims appear to be heroic, and to be engaged in a struggle, however unequal. In fact, the Jews went to their death like lambs to the slaughter. (Hilberg, "The Politics of Memory," p.135)

In the 1960's the Jewish philosopher Hannah Arendt was slandered and ostracized when she concluded from Hilberg that "almost without exception" the Jewish leadership co-operated with the Nazis.

In her book, "Eichmann in Jerusalem" she wrote, "In Amsterdam as in Warsaw, in Berlin as in Budapest, Jewish officials could be trusted to compile the list of persons, and of their property, to secure money from the deportees to defray the expenses of their deportation and extermination, to keep track of vacated apartments, to supply police forces to help seize Jews and get them on trains, until, as a last gesture, they handed over the assets of the Jewish community in good order for final confiscation. They distributed the Yellow Star badges [and sometimes sold] cloth and fancy plastic armbands which were washable." (p.117)

Had the Jews been totally unorganized and leaderless, Arendt writes, there would have been chaos and misery aplenty but the total number of deaths would have been far less. (p.125)

The reason Jews went quietly is not a mystery. Jewish leadership betrayed them. Hilberg attributes it partly to an age-old Jewish habit of persevering in the face of overwhelming odds. But a more important factor is that both Jewish world leadership and the Judenraten were dominated by Zionists.

Zionists did not believe in the Jewish Diaspora and actively sabotaged rescue attempts. If Jews could escape to other countries, what would be the purpose of Israel? Thus the Zionist Rabbi of Sweden Dr. Ehrenpreis scuttled a Swedish attempt to rescue 10,000 Jews. Zionists torpedoed a similar move by the British parliament. They also rejected numerous legitimate ransom attempts and discouraged resistance.

Generally the Zionists served the globalist elite agenda, suppressed news of the holocaust and didn't agitate for special measures. The Allies bombed factories a few kilometres from Auschwitz but the crematoriums and railroad tracks were untouched. The Zionists believed that the greater the Jewish losses, the greater the world's moral obligation to them.

WE WERE LIED TO

Young Jews like myself were told that Arab countries attacked peace-loving Israel after the 1948 U.N. Partition. They broadcast messages for the Palestinians to leave until the Jews were cleaned up.

In fact, Israel was given 57% of Palestine but immediately took more land and caused 700,000 Palestinians to flee in terror by slaughtering over 250 at Deir Yassin and another 250 at Lydda. The Arab radio broadcasts were a fable. Arab broadcasts encouraged the population to stay put. (Michael Prior, "Zionism and the State of Israel: A Moral Inquiry," 1999, pp.16-29, 187-205)

David Ben Gurion, the first Prime Minister of Israel, told TIME magazine (Aug. 16, 1948) that he envisaged a Jewish state of ten million souls. Asked if that many could be accommodated within the U.N. partition boundaries, he replied: "I doubt it."

Unknown to its citizens, Israel has always been designated to colonize the Middle East and be a linchpin in the new world order.

"Our policy must be the unity of the human race," Ben Gurion told the TIME reporter. "We consider the United Nations to be a Jewish ideal."

Look at how the Mossad website "Debka Weekly" characterized the Iraq war:

"Washington will have its hand on the oil lever and the ability to make Iraq's neighbors dance to its plan for reshaping the national borders and governments of the Middle East." (Vol. 2, Issue 94, January 23, 2003)

In conclusion, the holocaust gave the globalists the "moral authority" to invade Palestine, and enlisted unwitting Jews worldwide to their cause. In fact, they betrayed the trust of European Jewry in the most heinous fashion. Israelis and Jews in general can blindly follow their leaders, as European Jewry did. Americans can trust Barack Obama. But the results are certain to be the same.

Mightier than the nuclear bomb, the Lie is Satan's most powerful weapon. The bomb merely devastates. The Lie steals souls. It enlists millions of naïve people to Satan's cause.

Are Jews Being Set Up for Another Holocaust?

In 1938-39, just before Europe erupted in an inferno for Jews, all the exits were sealed shut. The Nazis had no problem allowing Jews to leave. The problem was that no country allowed them to enter.

In May 1939, the passenger liner "St. Louis" carrying 900 German Jewish refugees was turned away from Havana. The passengers' costly tourist visas had been revoked by Cuban authorities. The liner lingered near the coast of Florida but FDR refused to let it dock. Reluctantly, the ship returned to Europe where the refugees were divided among four Allied countries, of which three soon were overrun.

The image of unwanted Jews was seared into the collective Jewish psyche. It argued the necessity of a homeland in Israel as insurance against anti-Semitism. Millions of Jews devoted their money and lives to wresting Israel from its rightful owners and building a Jewish sanctuary there. Millions of non-Jews were recruited to this cause. World peace has hung in the balance ever since. The Third World War is being prepared on this battleground.

FDR famously said nothing in politics happens by accident. The possibility that the holocaust was staged to manipulate Jews, and give them a kind of moral impunity, is repugnant to consider.

However, a book, "The Holocaust Conspiracy" (1989) shows how Allied and neutral governments ensured that most Jews would remain in Europe and would die. The author William R. Perl argues that a parallel Nuremberg Trial is necessary for "those leading figures in the Allied and neutral camps" who "knowingly and willingly co-operated in the German annihilation scheme." (34)

William Perl (1906-1998) was not some armchair conspiracy theorist. He was a lawyer in Vienna in the 1930's who helped organize illegal transits to Palestine for the Revisionist Zionists. He negotiated with Adolf Eichmann face-to-face; and after the war, he prosecuted Nazi war criminals.

In this book, Perl argues that the Jewish holocaust was part of an international conspiracy. But of course, he didn't understand that the perpetrators were the Illuminati, a secret network comprising the highest rung of Freemasonry (including Communists, Zionists and Nazis) empowered by the world central banking cartel. Their goal is to create a world government tyranny dedicated to Lucifer with its capital in Jerusalem.

Holocaust means "burned offering." By what logic can we call this genocide a "sacrifice"? By Illuminati logic of course. They sacrificed Jews to hoodwink the world into establishing a Masonic state in Israel. The design of the Israeli Supreme Court is proof that this has transpired. Modern Israel was Masonic from conception.

This begs the question: If the Jewish holocaust was contrived by the people who run the world, would they do it again? I'll address this question at the end.

PERL'S CASE

William Perl states that there were "deliberate, concerted steps to thwart rescue actions...not only by individuals in power but by governments." He says this failure to rescue was more than a simple lack of action but a "deliberate set of actions bound to ensure the success of the German annihilation plans." While this seems "unbelievable," he says the documents available make this conclusion "not only logical but inescapable"(16.)

For example, Morgenthau's Treasury Dept. investigated the State Department and identified a half dozen top officials as "an American underground to let the Jews be killed." The report was especially critical of John J. McCloy, assistant Secretary of War, who later became the Rockefeller's lawyer, U.S. High Commissioner for Germany, the President of the World Bank and a member of the Warren Commission. Yes children, he was Illuminati.

Perl says that next to the Nazis, the British "carry the heaviest guilt" for the Jewish holocaust because they blocked the escape route to Palestine. In fact, the first person killed by the British in WWII was a Jewish refugee on the vessel "Tiger Hill."

Now you ask, if the Rothschilds control England, and wanted to set up a national home for Jews, why wouldn't England let all these Jews go to Israel? The answer is that this action would demonstrate to Jews that they didn't need a state and didn't need to become the lethal weapon they have become for the Rothschilds.

The Soviets were supposed to be a Jewish front. But Perl also blames the U.S.SR. Information was tightly controlled in Russia and the Soviets did nothing to warn the Jews of what they could expect from the Nazis. (In his biography of Hitler, John Toland describes non-Communist Jews in the Ukraine greeting the Nazis as saviours.)

Just to illustrate the transnational nature of the Illuminati, in Feb 1942, a Soviet submarine torpedoed the "Struma" a disabled cattle boat crammed with 760 Romanian Jewish refugees. There was one survivor. Why this gratuitous murder of Jews? More souls sacrificed for the future capital of the Luciferian New World Order. More reasons to tug on the heart strings of humanity.

The Allies also blocked Nazi attempts to ransom Jews and calls to bomb the concentration camps, although in 1944 factories five miles from Auschwitz were demolished. In all this, the Allies were supported by the Zionist establishment, which is directed by the Illuminati.

COULD IT HAPPEN AGAIN?

History teaches that the Illuminati consists of Satan-loving Jews and non-Jews; and exploits and kills anyone who doesn't fit into its plan for a Luciferian NWO. At first glance, Israel would be a prime candidate for a repeat of the Jewish holocaust as most Israelis probably don't see themselves in Masonic NWO terms.

Fellow Winnipegger Barry Chamish believes that the Illuminati, through its CFR arm, controls Israel and intends to spare Jerusalem, but sacrifice the rest to its ultimate goal.

In America, the Jewish role bears a remarkable resemblance to their position in the Weimar Republic. Their role in government, culture and the economy is well out of proportion to their numbers. As witting and unwitting tools of the Illuminati, they are seen by many as undermining Christian and American interests.

Pastor Chuck Baldwin made the comparison with Jesus and the "moneychangers."

"It is too bad that today's pastors and Christians do not share Jesus' disdain for the current generation of moneychangers, because it is the moneychangers who are in the process of destroying these United States of America--and our pastors and Christians either do not see it, or, if they do see it, do not seem to care."

Americans, like the Germans before them, are not anti-Semitic by nature. The economic situation in Germany had to deteriorate before Hitler could come to power. The economic situation in America is beginning to deteriorate. The real question is, does the Illuminati have anything to gain from an attack on Jews?

In the short term, as long as they need Zionists to control America, no. But as the New World Order becomes more onerous, and the position of Americans more perilous, the Illuminati may be happy to use Jews as their scapegoats once again. After all, pawns are made to be sacrificed.

The Other Side
of Holocaust Denial

Although I am the grandson of holocaust victims, I am embarrassed by Jewish organizations that want to make the Jewish holocaust the defining event of World War Two. This is seen in the boom in "Holocaust Studies Programs," Holocaust Museums and Hollywood movies like "The Pianist."

The Second World War was a human calamity. Over 60 million people died. Why focus on the Jewish experience? The purpose is to "own" the victim status. Guilt is a very effective psychological weapon. The Illuminati use it to elevate Jews to a special status. They do the same with Blacks, women and homosexuals.

Ethnocentrism is the cause of anti-Semitism in the first place. Jews are accused of always "taking over." Jewish power brokers are perpetuating a vicious cycle.

I am also troubled by the attempt to classify people like Ernst Zundel as a "hate criminal." Zundel's website claims only one million Jews were murdered; there were no gas chambers; and Hitler didn't intend genocide. Zundel's claims are wrong, but he has a right to be wrong. Society needs people to dispute the historical record. One may be right. If spreading false information is a crime, shouldn't we also lock up the announcer at NBC Nightly News?

Canada locked up Ernst Zundel. According to his wife, he was mistreated in prison. He was deported to Germany as a "security risk." Bernie Farber of the Canadian Jewish Congress conceded Zundel didn't "actually wield the stick" but "provided oxygen" to extremists. That definition would curb everyone's freedom of speech. The CJC is trying to curb mine.

When questioning what is true becomes "hate", we have entered Orwell's "1984" era of thought crime. Don't kid yourself. This is the slippery slope to tyranny and Jewish organizations like the CJC are leading the way.

The definition of hate is used selectively to re-engineer and brainwash society. For example, lesbian and feminist professors teach impressionable girls that males are potentially violent sexual predators and all families are oppressive. That's OK. The Talmud is full of hatred against Christ and Christians, but that doesn't count either.

Canadian MP Svend Robinson wanted to make "gay bashing" a hate crime. He isn't talking about violence against gays, which is a genuine crime. He would prevent society from defending itself from activists who teach children that heterosexual roles are not natural but homosexual ones are. (Robinson's career ended after he was arrested for shoplifting a gold ring for his male lover.)

Many so-called "Anti-Semites" have written me and most are not hateful or racist in the least. They are trying to defend their legitimate interests from an insidious attack. The arch anti-Semite Henry Ford, author of "The International Jew" employed thousands of Jews in his factories. He worked closely with a Jew, Mme. Rosika Schwimmer on his Peace Ship crusade. Ford's Jewish architect Albert Kahn designed scores of buildings for him.

Jewish power brokers use anti-Semitism to disarm opposition to their political agenda. The promotion of the Jewish holocaust maintains the Jews' status as the world's premier "victims." This gives them immunity from criticism. It makes people feel more favourable to them and willing to accede to their direction and influence. (The same strategy is used to paint homosexuals and women as "victims.")

Jewish power brokers use victim status to manipulate Jews and extract their donations. Victimhood turns some Jews into moral zombies. For most of my life, I didn't consider the right of Palestinians to their homeland. "We suffered, we deserve a homeland," the logic went.

The holocaust also serves their New World Order agenda. It is a constant reminder of the pitfalls of nationalism or racial consciousness, two things the financial elite is trying to bury for everyone in the West but Jews.

"ALSO RAN" HOLOCAUSTS

To maintain victim priority, it's necessary for the Jewish establishment to practise "holocaust denial" when it comes to other people.

In his book "Crimes and Mercies" (1997) James Bacque describes how he confronted "New York Times" reporter Drew Middleton with evidence that after the war, the U.S. starved to death over one million German POWs. "What Middleton told me basically was that, yes, he had lied in 1945 and no, it did not matter to him or the "New York Times" if I exposed this." (183)

"Middleton's sense of security, his sense of the New York Times' power, took my breath away", Bacque writes. "But worse than that, Middleton did not care about this atrocity... the New York Times witnessed it, then denied that it happened. And has gone on denying it into the 1990's." (184)

Bacque estimates that, during the Allied Occupation (1946-1950) an additional eight to twelve million Germans were deliberately starved to death. The war did not end in 1945. For five additional years, Germany was subjected to "physical and psychic trauma unparalleled in history." (93)

Red Army soldiers raped up to two million German women during the last six months of the Second World War, around 100,000 of them in Berlin. They also raped Russian women released from German labour camps. We live in a Feminist era. Have you seen any movies about these women?

At Potsdam in 1945, the Allies ratified the 1939 Soviet-Nazi Pact that gave U.S.S.R. half of Poland. Poland was compensated with the eastern quarter of Germany, in effect another gift to the Russian empire. This required the expulsion of about 12 million Germans, the largest forced migration in history.

Jews were prominent in the Polish Communist regime. In a stunning reversal of roles, Jewish policemen ordered Germans out of their homes and into cattle cars. In his book, "An Eye for An Eye" Jewish writer John Sack relates that about 1.5 million of these Germans died in the removal. He quotes a German woman from Gleiwitz: "What happened to the Jews was sad. But there was another holocaust too." (138)

According to Sacks, Jewish Communists extracted another cruel revenge. They filled 1250 Nazi concentration and labour camps and brutally tortured and murdered tens of thousands of Germans. (101 ff.)

Have you seen a movie where concentration camp guards and commandants were Jews? Since 1948, the American Jewish Committee and the Anti Defamation League have censored all Hollywood scripts involving Jews. Since these bodies are extensions of Jewish finance, what other topics have they censored? (Gabler, "An Empire of the Own: How Jews Invented Hollywood" 1988, p.303)

In his book, "Victims of Yalta", Nicholai Tolstoy documents "Operation Keelhaul," the Allies' forced repatriation of two million Russians who were German slave labourers, prisoners of wars, or soldiers. These people were sent to the Gulag and were liquidated. Where is the museum dedicated to them?

The mass media is unusually coy when it comes to reporting Communist atrocities. Nine million people died in the Russian Civil War (1917-1922). The Communists targeted Czarist society and Christians in particular. Stalin's purges and famines accounted for 20 million more deaths. In China, Mao Tse-tung is blamed for 60 million. More recently, let's not forgot Tibet, Cambodia and Rwanda.

In "The Holocaust Industry" (2000) Norman Finkelstein describes how Israel helped its ally Turkey deny the massacre of one million Armenians in 1915. "Acting at Israel's behest, the U.S. Holocaust Council practically eliminated mention of the Armenians in the Washington Holocaust Memorial Museum, and Jewish lobbyists in Congress blocked a day of remembrance for the Armenian genocide." (p.69)

CONCLUSION

Jewish organizations dishonor holocaust victims by using them for political purposes. It is tasteless to cast Jews as the world's premier victims. Humanity is one family and no genocide is more important than another.

For Ernst Zundel to understate the Jewish holocaust is distasteful. But it is not a crime. In these questions, only the truth matters. Let the truth speak for itself. Let Zundel be judged by it.

The reason other holocausts are suppressed and Zundel is jailed, is because the Jewish holocaust is a valuable tool in advancing the New World Order agenda. It gives their Jewish pawns moral immunity and allows them to vilify any opponents as Nazis.

Israel's Descent
Into a Moral Abyss

"God's chosen people" have been Satan's chosen people. Zionists took control of them using the holocaust and the 1948 "War of Independence" as ruses.

1) Jews did not need a "national homeland" because of the holocaust. Instead, Jews were sacrificed in the holocaust so they would build Israel. The Illuminati want it as capital of their New World Order. The blatant Masonic symbolism in the Rothschild-built Israeli Supreme Court is a tip-off. Also, Israel is the fortress for their invasion of the Islamic world.

2) In the "1948 War of Independence," Israelis did NOT face a second holocaust from blood-thirsty Arab armies, as Jews are taught. The war was in fact a brutal ethnic cleansing of Palestinians by Zionists, the "Nakba" ("Cataclysm") reminiscent of what Nazis did to Jews.

I'll deal with the second lie first.

THE "PHONEY WAR"

According to Israeli historian Ilan Pappe, 1948 was a pretext and cover for the pre-planned expulsion of a million mostly defenceless Palestinians from their ancestral homes, orchards, fields and businesses. ("The Ethnic Cleansing of Palestine," 2006)

The Zionist leadership knew the neighboring Arab states did not constitute a threat. The Palestinians did not flee willingly as Jews are taught, but were driven out.

The British and UN were accomplices. With 75,000 soldiers present, the British permitted the massacres and pillage in spite of their promise in the Balfour Declaration to uphold Palestinian rights.

The UN ceded to 600,000 Jews a territory containing one million Palestinians, leaving them at the mercy of David Ben Gurion who said, "Only a state with at least 80% Jews is a viable and stable state." (Pappe, p.48)

Eighty-nine percent of the cultivated land in the UN designated Jewish state belonged to Palestinians. (30)

General Sir John Bagot Glubb, the British chief the (Jordanian) Arab Legion called 1948 "a phoney war." Like most wars the outcome was determined in advance. The leader of Arab forces, King Abdullah of Jordan, had a secret deal with the Zionists to offer only token resistance in return for the West Bank and East Jerusalem. In addition, the English controlled the Arab armies and curtailed supplies.

Far from being "a rag tag group of defenders", Israel had 50,000 soldiers, half of whom had served in the British army. It had a small air force, navy, tanks, armoured cars and heavy artillery. Facing them were the real "rag tag defenders," perhaps 10,000 poorly trained and equipped Palestinian paramilitary outfits and volunteers from the Arab world. (44)

Despite rhetoric from Arab capitals, there was never any chance of driving the Jews into the sea. The Palestinians were passive and underestimated their danger. They had lived under Ottoman and British rule, and somehow would manage under the Jewish regime. Many villages made "non-aggression pacts" with the Jews.

In March 1948 Ben Gurion told the Jewish Agency Executive: "I believe the majority of the Palestinian masses accept the partition as a fait accompli...[they] do not want to fight us." (61)

The (British-controlled) Arab Legion was the only potential real opposition. It was used to repulse the Zionists when they reneged on their bargain and attacked the Old City of Jerusalem.

The other Arab nations were so feeble that the Zionists occupied Southern Lebanon and expelled Arabs from there. On May 24, 1948, David Ben Gurion did not sound like the leader of a beleaguered people when he confided in his diary: "We will establish a Christian state in Lebanon, the southern border of which will be the Litani river. We will break Transjordan, bomb Amman and destroy its army, and then Syria falls, and if Egypt will still continue to fight, we will bombard Port Said, Alexandria and Cairo." (144)

Yes, the Palestinians did attack some convoys and isolated Jewish settlements at considerable loss of Jewish life. These attacks played into the hands of the Zionists who always portray resistance to their aggression as "anti-Semitism."

THE NAKBA

Arabic speaking, Ilan Pappe interviewed survivors in Palestinian refugee camps. He compared their accounts to those in the IDF Archives.

Over 200 Arab villages were destroyed before a regular Arab soldier set foot in Palestine. Their ethnic cleansing program was called "Plan D". (82) A detailed inventory of all Palestinian settlements and property had been made for it. (Often the unwary Palestinians extended hospitality to the takers of this macabre "census.")

The Zionists attacked Palestinian villages at night and dynamited houses while residents slept inside. Then they rounded up males between age 10 and 50 and shot them or sent them to prison camps. The women, children and elders were made to leave. Eventually about 750,000 ended up in refugee camps in Gaza, the West Bank or neighboring countries. There were many instances of rape and plunder.

In the big cities like Jerusalem, Jaffa and Haifa, the Palestinian districts were shelled and people terrorized and killed. Altogether, 530 of about 1000 Palestinian villages were physically demolished. About a dozen cities and towns were also emptied. Some villages had forged economic or personal ties with the Jews and escaped this fate. Many of these "deals" were not honoured by the Zionists.

Deir Yassin was bad but the events that unfolded October 28 1948 in the village of Dawaymeh between Beersheba and Hebron were even worse. I cite Pappe:

"Venturing into the village the next day the Muktar (Hassan Mahmoud Ihdeib) beheld with horror the piles of dead bodies in the mosque—with many more strewn about in the street—men, women and children, among them his own father....455 people were missing among them around 170 children and women. The Jewish soldiers who took part also reported horrific scenes, babies whose skulls were cracked open, women raped or burned alive in houses, and men stabbed to death. These were...eye-witness accounts sent to [Israeli] High Command within a few days of the event." (197)

THE HOLOCAUST

The day before a Palestinian village was attacked, Israeli political officers (like Soviet commissars) would incite the troops with a talk about the holocaust. The Zionists also used the holocaust to give themselves moral impunity. The whole world watched and said nothing.

But were Zionists themselves also partly responsible for the holocaust? Did Zionists first do to Jews what they later did to Palestinians?

In 1943 Rabbi Dov Weissmandl of the Jewish Rescue Committee in Slovakia arranged for Nazi officials to stop transports to concentration camps in exchange for $50,000. They in fact stopped them while waiting for the money which had to come from abroad.

Weissmandl appealed to the Zionist Jewish Agency HQ in Switzerland and was told Zionists "must turn a deaf ear to the pleas and cries emanating from Eastern Europe" in order to establish the state of Israel.

" Remember this: all the allies have suffered many losses, and if we also do not offer human sacrifices, how can we gain the right to sit at the conference table when the territorial boundaries are reshaped? [Israel] Eretz Yisroel will be ours only by paying with blood, but as far as our immediate circle is concerned, ATEM TAJLU. The messenger bearing this letter will supply you with funds for this purpose".

Weismandl interpreted the letter as follows: "The price of Eretz Yisroel is the blood of the men and women, hoary sages, and babes in arms - but not YOUR [Zionist] blood! Let us not spoil this plan by giving the Axis [i.e. Nazis] powers to save Jewish lives. But for you, [Zionist] comrades, I have enclosed carfare for your escape. What a nightmare! The Zionist agent "diplomat" comes to Czechoslovakia and says "Shed your blood cheerfully, for your blood is cheap. But for your blood, the Land (of Israel) will be ours! ("Min Hametzar" (p. 92) by Rabbi Michael Dov Weissmandl , Dean of Nitra Yeshiva)

If you don't think this philosophy actuated the rise of Nazism, anti-Semitism and the holocaust, you are kidding yourself. Nazism was a fraud on the German people, just as Zionism is a fraud on Jews. Both turned good people into cold blooded killers, pawns of the "Prince of Lies."

CONCLUSION

Today the Nakba continues in Gaza Strip, the West Bank and along the partition wall. (One could argue it continues in Lebanon, Afghanistan and Iraq.) New settlements are being built to strengthen Israeli claims, as "fait accompli."

The majority of Israelis and their supporters are faced with a moral "fait accompli." Having been deceived about the holocaust and "War of Independence," they have been tainted by a moral abomination. Many have built their lives accordingly. What can they do now?

When you have travelled down the wrong road, there is no use pretending it is the right one. You have to make a U-turn and retrace your steps, the sooner the better. If I were living in Israel, I would work to expose the truth or leave.

I believe Zionists should acknowledge the truth and pursue a two-state solution providing apologies and generous restitution to the Palestinians. There should be a limited right of return.

Ilan Pappe says Palestinians would accept this. Pappe is a rare historian: honest, courageous and moral in the true Jewish spirit. He says his research "fully vindicates" the Palestinian version of events denied for so many years. (Yet "Nakba denial" is not a crime anywhere.)

Israelis need to make a 180-degree turn before they burn in hell, and take the rest of us along. The Illuminati controls Israel through Israeli leaders who are Masons. It has already betrayed the Jewish people more than once.

Pappe is not optimistic. The premeditated attack on Lebanon in July 2006 was the last straw. A professor at Haifa University, he watched his dovish colleagues accept the government rationale. They are prisoners of a Satanic "fait accompli." If anything Israelis now are more fanatical. Pappe has left Israel to become Chair of History at Exeter University in England.

There is only one way the human race will flourish in peace: by acknowledging the truth no matter how self-incriminating or painful it is.

Zionists "False-Flagged" Iraqi Jews

In 1950, a wave of anti-Semitism and terrorism in Iraq made Naeim Giladi, 21, join the Zionist underground.

Giladi was imprisoned, tortured and sentenced to death by Iraqi authorities. He escaped and fled to Israel only to discover that the anti-Semitism and bombings had been engineered by his fellow Zionists to dupe Iraqi Jews like him into going to Israel.

Giladi's family was part of a Jewish community that settled and prospered in Babylon 2600 years ago, 600 years before Christianity, 1200 years before Islam.

Then in the late 1940's, the Prime Minister Nouri-el-Said fired Jewish government employees, denied permits to Jewish merchants, and finally, in March 1950, deprived Jews of their citizenship. Still they did not leave.

A month later, a series of terrorist bombings started the wave of emigration. By January 1951 when a bomb thrown at a synagogue killed three and wounded 30, the exodus of frightened Jews jumped to 600-700 per day.

When Giladi's father discovered his son had joined the Zionists, he was sceptical. "You'll come home with your tail between your legs," he said.

But Giladi was young and idealistic. Jews were being killed and Zionism represented a chance to build a national home. "I was a true believer," he writes.

In an online essay "The Jews of Iraq," Giladi describes his bitter realization that Zionists were behind the anti-Semitism and bombings.

Unknown to Giladi, two members of the Zionist Underground had been arrested and confessed that they had carried out the terrorist attacks. A book, "Venom of the Zionist Viper," by an Iraqi investigator names Zionist "emissary" Mordecai Ben-Porat as the organizer. The book was banned in Israel.

Iraqi Prime Minister Said was a British pawn. He met Israeli PM David Ben Gurion in Vienna in 1948 and agreed to transfer the Iraqi Jews to Israel as part of the elite geopolitical program.

This and other Zionist crimes against Jews are documented in Giladi's book, "Ben Gurion's Scandals: How the Mossad and the Haganah Eliminated Jews,"(1992) which has been republished by Dandelion Books.

By January 1952, all but 6,000 of 125,000 Iraqi Jews had fled to Israel where as "Arab Jews," they were treated worse than in Iraq. Israel wanted them to perform the menial jobs vacated by the Palestinians. Between the Iraqi and Israeli governments, the Iraqi Jews lost much of their wealth.

Of his people, Giladi concludes: "An ancient, cultured, prosperous community had been uprooted and its people transplanted to a land dominated by East European Jews, whose culture was not only foreign but entirely hateful to them."

Their fate was typical of all 500,000 Jews from Arab countries. This belies the Zionist argument that these Jews were expelled from Muslim countries and make up for displaced Palestinians.

Giladi discovered that Israel had spurned many sincere Arab peace overtures because of its expansionist plans. He met Prime Minister Ben Gurion and asked him why Israel didn't have a constitution.

'If we had a constitution, we'd have to have a border, and this is not our border," Ben Gurion told him. "Where the army conquers, that will be our border.'

Giladi served in the 1967 and 1973 wars. But after the Israeli invasion of Lebanon in 1982, he renounced his Israeli citizenship and moved to New York City.

'TRUE BELIEVERS'

Giladi's story confirms that the modus operandi of Zionists is the "false flag" operation and "protection" racket. They attacked Iraqi Jews pretending to be Muslim terrorists. In 1954, they bombed American establishments in Cairo (the "Lavon Affair") to sabotage Egyptian-American relations. The Israeli attack on the U.S.S Liberty was an attempt to blame Egypt and draw the U.S. into the 1967 War.

I won't dwell on September 11, which I think was perpetrated by the CIA and Mossad. I'd rather focus on the irony that Naeim Giladi almost died for a cause he later repudiated. Tens of millions of "true believers" have been similarly conned.

Zionism cons all Jews. Israelis have been con-scripted in a never-ending colonial war against Muslims. Their supporters in the Diaspora are being compromised morally. But try to warn Zionist "true believers" and you will meet with abuse and ostracism. Zionism is their religion and identity.

BOOK FOUR

Hidden History

Illuminati Murdered
at Least Two Other Presidents

"The bane of our civil institutions is to be found in Masonry, already powerful and daily becoming more so. I owe to my country an exposure of its dangers." - Captain William Morgan, murdered Sept. 11, 1826

A curious but very credible Internet document called "The Mardi Gras Secrets" states that Illuminati agents poisoned and killed Presidents William Henry Harrison (1773-1841) and Zachary Taylor (1784-1850). They also poisoned James Buchanan in 1857 but he survived. All three were obstructing Illuminati-Rothschild plans for the U.S. Civil War (1860-1865.)

The document also describes the Illuminati role in the murders of Abraham Lincoln and Senator Huey Long. We know they killed Presidents Garfield, McKinley and Kennedy and probably Warren Harding and possibly FDR. If George W. Bush hadn't done such an awful job, he probably would have been murdered as well.

The Mardi Gras Secrets website was created in Dec. 2005 by Mimi L. Eustis, the daughter of Samuel Todd Churchill, a high level member of the secret New Orleans Mardi Gras Society called "The Mystick Crewe of Comus."

This Society, which reorganized the Mardi Gras festivities in 1857, was a chapter of the "Skull and Bones." It began as a front for the activities of Masons Albert Pike, Judah Benjamin and John Slidell who became leaders of the Confederacy.

This information is based on Samuel Churchill's deathbed confessions. He was dying of lung cancer. Mrs. Eustis later decided to make them public after she also contracted the terminal disease.

The Illuminati ringleader was Caleb Cushing (1800-1879), the partner of William Russell, the opium smuggler who founded the Yale "Skull and Bones" society in 1832. In order to rise in this society, one had to participate in a "killing of the king" rite of passage.

According to Eustis, the "Skull and Bones" (or "Brotherhood of Death") is "nothing more than a political assassination hit team against those United States politicians who [oppose] the House of Rothschild's plans for a blood elitist domination and control over the world's economy...For example Caleb Cushing was involved in the arsenic poisoning deaths of United States presidents William Henry Harrison on April 4, 1841 and Zachary Taylor on July 9, 1850. These two Presidents had opposed admitting Texas and California as slave states."

William Henry Harrison was the first President ever to die in office, serving only 31 days. According to Wikipedia he died of "pneumonia."

On July 3, 1850, Zachary Taylor threatened to hang those "taken in rebellion against the Union." The next day the President fell ill, vomited blackish material, and died July 9. (Kentucky authorities recently dug up Taylor's body looking for evidence of arsenic poisoning.)

THE ASSASSINATION OF ABRAHAM LINCOLN

I paraphrase Mrs. Eustis: During the Civil War (from 1861-1865), President Lincoln needed money to finance the War . The loan shark-bankers wanted 24% to 36% interest. Instead, Lincoln got Congress to authorize the printing of 450 million dollars worth of "Greenbacks" debt and interest-free money. It served as legal tender for all debts, public and private.

The House of Rothschild recognized that sovereign governments printing interest-free and debt-free paper money would break their power. Lincoln's assassin, John Wilkes Booth, was a member of Pike's "Knights of the Golden Circle." He was in New Orleans during the winter of 1863-64 and conspired with Pike, Benjamin, Slidell and Admiral G.W. Baird to assassinate Lincoln.

Eustis says her father emphasized that most Masons below the 3rd degree were good, hardworking people. The Illuminati-Skull and Bones used the Masons as a disguise. Those who rose past the 33 degree level did so by participating in the "Killing of the King" ritual. The lower levels did as they were told without realizing their part in the "Killing of the King."

For assassinating Abraham Lincoln, Pike, Benjamin, Slidell and August Belmont (Rothschild's Northern agent) were made secret "Kings of the Mystick Krewe of Comus." Andrew Johnson, the Vice -President became President and pardoned Albert Pike. Albert Pike awarded Andrew Johnson the thirty-third degree rite of passage.

"Doctors were an essential part of the Illuminati plan to kill U.S. political leaders [who] hindered the take over of the U.S. Republic by the international banking elite," Eustis writes.

"Illuminati doctors eventually did in both U.S. President William Henry Harrison and Zachary Taylor. They also played a death role in the shooting assassinations of U.S. Presidents Abraham Lincoln on April 14, 1865 (died April 15, 1865), James Garfield on July 2, 1881 (died September 19, 1881), and William McKinley Jr. on September 6, 1901 (died September 14, 1901.)"

"Teddy Roosevelt became President after William McKinley was shot. Roosevelt received passage into the 33rd. degree and became a secret king of the Mystick Krewe of Comus. During his presidency, the "Skull and Bones" became firmly entrenched and controlled the U.S. Republic."

HUEY LONG

Huey Long ("Kingfish") was a populist who mounted a powerful challenge to FDR as Governor of Louisiana and later as a U.S. Senator. Unlike FDR, he was not a

Mason and not a shill for the bankers. His "Share Our Wealth" program represented a genuine threat to the Illuminati.

An Illuminati member, Dr. Carl Austin Weiss shot Long on Sept 8, 1935 and Dr. Arthur Vidrine ensured that Long did not recover. According to Eustis, Weiss was supposed to hit Long in the face, and Long's bodyguard Murphy Roden was supposed to shoot both Weiss and Long. This may indeed be what happened.

Roden, "a spy for J. Edgar Hoover," pumped 60 bullets into Weiss' body. Dr. Weiss was told his baby would be killed if he reneged on the mission.

Both FDR and J. Edgar Hoover won their 33 degree rite of passage for their participation in this murder.

"Franklin Delano Roosevelt was made King of Comus in 1937. When J. Edgar Hoover came down to New Orleans to act out his reign as King of Comus, he was involved in a sexual revelry of homosexuality and cross-dressing with various elitist bloodline members of the Mystick Krewe of Comus."

LINDBERG AND HARDING

"Agents of 'Skull and Bones' with blessing and involvement of J. Edgar Hoover, 33rd level executioner-cover up specialist for the elitist bloodline of the House of Rothschild murdered Freemason Charles Lindbergh's son. This killing of Freemason Charles Lindbergh's son was to set an example that the isolationist stand was not the will of the Illuminati."

Mrs. Eustis doesn't touch upon the poisoning death of President Warren Harding (1865-1923) but this is how Wikipedia describes it:

"At the end of July, while travelling south from Alaska through British Columbia, [Harding] developed what was thought to be a severe case of food poisoning. At the Palace Hotel in San Francisco, he developed pneumonia. Harding died of either a heart attack or a stroke at 7:35 p.m. on August 2, 1923, at the age of 57. The formal announcement, printed in the New York Times of that day, stated that 'a stroke of apoplexy' was the cause of death.' He had been ill exactly one week."

For FDR, see Emanuel Josephson, "The Strange Death of Franklin D. Roosevelt." (1948)

CONCLUSION

The "Mardi Gras Secrets" suggest that, given the depth of corruption, the U.S. cannot be taken seriously as a democracy. There is a pattern of Illuminati-Rothschild control throughout U.S. history. People who deny this are living in a fantasy.

The United States was created to advance the Illuminati New World Order based on Rothschild control of credit. American ideals were designed to dupe and convert the masses, not to be ultimately realized.

The founders and heroes of the U.S. were mostly Masons including Paul Revere,

John Paul Jones and Benjamin Franklin. Francis Scott Key who wrote the national anthem was a Mason. John Hancock and most of the signatories of the Declaration of Independence were also Masons.

More than half the Presidents were Masons. These include Washington, Madison, Adams, Jefferson, Monroe, Jackson, Van Buren, Tyler, Polk, Taylor, Pierce, Buchanan, Johnson, Garfield, McKinley, TR, Taft, Harding, FDR, Truman, LBJ, Ford, Reagan, Clinton, Bush I and II and Obama.

Some of these really thought Masonry was about "making good men better" and had to be assassinated. Other Presidents who weren't Masons, like Eisenhower, Nixon and Carter, were still controlled by the same dark forces.

Throughout its history the United States has been in the clutches of a Satanic cult empowered by the Rothschild central banking cartel. Many heroic Presidents and other politicians tried to free their countrymen and died unrecognized and unmourned, while their killers thrived and were honored. This is the way in a Satanic dispensation.

The U.S. is a nation decapitated, a headless giant led by demons.

Are World Wars Orchestrated?

Muslims were rioting in Afghanistan because U.S. interrogators at Guantanamo Bay flushed copies of the Koran down the toilet.

How do the rioters know this? It was reported in Newsweek, of course. Oh no, they couldn't suppress this one.

Newsweek is owned by the family of Eugene Meyer, a past Director of the War Finance Board (WW1), Governor of the Federal Reserve and President of the World Bank. His "Washington Post" company has had a long relationship with the CIA.

Nothing appears in the mass media without an ulterior purpose. The Illuminati is promoting a clash of "civilizations" between Islam and the U.S..

In the present run-up to World War Three, it is worth asking if this sinister cabal also orchestrated World War Two, which saw the genocide of 70 million human beings.

A detail in Prince Michel Sturdza's aptly titled "The Suicide of Europe" (1968) set off my alarm bells.

Sturdza was Romanian Foreign Minister from Sept.-Dec. 1940. He was a leader in the pro-Nazi, anti-Communist, nationalist Christian "Legionary" movement. The Nazis, who like their Communist counterparts were Illuminati, were opposed to all "nationalist" movements. They soon overthrew the Legionaries and put these patriots in concentration camps.

Before assuming his post in 1940, Sturdza was visiting Berlin. No one wanted to speak to him with the exception of Admiral Wilhelm Canaris, the wily chief of the Abwehr, German Army Intelligence.

Canaris had a request that surprised Sturdza. He asked him to co-operate with Canaris' man in Bucharest, a certain Moruzov who Sturdza suspected was a Communist agent.

Pressed on this, Canaris said Moruzov was providing the "best information concerning Soviet Russia's military preparations."

Before leaving Berlin, Sturdza received a visit from Canaris' deputy, a Captain Muller, "bearer once more of his chief's insistences, which left my wife and me perplexed."

"Captain Muller informed us that Great Britain had never been and would never be defeated. He added: "What I am about to tell you, coming from a Prussian officer, might perhaps be considered an act of high treason. Pay attention however. Don't under any circumstances take the responsibility as Minister of Foreign Affairs in your country, for pushing it into a war where you have Great Britain as an adversary. You will be crushed. Great Britain is always victorious."

This was a peculiar thing for an Abwehr official to say in August 1940, when Germany had just conquered France and much of Europe and appeared invincible.

Sturdza thought he was being tested and was non-committal. "I had not the faintest idea that I had been in contact with the greatest spy ring and traitors known to the military history of any country." (p. 162)

Canaris, who may have been of Greek-Jewish origin, did indeed sabotage the Nazi war effort. Sturdza believes his spy ring was the main cause of the Nazi defeat. After a failed attempt to assassinate Hitler, its members were tortured and brutally murdered by the Gestapo.

Naturally, they are portrayed as courageous heroes: principled humanists who resisted fascist tyranny. I hope this is the case.

Yet, the statement, "You will be crushed. Great Britain is always victorious," suggests a different agenda, a larger design.

The headquarters of the Communist-Capitalist International is in the City of London. The Bank of England financed the Nazi war machine just as they financed the Bolshevik revolution. The bankers orchestrated World War Two to destroy the great nation states of Europe and wipe out the cream of the new generation.

Was Canaris Illuminati or an illuminati dupe? Apparently he wanted to overthrow Hitler and end the war early, but the Allies insisted on "unconditional surrender," i.e. maximum slaughter. No nationalist forces, including Germans, were to remain. Only "internationalists." The German army had no choice but fight to the end.

I don't see the Second World War as "the good war." It was fabricated to concentrate wealth and power in the usual hands, and to degrade and demoralize humanity. Both sides were guilty of unspeakable atrocities.

The two great wars, and the potential third are designed to advance Illuminati one-world dictatorship and mind control. Mankind is in the grip of a multigenerational diabolical conspiracy, and is too mesmerized by sex and money to realize it.

Bankers Extended
World War One by Three Years

On Oct. 12, 1915, Edith Cavell, 50, a British nurse and head of a teaching hospital in Belgium, was shot by a German firing squad. Her death inflamed anti-German feeling in the U.S. and caused enlistment in England to double.

She had helped some British POW's escape. Normally her crime was punished by three months imprisonment. Why was she killed?

According to Eustace Mullins, Edith Cavell had stumbled upon some damaging information. On April 15, 1915, "The Nursing Mirror" in London published her letter revealing that the Allied "Belgian Relief Commission" (charged with feeding Belgium) in fact was channelling thousands of tons of food to Germany.

Sir William Wiseman, head of British Intelligence and a partner in the bankers Kuhn Loeb, demanded the Germans execute Cavell as a spy. Wiseman believed that "the continuance of the war was at stake." The Germans reluctantly agreed thus creating "one of the principal martyrs of the First World War." ("The Secrets of the Federal Reserve," pp. 72-73)

Pretty cynical you say? No more cynical than demolishing the World Trade Centre, and murdering over 3000 Americans to start a bogus "War on Terror."

This example of co-operation between belligerents was accomplished because Wiseman worked closely with the head of the U.S. Federal Reserve, Paul Warburg. Warburg's brother Max was Chief of German Intelligence and a close friend of Kaiser Wilhelm.

The London-based central bankers use wars to weaken nations and colonize the world (incl. UK, U.S. Israel etc.). The difficulty executing WWI was that they had already bankrupted the European states by selling them battleships etc. Europe couldn't afford a war!

The introduction of the U.S. Federal Reserve and the Income Tax Act in 1913 solved this problem. U.S. government loans financed World War One. The American people were on the hook for both sides of the conflict.

HOW THEY PROPPED UP GERMANY

Germany and her allies did not have the resources to fight for more than a year.

As Edith Cavell's discovery suggests, the banksters solved this problem by trading with "neutral" states: Switzerland, Belgium, Holland, Denmark, Norway and

Sweden. Thus the banksters allowed essential resources from England, the U.S. and the British Empire to reach Germany indirectly.

The whole thing is documented in a book entitled, "The Triumph of Unarmed Forces 1914-1918" (1923) by Rear Admiral M.W.W.P. Consett, who was British Naval Attache in Scandinavia. His job was to keep track of the movement of supplies ("unarmed forces") necessary for the continuation of the conflict.

For example, Scandinavia was completely dependent on British coal. So the Swedish iron ore that became German submarines that sank Allied shipping reached Germany on vessels powered by British coal.

Germany needed glycerin (animal fat) for the manufacture of explosives. England had no trouble securing this substance because it controlled the seas. After the war began, the demand for these products from neutral countries "exploded." The British continued to fill these orders. They could have restricted them.

The same applies to copper, zinc, nickel, tin, and many other essential products. Consett believes that had they been embargoed, the war would have been over by 1915.

The trade of tea, coffee and cocoa to neutral countries also increased dramatically but these products often weren't available there. They all went to Germany for huge profit.

Consett's protests fell on deaf ears. The Minister of Blockade was Robert Cecil, a member of the Round Table (i.e. central banker) cabal.

Similarly, the central bankers financed the German side through their Scandinavian banks to the tune of 45 million pound sterling. (p. 146)

The Allied nations became the banksters' debt slaves: "Despite the huge revenues raised from taxation, the British national debt rose tenfold. The government failed to use its bargaining power as the only really massive borrower in wartime to get money at low rates of interest. The French national debt rose from 28 billion to 151 billion francs ..." (Davies, "The History of Money") The U.S. debt soared from one billion to $25 billion.

According to the book "The Merchants of Death," World War I was waged by 27 nations; it mobilized 66,103,164 men of whom 37,494,186 became casualties (about 7 million dead.) Its direct costs are estimated at $208,000,000,000, its indirect costs at $151,000,000,000. And these figures do not include the additional billions in interest payments, veterans' care and pensions, and similar expenses..."

Can there be any doubt that mankind is in the thrall of a cult of Satan-worshippers??

MISSION ACCOMPLISHED

As mysteriously as it began, the war ended. In Dec. 1918, the German Empire suddenly "collapsed." You can guess what happened. The banksters had achieved their aims and shut off the spigot. (Hence, the natural sense of betrayal felt in Germany, exacerbated by the onerous reparations dictated by the banksters at Versailles.)

What were the banksters' aims? The Old Order was destroyed. Four empires (Russian, German, Austro-Hungarian and Ottoman) lay in ruins.

The banksters had set up their Bolshevik go-fers in Russia. They ensured that Palestine would become a "Jewish" state under their control. Israel would be a perennial source of new conflict.

But more important, thanks to bloodbaths such as Verdun (800,000 dead), the optimistic spirit of Christian Western civilization, faith in man and God, were dealt a mortal blow. The flower of the new generation was slaughtered. (See, "The Testament of Youth" by Vera Britain for a moving first-hand account.)

The broad sweep of history reveals the pattern. The murder of the Austrian heir Arch Duke Ferdinand by the Masonic "Black Hand" group (which began WWI) was a staged event, an "excuse," i.e. the equivalent of Sept. 11, 2001.

CONCLUSION

Modern history is the account of how the central banking cartel converts its monopoly of credit into a monopoly of power. This entails destroying our connection with nation, religion (God), race and family. It means substituting objective truth (God, nature) with their Diktat (political correctness, etc.)

It takes courage and clarity to understand we are mice in their lab experiment. We have been sold out by our "leaders," dumbed down by our media/education and spoiled stupid by the welfare state. (Everyone can be bought.) We can't even recognize what is happening, let alone act.

For now, we have prosperity and think we are free. As Aldous Huxley said:

"A really efficient totalitarian state would be one in which the all-powerful executive of political bosses and their army of managers control a population of slaves WHO DO NOT HAVE TO BE COERCED, because they love their servitude. To make them love it is the task assigned, in present day totalitarian states, to ministries of propaganda, newspaper editors and schoolteachers." ["Brave New World," Bantam Books, 1967, p. xii. Caps added.]

On the bright side, the knowledge that our society is a fraud is liberating. No longer do we genuflect to its plastic gods. "The truth will make you free!"

The U.S. is a Crown Financial Colony

The U.S. has been a financial colony of Britain for at least 100 years. This is confirmed by the "Col. E.M. House Report", a chilling 10-page "progress report" dated June 10, 1919, which portrays the United States in these terms.

The author is Col. Edward Mandell House (1858-1938), the Rothschild agent who secretly directed U.S. affairs during the Woodrow Wilson administration. Col. House was known as Wilson's friend and "alter ego." (He had not served in the military and the term "Colonel" was merely pretension.) The report is addressed to British Prime Minister David Lloyd George, whose career was made as a lawyer for the World Zionist Organization.

The report details Col. House's progress in preparing "for the peaceful return of the American colonies to the dominion of the Crown." The League of Nations was a façade for British hegemony. "Crown" means the hegemony of London-based international bankers and their aristocrat allies.

House writes: "We have wrapped this plan in the peace treaty so that the world must accept from us the League or a continuance of the war. The League is in substance the Empire with America admitted on the same basis as our other colonies."

The report oozes contempt for Americans. "The plain people of this country are inveterate and incurable hero worshipers," Col. House explains. A man with a slogan that expresses their "undefined aspirations" can manipulate them easily.

Afterwards, they will trust the sloganeer no matter what he does. [Woodrow] Wilson has gained this trust and this accounts for "his exceptional usefulness to us."

Rep. Jacob Thorkelson (1876-1945) introduced "The House Report" to Congress in Oct.1939 and published it in the Congressional Record (Oct. 13 1939, pp.598-604). Attempts to delete it were thwarted. The complete text is available on line.

THE "CROWN"

British bankers took over the U.S. during the Teddy Roosevelt Administration (1901-1909) when Rothschild front J.P. Morgan alone controlled 25% of American business.

"Crown" refers to the owners of the Bank of England. Their identities are an official secret. According to E.C. Knuth, the "international financial oligarchy uses the allegoric 'Crown' as its symbol of power and has its headquarters in the ancient city of London...the giant Bank of England, a privately owned institution... is not subject to regulation by the British parliament and is in effect a sovereign world power." ("The Empire of the City," p. 59)

It is foolish to talk of British, American, German, Japanese or even Zionist imperialism. They are all sock puppets for this one imperialism that is colonizing the whole earth, including the U.S., UK and Israel. This is the New World Order.

Col. House continues: The "peaceful return of the American colonies" can only be brought about with "the consent of the dominant group of the controlling clans."

Col. House relates how Americans are being taught to accept "British" leadership. He details how the universities and press are staffed by "British-born" or Canadians.

"Through the Red Cross, the Scout movement, the YMCA, the church, and other humane, religious, and quasi-religious organizations, we have created an atmosphere of international effort which strengthens the idea of unity of the English speaking world."

The Overseas Clubs, service clubs, and war charities "enable us to pervade all sections and classes of the country." This is an indication of how pervasive Illuminati influence really is.

We "hold all American newspapers as isolated from the non-American world as if they had been in another planet instead of another hemisphere. The realization of this by the Associated Press and the other universal news gatherers, except Hearst, was most helpful in bringing only our point of view to the papers they served."

He boasts that the United States, "while still maintaining an outward show of independence," is identical with other colonies in its relationship to the Crown. "Has not President Wilson cancelled the big Navy program and dutifully conceded to us the command of the seas?"

He boasts that "the Anglo American alliance" has become "the unchallenged financiers of the world."

He congratulates "our fiscal agents Messrs Pierpont Morgan & Company" for "putting this country into the war." They exert "widespread influence on newspaper policy" through advertising and lent $200,000,000 to Japan to build a fleet to compete with America (making the U.S still more dependent on England.)

Col. House boasts that the "Crown" used money lent by the U.S. government for war purposes to buy up oil fields in California, Mexico and Latin America.

"The war has made us custodians of the greater part of the world's raw materials... [We] now largely control the oil fields of the world and thereby the world's transportation and industry."

THE LEAGUE OF NATIONS RUSE

The pressing issue now is to "transfer its dangerous sovereignty from this colony to the custody of the Crown. We must, in short, now bring America within the Empire."

The first step was Wilson's plan for the League of Nations "which we prepared for him."

"Any abrupt change might startle the ignorant American masses and rouse them to action against it. And us. Our best policy therefore would be to appoint President Wilson the first president of the League... he will be able to satisfy [Americans] that far from surrendering their independence to the League, they are actually extending their sovereignty by it..."

Foreshadowing The Patriot Act, Col. House says Woodrow Wilson "alone can father an anti-Bolshevik act which judicially interpreted, will enable appropriate punitive measures to be applied to any American who may be unwise enough to assert that America must once again declare her independence."

Col. House goes into great detail about how Wilson must be massaged and manipulated. Many people think someone else wrote this Report but only Edward Mandell House knew Wilson this well.

For example he says Wilson "is easily slighted and remarkably vindictive." The new British ambassador should be a "Wilson worshipper" and "a gentleman-in-waiting to the President." He lists the gifts Wilson already has been given.

"OUR ENTIRE SYSTEM OF THOUGHT CONTROL" IS AT WORK

Col. House suggests staging the first session of the League of Nations in Washington.

"This will convince these simple people that they are the League and its power resides in them."

He recommends a "series of spectacles by which the mob may be diverted from any attempt to think too much of matters beyond their province."

"While awaiting these diversions for the vulgar, we are incessantly instructing them in the wonders of the League. Its praises are thundered by our press, decreed by our college presidents, and professed by our professors. Our authors, writers and lecturers are analysing its selected virtues... we have enlisted 8000 propagandists for the League. We have organized international and national synods, committees, conferences, convocations, conventions, councils...to herald the birth of the League as the dawn of universal peace."

"Agriculturalists, bankers, brokers, accountants, chemists, and all other functional groups capable of exerting organized professional, business, financial or social pressure are meeting to endorse the League in the name of peace, progress and prosperity...Our film concerns are preparing an epoch-making picture..."

"In short, our entire system of thought control is working ceaselessly, tirelessly, ruthlessly, to ensure the adoption of the League. And it will be adopted, for business wants peace, the righteous cannot resist a covenant, and the politicians, after shadow boxing for patronage purposes, will yield valiantly lest the fate of the wanton and wilful pursue them."

CONCLUSIONS

The House Report unveils the reality behind globalization and the United Nations. If ever we needed proof of a long-term conspiracy to subvert national sovereignty and ensnare humanity, this is it.

Thanks to the valiant opposition of Republican Senators, the United States rejected the Peace Treaty and with it the League of Nations on Nov. 19, 1919. The plot was temporarily foiled.

But the British bankers' covert campaign to impose world tyranny has not abated. They financed Hitler and engineered the Depression and World War Two. The League of Nations was resurrected as the United Nations in 1945 and the "Cold War" hoax initiated. Now we have the 9-11 and the "War on Terror."

The New World Order, world government and globalization are all extensions of British imperialism which itself is the expression of the financial hegemony of central bankers and their minions.

Americans are helping to build the New World Order for their master, "the Crown." In Col. House's words, Americans will be colonists who have to "petition at the foot of the throne."

The references to control of oil fields suggest that oil is first and foremost an instrument of world domination. The final stage of world tyranny involves gaining complete control of Middle Eastern oil. This explains Iraq and portends an invasion of Iran.

The threat cannot be characterized as strictly "Jewish." The Rothschilds have received such a degree of collaboration from the world's financial, cultural and political elite so as to render this point mute. [Essentially collaboration is the price of admission.]

Lemming-like, the Western elite has embraced a death-wish for civilization. They have sold their soul (and us) to the devil.

The 1933 "Bankers' Coup" Was a Ruse

The story that Wall Street bankers planned to overthrow FDR in 1933 still makes the rounds in 2007.

Recently, the BBC named "Dubya's" grandfather, Prescott Bush as one of the conspirators. The NWO apparently still considers Roosevelt and the New Deal as propaganda assets. They want us to think the bankers don't run the government and fascism doesn't also take the form of Liberalism, Socialism and Communism.

The Illuminati bankers staged the coup to give FDR credibility as Wall Street's nemesis. As I will show, they routinely used such tricks to build up their Presidential puppet.

The conspirators (members of the "American Liberty League") approached retired Major General Smedley Butler to use 500,000 veterans to remove FDR and become a Mussolini-like figure.

Smedley Butler was absolutely the LAST man you would ask if you were serious. The most decorated Marine in history; Gen. Smedley Butler recently had been forced to resign by Herbert Hoover for calling Mussolini a "mad dog" and warning that his fascist cohorts "were about to break loose in Europe." Butler refused to retract his remarks and thus became a national hero overnight.

They asked this man to become the American Mussolini. However, if you wanted someone sure to expose your coup (as he did; thought it "smacked of treason,") Butler was the "go-to" person.

Nor was Butler any friend of Wall Street. He was touring the nation with a speech stating that the bankers used the U.S. army as "gangsters for capitalism" -- thugs and debt collectors: "Looking back on it, I feel that I could have given Al Capone a few hints," Butler said. "The best he could do was .. operate his racket in three districts. I operated on three continents." ("War is a Racket" 1933)

"There was definitely something crazy about the whole affair," remarked Curt Gentry. "Butler who had gained prominence for speaking out against fascism, being asked to become an American Duce." ("J. Edgar Hoover" p. 203)

Nevertheless, Gentry and most other historians accepted the tale, indicating their function as highly paid flacks.

The story received its widest currency in Jules Archer's book "The Plot to Seize the White House" (1973). Judging from Archer's other works, he is either the

Illuminati's best propagandist or biggest dupe (or both.)

His other subjects include such "defenders of the people" (Illuminati front-men) as: Trotsky, Mao Tse Tung; Chou En Lai; and Ho Chi Minh. He has also penned books about such elite-sponsored movements as feminism, civil rights and environmentalism.

WHO WAS FDR?

For the answer, we are indebted to a book by a courageous, honest, public-spirited New York doctor, Emmanuel Josephson: "The Strange Death of Franklin D. Roosevelt" (1948.)

FDR was the scion of two Illuminati families, the Delanos and the Roosevelts. He was related to a dozen U.S. Presidents: four on the Roosevelt side and eight on the Delano side. He was a third cousin of King George VI and Queen Elizabeth.

These families have some Jewish antecedents but they also have Dutch, German, Swedish and principally English blood. FDR's mother's father, Warren Delano made a fortune in the opium trade. His father James Roosevelt was Vice President of a railway and director of several companies.

FDR was a spoiled brat who always changed the rules to suit his whims. He was tutored privately, and failed law school but allowed to enter the bar anyway. He never held a real job. In the 1920's, he helped float some stock market scams. As Governor and later President, he was extremely suggestible, evasive and shifty. Louis Howe created his public persona and did his thinking for him. Howe was FDR's "alter and wiser ego." (102)

FDR had a small army of speech writers and sometimes there were screw-ups. For his Democratic nomination acceptance in 1932, he was handed two speeches with diametrically opposed views and read them both. (157)

After his attack of encephalomyelitis, the Rockefellers gave him a health spa at Warm Springs, Georgia. They subsequently funnelled millions of dollars to FDR in the guise of charitable contributions to his "foundation." (Dr. Josephson found that the institution did not accept charity cases and didn't issue financial statements.) (118-ff)

In Josephson's words, "Roosevelt was magnificently bribed to run for office. By the end of 1930, some $700,000 was poured into the coffers of the foundation ...[FDR] was the pathetic puppet of conspirators scheming the destruction of democracy and the establishment of an American monarchy." (95, 124)

In return , the U.S. Treasury under FDR spent hundreds of millions bribing Saudi King Ibn Saud and building oil infrastructure in Saudi Arabia to benefit Standard Oil. (262-263)

Josephson said the basic doctrines of the Rockefeller Empire are "feudalistic monarchic government" ... "monopoly of every necessity of life and of national existence, and absolute dictatorship..." (86-87)

The rich must "divide and rule": " The people must be dealt with not as Americans but as minorities set at each other's throats, Labor vs. Capital, Black vs. White, Catholic vs. Protestant, Christian vs. Jew for e.g." (87) He could have added male vs. female and gay vs. straight.

FEIGNED OPPOSITION FROM WALL STREET

Rich inbred degenerates running for President naturally pretend to defend the public good. Naturally their banker-sponsors are willing to feign displeasure and opposition.

FDR learned the game from his cousin Theodore Roosevelt who pretended to be a "trust buster" while remaining a creation of the trusts and giving the country to them.

The contributors to FDR's 1932 campaign include a "Who's Who" of the U.S. business elite, the same people who supposedly tried to overthrow him a year later: Hearst, Rockefeller, Morgan, Baruch, Du Pont, Astor.

In 1933, a group of "publicity men" advised that fascism was becoming unpopular in America and FDR could score points by opposing the Nazis. "They suggested that Hearst and his publications launch a sham attack on Roosevelt and at the same time pretend to support Nazism and Fascism, thus throwing the Anti-Nazis and Anti-Fascists into the Roosevelt camp." (167)

"As the perverters of public opinion expected, the gullible public raged at Hearst and flocked to the standards of Roosevelt, blind to the fact that he was giving them another of the same brand of dictatorship." (167)

The antagonism was an utter sham. Hearst employed FDR's son Elliot, his daughter and her husband! Similarly the public enmity of the munitions manufacturing Duponts was also a sham. Ethel Dupont married FDR Jr. !

"The Liberty League was then set up for the ostensible purpose of attacking Roosevelt and fighting his re-election. This served to throw the entire pacifist vote into Roosevelt's camp and helped reassure his re-election." (169)

Clearly the "Fascist Coup" was just another clever ploy invented by the "publicity men."

CONCLUSION

Curtis Dall was a banker and FDR's son-in-law. He portrays the President not as a leader but as a "quarterback" with little actual power. The "coaching staff" consisted of a coterie of handlers ("advisers" like Louis Howe, Bernard Baruch and Harry Hopkins) who represented the international banking cartel. For Dall, FDR ultimately was a traitor manipulated by "World Money" and motivated by conceit and personal ambition. (Dall, "FDR: My Exploited Father-In-Law" 1970)

The 1933 "Banker's Coup" is indicative of the trouble the financial elite takes to deceive the public. Until George W. Bush, no President did more than FDR to take America down the road to tyranny.

Was Victor Rothschild
an Illuminati Agent?

In 1942, Sir Mark Oliphant, a leading British physicist was shocked when a messenger delivered a part from his new radar technology with a warning from MI-5 Security Inspector Victor Rothschild to "tighten up your security."

A few days earlier Rothschild had visited Oliphant's Birmingham University lab, quizzed him on his research, and pocketed the three-inch diameter magnetron.

Talk about chutzpah! Baron Rothschild was himself a Soviet agent. Before returning the magnetron, he had transmitted detailed drawings to Moscow, a fact later confirmed by his KGB handlers.

Oliphant related this story in 1994 to Roland Perry, the Australian author of "The Fifth Man" (1994, Sedgwick and Jackson, 475 pp). This report is based on this book.

Between 1935 and 1963, the Soviet Union knew all of Britain's military and scientific secrets thanks to "The Cambridge Five," a spy ring that operated in M1-5, MI-6 and the Foreign Office. Western intelligence agencies were rendered ineffective and Allied secrets including the design of the atomic bomb were stolen.

The traitors were Kim Philby, Donald Maclean, Guy Burgess and Anthony Blunt. But there is a natural reluctance to admit that "the Fifth Man" was Nathaniel Meyer Victor Rothschild (1910-1990), the Third Baron Rothschild, the British head of the world's richest banking dynasty , which controls the Bank of England.

In 1993, after the dissolution of the Soviet Union, six retired KGB Colonels in Moscow confirmed Rothschild's identity to Roland Perry. Col. Yuri Modin, the spy ring's handler, went on the record.

Perry writes: "According to ...Modin, Rothschild was the key to most of the Cambridge ring's penetration of British intelligence. 'He had the contacts,' Modin noted. 'He was able to introduce Burgess, Blunt and others to important figures in Intelligence such as Stewart Menzies, Dick White and Robert Vansittart in the Foreign Office...who controlled Mi-6." (p. 89)

You can understand the reluctance. The Rothschilds are undoubtedly the largest shareholders in the world's central bank system. Victor Rothschild's career as Soviet agent confirms that these London-based bankers plan to impose a "world government" dictatorship akin to Communism.

It adds credence to the claim they were behind the Bolshevik Revolution, and used the Cold War and more recently the 9-11 hoax and "war on terror" to advance their world hegemony.

Which is more plausible? One of the richest men in the world, Victor Rothschild espoused Communist ideals so his own fabulous wealth and position would be taken away? Or that Communism in fact was a deception designed to take away our wealth and freedom in the guise of "economic equality" and "brotherhood"?

MAN OF ACTION

According to "The Fifth Man", Victor Rothschild had an IQ of 184. He was a gifted jazz pianist with an intuitive understanding of many scientific disciplines. He saw banking as a dreary affair and preferred the exciting example of his great grandfather Lionel Rothschild (1808-1879) who Benjamin D'Israeli immortalized as "Sidonia" in the novel "Coningsby." (1844)

"No minister of state had such communication with secret agents and political spies as Sidonia. He held relations with all the clever outcasts of the world. The catalogue of his acquaintances in the shape of Greeks, Armenians, Moors, secret Jews, Tartars, Gypsies, wandering Poles and Carbonari, would throw a curious light on those subterranean agencies of which the world in general knows so little, but which exercise so great an influence on public events. The secret history of the world was his pastime. His great pleasure was to contrast the hidden motive, with the public pretext, of transactions." ("Coningsby" pp. 218-219)

Rothschild studied Zoology at Cambridge where he recruited Anthony Blunt for the KGB in 1936. Rothschild later joined MI-5 and was in charge of counter sabotage. He instructed the military on how to recognize and defuse bombs. Rothschild was a personal friend of Winston Churchill. Perry writes:

"The two socialized often during the war years. Rothschild used his wealth and position to invite the Prime Minister to private parties. His entree to the wartime leader, plus access to all the key intelligence information, every major weapons development and his command of counter-sabotage operations in Britain, made Rothschild a secretly powerful figure during the war years...The result was that Stalin knew as much as Churchill about vital information, often before the British High Command were informed." (xxviii-xxix)

Rothschild helped neutralize enemies of the Soviet Union who came to the British for support. For example, he was involved in covering up the assassination of Polish war leader Wladyslaw Sikorski, whose plane was blown up in July 1944. Sikorski had become burdensome to Stalin after he discovered the KGB had massacred 16,000 Polish officers in the Katyn Woods and elsewhere in 1940.

In 1944, Blunt, Burgess and Philby all stayed with Victor at the Rothschild mansion in Paris. Rothschild was briefly in charge of Allied intelligence in Paris and interrogated many prisoners.

After the war Rothschild spent time in the U.S. overseeing attempts to learn the secrets of the atom bomb. Due in part to the "Cambridge Five," Perry says "the Russians knew about every major intelligence operation run against them in the years 1945 to 1963." (xxxi)

CONCLUSION

Victor Rothschild held many jobs that served to disguise his true role which I suspect was that of a member of the Illuminati Grand Council. (The Illuminati represent the highest rank of Freemasonry.) He was not a lowly agent. He probably gave orders to people like Winston Churchill, FDR and Stalin.

For example, he ensured that the U.S.SR supported the establishment of the State of Israel. "He knew the proper back-channels to reach decision-makers in Moscow," a KGB Colonel told Perry. "Let us just say he got things done. You only did that if you reached the top. He was very persuasive." (176)

When you control the money supply, you can be very persuasive, as Americans have learned.

The super rich have more in common with each other than they have with the rest of humanity. It appears they have abandoned their natural role as leaders and benefactors of humanity, and instead conspire to enchain us. It's too bad because the only thing they don't already have is love.

The fact that Rothschild was protected until his death suggests a ruling class conspiracy. According to Greg Hallett, Anthony Blunt, a fellow spy, was an illegitimate son of George V, half-brother and look-alike to Edward VIII, the Duke of Windsor. Until his exposure in 1964, Blunt was Knighted and Curator of the Queen's art collection. He received immunity from prosecution in exchange for his confession.

Many believe this conspiracy is "Jewish." Certainly Zionism, Neo Conservatism and Communism (in all its forms) play an important part. But consider this: the current Lord Jacob Rothschild, the Fourth Baron Rothschild is Victor's son by his first wife Barbara Hutchinson, a non-Jew who converted. In Jewish law, Jacob Rothschild is not a Jew. He married Serena Dunn. By the way, Meyer Amschel, Victor's only son by his second marriage to Theresa Mayor, also a non-Jew, 'committed suicide' in 1996. He probably rebelled against the Satanic agenda.

While Victor Rothschild pretended to "socialist ideals," the banker was a conspicuous traitor. Treason is the template for contemporary politics. The central banking cartel is stealthily erecting its "world governance" dictatorship by fomenting wars in which it stands on both sides.

"As flies to wanton boys, are we to the gods. They kill us for their sport." (King Lear)

The Illuminati Tricked Hitler With "Appeasement"

In Dec. 1942 Heinrich Mueller, Chief of the Gestapo, rolled up the Soviet spy network in mainland Europe and secured a list of Soviet agents and informants in England that reads like a "Who's who" of the British establishment and lifts the veil from modern history. It indicates that not just Victor Rothschild, but a large swath of the British establishment was sympathetic to Russian Communism, and were considered "assets."

These assets include Edward Wood, Lord Halifax, who was Neville Chamberlain's Foreign Secretary and leading architect of the "Appeasement" policy.

Appeasement encouraged Hitler to think England wanted him to attack the Soviet Union. In fact, Halifax was working indirectly for the Communists. Appeasement was designed to trap Hitler in a two-front war which would level Germany (and Europe) and kill sixty million people.

Mueller's list includes Victor Rothschild, the head of the central banking dynasty, long suspected as one of the "Cambridge Five." Curiously, the other four (Burgess, Maclean, Blunt and Philby) aren't on this list. Halifax's son married a Rothschild.

It includes Charles Hambro, another banker of Jewish origin who was part of a Bank of England decision to continue financing Nazism in 1934 as a "stabilizing influence." Obviously, as a Soviet asset, this man was not pro-Nazi.

It includes Sir Robert Waley-Cohen and many members of the anti-appeasement "Focus" group that funded Winston Churchill. Waley-Cohen was the Chairman of the Rothschild-controlled Shell Oil and the leader of the British Jewish Community.

Other bankers and industrialists include Eugen Spier, Maurice Baring, Leonard Montefiore, Edward Guggenheim, Sir Robert Mond and Sir Phillip Sassoon. All but Baring are of Jewish origin.

Prominent Labor Party and trade union leaders included Ernest Bevin, Harold Laski, Herbert Stanley Morrison and Sir Walter Citrine. Members of ancient aristocratic families include Richard Combe Abdy, Baron Strabogli, and Admiral Reginald Plunkett-Ernle-Erle-Drax. There was press mogul J.S. Elias, cartoonist Victor Weisz and Daily Express Chairman Ralph D. Blumenfeld.

Prominent civil servants include Rex Leeper of the Foreign Office ruling clique and Sir Maurice Hankey, who as cabinet secretary and Clerk of the Privy Council (1919-1938) knew all the secrets. There was Slavonic scholar Bernard Pares and Jurist Sir

Hirsch Lauterpacht.

What did this disparate group have in common? About half of them are recognizably Jewish. But the connection that binds them all likely is Freemasonry. Dupes or conscious agents, their aim is to establish a Masonic or "Illuminist" world dictatorship dedicated to the "light giver" Lucifer (their alter ego.) Today, Bush, Clinton, Kerry, Obama and McCain etc. are all members.

Heinrich Mueller died in California in 1983. The CIA recruited Mueller in Switzerland in 1948 and paid him $1 million for an Interrogation running 1000-pages that includes this list. Mueller left his microfilmed archives to his nephew, "Gregory Douglas " who has published a part.

BAIT AND SWITCH

The Bank of England funded the rise of Adolf Hitler through the Schroder Bank. F.C. Tiarcks, the Managing Director of the Schroder Bank, was also a Director of the Bank of England.

Eustace Mullins writes: "Because his own financial backers, the Schroders, were sponsoring the Appeasement Party, Hitler believed there would be no war [with England.] He did not suspect that the backers of the Appeasement Party, now that Chamberlain had served his purpose in duping Hitler, would cast Chamberlain aside and make Churchill the Prime Minister." ("The Secrets of the Federal Reserve," pp.76-78.)

While history portrays Hitler as duping the naive Neville Chamberlain and Lord Halifax, it appears Hitler himself was tricked into thinking he could expand eastward with impunity. Neville Chamberlain wasn't in on the secret. (He died prematurely "of cancer" just months after leaving office.) But as a Soviet informant, Halifax certainly was instrumental.

As an early opponent of British rearmament, Halifax encouraged Hitler's expansion and later complimented the dictator for being a "genuine hater of Communism." In 1937, Halifax actually offered Hitler changes in the "European Order" in regard to Danzig, Austria and Czechoslovakia.

"It was Halifax not Hitler who first mentioned by name the areas where the Versailles Treaty might be reinterpreted to Germany's benefit," writes historian Andrew Roberts. "Halifax did the one thing which Eden had told him not to, and which Vansittart warned would 'bring the European card-castle tumbling down.' Moreover he did it not once but thrice in the course of the conversations." ("The Holy Fox: A Biography of Lord Halifax," 1991, pp. 67, 70-71.)

Halifax's closest adviser was Philip Kerr, Lord Lothian, a member of the Rothschild-Milner-Rhodes Round Table secret society (i.e the Illuminati). According to Andrew Roberts, Lothian was "a friend of Halifax's and had non-parliamentary political influence of a type seldom seen in today's politics." (109)

Appeasement was designed to encourage Hitler to take action which would justify a declaration of war by the West. "What we want to secure is the certainty of a war on two-fronts," Halifax said in March 1939. (Roberts, 146) Halifax was responsible for the foolhardy British guarantee of Poland that led to this war declaration in Sept. 1939. The U.S.SR also invaded Poland but there was no declaration of war against it. Stalin was pre-primed to attack the Nazis in 1941. The trick was getting England into the war first.

The whole knuckle-biting drama of war and peace in 1939-41, including England as the lonely defender of freedom, was a charade. Germany was in the cross-hairs all along. Could the U.S.A be in the same position today?

The appeasers and their opponents were two Illuminati house teams pursuing common goals. Lady Astor's Cliveden Manor was supposed to be the HQ of the (pro-Nazi) appeasement party but, as Andrew Roberts points out, arch anti-appeasers like Duff Cooper, Anthony Eden and Russian Foreign Minister Maxim Litvinov (nee Meir Finkelstein) were regular guests. (67)

CONCLUSION

Wars are the artificial creation of the Illuminati, a Satanic cult that extends its tentacles over the whole planet. "Muller's List" provides a glimpse at the composition of this group: bankers, industrialists, aristocrats, military, scholars, trade unionists and media from all parts of the political spectrum.

There are a lot of Jews but it should be obvious that the Illuminati victimized Jews as much as anyone. Jews have been the canon fodder for Communism, Zionism and Nazism.

Possibly some listees didn't know what they were advancing. The Illuminati pretended to oppose fascism and advance "equality." Today they pretend to build a humanist utopia. Former World Bank President James Wolfensohn had the slogan "Plutocrat for the Poor" on his web site.

The Illuminati start wars to demoralize and destroy humanity, to consolidate power and produce huge profits and debt slavery. This cult, which has a stranglehold over thought and expression, pretty much defines realty. Our only course is to find our truth from different sources and define reality anew.

How the Bankers Frog-marched the U.S. Into WW2

After Britain's humiliating retreat from Dunkirk June 4, 1940, Winston Churchill defiantly declared, "We shall fight on the beaches...we shall never surrender..."

His bravado was based on his secret knowledge the United States would back Britain to the hilt.

The vast majority of Americans were against intervention. But a covert British "dirty tricks" campaign, employing almost 1000 people in NYC (mostly Brits and Canadians), had hijacked democracy with the full co-operation of the FDR administration. It illustrates how London-based central bankers control the American people to this day.

The Republican Party was against intervention. Thanks to the British, the Republican Presidential nomination June 28, 1940 went to an unknown pro-intervention pro-conscription "internationalist" Wendell Wilkie, a lifetime Democrat who had never held public office.

On the eve of the costliest war in U.S. history, (one million dead or maimed, $2 trillion in 1990 dollars), Americans were not given a choice. There wasn't an anti-war candidate. Does this remind you of 2004 or 2008?

More than propaganda was involved. The organizer of the Republican convention, Ralph Williams, an "isolationist" (doublespeak for nationalist) conveniently died May 16 and was replaced by a lifelong British agent Sam Pryor who packed the convention with Wilkie supporters shouting, "We want Wilkie."

True, Williams was 70 years old. But historian Thomas Mahl says that the British mandate included murder and he implies this is what took place. Heinrich Muller, the Chief of the Gestapo who worked for the CIA during the Truman administration confirms that the British killed many Americans who got in the way.

"[Wilkie's] nomination exempted President Franklin Roosevelt from the normal pressures of an election campaign," Mahl writes in his explosive book "Desperate Deception: British Covert Operations in the U.S., 1939-44." (1998)

Walter Lippmann wrote, "the sudden rise and nomination of Wendell Wilkie was the decisive event, perhaps providential, which made it possible to rally the free world...Under any other leadership but his, the Republican Party would ... have turned its back on Great Britain..." (164)

If a Republican nationalist like Robert Taft had won the nomination, Churchill was prepared to make peace with Hitler and abandon Stalin to his fate. The Jewish holocaust wouldn't have occurred because Hitler wanted good relations with England. In a repeat of World War One, American intervention prolonged the war with disastrous consequences for mankind.

The Illuminati game plan was for a long two-front war that the Nazis would lose. Although Mahl doesn't mention the Illuminati by name, his book exposes its modus operandi, which I will detail later.

CENTRAL BANKERS AND SPIES

The Rockefeller and Morgan empires are part of the central banking cartel. At the highest level, all intelligence agencies (MI-6, CIA, Mossad, KGB) answer to this cartel, not to their national governments.

MI-6's "British Security Coordination," (BSC) handled the Illuminati campaign to frog march the U.S.A into World War Two. It was financed by the Rockefellers and Morgans and housed rent-free on the 38th Floor of the "International Building" of Rockefeller Centre.

"This was a convenient address," Mahl writes. "Several British agencies promoting intervention were also housed here. The British Press Service was located on the 44th Floor. The British intelligence front group Fight for Freedom located its operations on the 22nd floor in the same building, also rent free." (11)

Wendell Wilkie had been an organizer at numerous Democratic conventions. He was the President of a Morgan-controlled insurance company and a member of the "Fight for Freedom" executive. His whole campaign was financed and organized by the Morgans and British intelligence but made to look homespun.

After losing the 1940 election, Wilkie worked closely with FDR to sabotage nationalist Republicans and was briefly considered for FDR's VP in 1944. Instead, his usefulness apparently at an end, he conveniently died in 1944 at age 52 of a "streptococcic throat infection" contracted in the hospital.

Defeating Nazism was not the immediate goal of American intervention. The goal was to have a long, devastating and lucrative war, leading to greater concentration of power in their hands and eventual "world government."

THE MODUS OPERANDI

In the 1930's the American people learned how the bankers had manoeuvred the U.S. into WWI for great profit. Congress passed a battery of legislation to prevent this from happening again. British PM Neville Chamberlain called the U.S. Congress "pig headed and self righteous nobodies."

The Illuminati had to change public opinion before FDR could commit the U.S. to war. Their main weapon was the mass media, literally owned by the central bankers or controlled by advertising from their cartels.

In 1940, publications owned by the central bankers and their front men included The New York Herald Tribune, The New York Times, PM, The Chicago Sun, The Cowles Group (Look), Time Life, The Washington Post and the Baltimore Sun. All were decidedly for intervention. Hollywood also produced war propaganda. Alexander Korda, director of "Lady Hamiliton" and "The Lion has Wings" was a British agent.

Journalists who achieved success as spokesmen for British Intelligence included Walter Winchell, Drew Pearson, Dorothy Thompson, Walter Lippmann, James Reston and Hubert Bayard Swope.

Public opinion polls were rigged or edited to give Americans the impression they favored intervention. For example, a British agent David Ogilvy put out the Gallup polls.

Nationalist politicians like Hamilton Fish, Martin Dies and Burton Wheeler were smeared as pro-Nazi and anti Semitic. They were hounded with false charges and eventually defeated. One, Senator Arthur Vandenburg changed his mind with the help of a beautiful socialite working for British Intelligence.

The British manufactured German atrocity photos and a phoney map purporting to be a Nazi plan to divide South America. This map helped FDR overturn the last remaining neutrality legislation. Phoney horoscopes forecasted ruin for Hitler and American "isolationists."

Like the Communists, the British formed numerous groups that masqueraded as grass roots organizations. They included "Friends of Democracy," "The League for Human Rights," the "Fight for Freedom Committee."

After the war, the Rockefeller's Council on Foreign Relations ensured that official histories of American intervention were written. They did not want a repeat of the embarrassing revelations of how the U.S. was tricked into World War One.

COMMUNIST JEWS

The British would have abandoned Stalin only as a last resort. British Freemasonry (i.e. the central bankers) was behind the Bolshevik Revolution but by pretending to be opposed, Britain was able to betray their allies, the nationalist White Russians. The bankers later created Nazi Germany partly because Stalin had become too nationalistic himself.

The bankers were going to let the two titans fight it out like monsters in a cheap Japanese horror but Hitler had to lose because he was more independent than Stalin.

Mahl's book provides glimpses into this confluence of interest between the central bankers, the British, Jewish leaders, and the U.S.SR.

For example, the BSC subsidized the Overseas News Agency, which was a branch of the Jewish Telegraphic Agency, founded by Jacob Landau. Banker Felix Warburg also subsidized the JTA, whose job was to publicize persecution of Jews. Landau was also on the executive of "Fight for Freedom."

Decrypted VENONA messages (wires between the Soviet embassy and Moscow) reveal that Landau was working for both the British and the Soviets. He travelled to Mexico City in 1943 and had several meetings with the Soviet ambassador.

Mahl writes: "the VENONA messages reveal...Soviet secret intelligence had thoroughly penetrated BSC and its offspring OSS" (which became the CIA.) (49)

William Stephenson headed BSC. His Second -in- Command was Col. Charles "Dick" Ellis a member of MI-6 who organized and ran the future CIA. According to Mahl, Ellis was "also suspected of working for German and Soviet intelligence services." (194)

This picture is consistent with the view that the central bankers secretly control all Intelligence agencies and wars are just a charade.

FINALLY

Freud's nephew Edward Bernays helped manipulate the masses for the Illuminati. In his book "Propaganda," he wrote:

"The conscious and intelligent manipulation of the organized habits and opinions of the masses is an important element in democratic society. Those who manipulate this unseen mechanism of society constitute an invisible government, which is the true ruling power of our country."

Clearly democracy and freedom itself are an illusion. The Illuminati provides the choices and controls the debate. Ultimately our "democracy" only legitimizes illegitimate power.

Americans are being frog marched into the next world war. The present period might be compared to the 1930's when both sides armed and rehearsed. The final conflagration, possibly in 2010-2012, would eliminate a large number of "useless eaters."

"I Was Hitler's Boss"

The man who became the personification of evil was probably the puppet of the invisible power still in control of the world.

Examine this curious little-known document entitled "I was Hitler's Boss" by Captain Karl Mayr published in the New York-based magazine "Current History" (November 1941.)

As Hitler's boss in the "Instruction Dept." of the Reichwehr in Munich, Capt. Mayr had "daily contact" with Hitler for 15 months (March 1919- June 1920). Corporal Hitler was charged with propaganda functions and infiltrating labor groups.

Mayr portrays Hitler as a "tired stray dog looking for a master," a mere factotum first of General Ludendorff and then of Goering, considered dispensable after fulfilling his purpose.

He "tried to enter the postal service as a mail carrier. His services were refused because he was unable to pass the intelligence test. His school education in his Austrian village would have been quite sufficient, but his mental capacity suffered after he was gassed in the war."

While I believe Captain Mayr, who opposed Hitler later (and was interned at Buchenwald and murdered) wrote the essay, it may be "black propaganda." Published the month before the U.S. entered the war, it may have been designed to create friction between Hitler and his designated successor Herman Goering, and to anger Hitler by belittling him.

The editor of "Current History" was "Spencer Brodney." His real name was Leon Brotzky, who was a long time Communist. "Current History" was published quarterly by the New York Times Company, the organ of the central banking cartel.

Nevertheless, the document has been suppressed which suggests it contradicted the bankers' policy of making Hitler look credible. Although black propaganda spins the truth, its effectiveness depends on including a considerable amount of fact. And much of what Mayr says is consistent with other sources. I will summarize his most plausible revelations and then briefly consider the implications.

HITLER A MISFIT BECOMES 'MAN ON THE HORSE'

Capt. Mayr says that in 1919, Hitler was "one of the many thousand of ex-soldiers who walked the streets looking for work. At this time, Hitler was ready to throw in his lot with anyone who would show him kindness...He would have worked for a Jewish or French employer just as readily as for an Aryan." He was "totally unconcerned about the German people and their destinies."

Hitler "talked and walked in his sleep and made himself generally a nuisance." He had no friends, and was shy and self conscious because of a "deformity [which] made him unlike other men--in my opinion this infliction made Hitler a lone wolf and outsider." [Hitler apparently had only one testicle. Funny Mayr doesn't mention this detail if he is trying to discredit Hitler. Perhaps the era forbade it.] Hitler was "continually chaffed by his comrades."

According to Mayr, General Erich Ludendorff (1865-1937) the hero of World War One met weekly with a coterie of industrialists at the Hotel Four Seasons in Munich and plotted vengeance for Germany's war loss.

The challenge was to mobilize the dispirited German worker for another fight. Ludendorff decided they needed a Joan D'Arc figure, a common person who heard God's voice, to lead them into battle. He even roamed the Bavarian Alps looking for a "red headed peasant girl" who could be sold as a divine messenger.

Ludendorff and his friends "were like Hollywood scouts looking for talent..." At the same time Hitler was involved in an army "experiment." He was given money to hold meetings of the German Workers Party in taverns and buy everyone beer, sausages and pretzels. After some rousing songs, when everyone felt "happy and grateful," Hitler would jump on a chair or a table and started with "fellow-workers, Germany, awake!"

"In such a genial atmosphere it was a pleasure for workers to awake and manly applaud everything." Mayr writes. "The experiment with Hitler was considered highly successful by his sponsors" and Hitler got the Joan D'Arc job.

"The program was carefully concocted to fit with the wishful thinking of the majority."

The leaders knew that "a minority must suffer, and so the German Jews were made the chief scapegoats because their destruction would gain millions of votes for the Nazis. Small shopkeepers hated Jews because they owned the chain stores; farmers wished their destruction because they were indebted to Jewish bankers; even intellectuals were jealous because Jews held lucrative positions in the arts and sciences and professions. The Communists also had to be destroyed, but that was because they took their orders from Russia and would never vote for an Imperial Germany."

"The "Nazi salesmen" offered anything and everything to make the people war minded... Therefore, their sales talk was: Germany is a have-not country; other nations have all the wealth; Germany must fight them successfully, and so be entitled to that wealth."

Thus the Nazis catered always to the desires of the majority. "No one cared what happened to Germany as long as the result was the restoration of the good old days ..."

Hitler was looked upon as "a good salesman for the Nazi ideology, who would be paid off when he was no longer needed."

HITLER THE FIGUREHEAD

Mayr maintains that Hitler never was the real leader of the Nazis. "As a leader, Hitler is probably the greatest hoax ever played on the world... His reports always had to be rewritten... His intellect was not higher than that of an eight-year-old child... Hitler has never been capable of making a decision of his own...he certainly never wrote a line of Mein Kampf; ...[but] was of course proud to sign his name as author of a book."

"Before every important speech Hitler was, sometimes for days, closeted with Hess who in some unknown way, got Hitler into that frenetic state in which he came forth to address the public. Just before Hitler had appointments to receive statesmen or foreign correspondents, he was minutely coached as what to say. Sometimes when unexpected questions were put to him, he just walked away, or started his senseless political ranting."

Ludendorff soon lost control of Hitler to Ernst Roehm and Hermann Goering who engaged in a bitter war for Nazi supremacy. Finally Goering won the battle "in the blood purge" of June 30, 1934. By this time, Mayr had become associated with Roehm, who represented the original socialist goals of Nazism.

"The way was now clear for Goering and he lost no time. Conscription; occupation of the Rhineland; total rearmament; intervention in Spain; invasion of Austria, Czechoslovakia, Poland and other countries followed."

"Germany has many Fausts, but their Mephistopheles is Goering who was able, through crafty propagandists like Goebbels, to sell Hitler to the entire world as a patriotic superman. Goering alone engineered the burning of the Reichstag and had a feeble minded boy executed for it...It was he that arranged Hitler got the false material to convince him that Roehm intended to kill him unless he killed Roehm first. Goering's fawning on Hitler was sheer hypocrisy designed to mislead public opinion."

[The view purveyed by most historians is that Goering was an ineffectual leader, who preferred to hunt or collect (or steal) art rather than run the Luftwaffe. Supposedly he lived in fear of Hitler.]

CONCLUSION

Mayr's view is in stark contrast with the conventional view of Hitler. Either Mayr is lying or the majority of modern historians are engaged in building Hitler up to seem like a credible leader and personification of evil.

I believe that Hitler was stage managed by the Illuminati, i.e. Masons organized around the Rothschild's desire for world tyranny to protect their monopoly on credit.

In the "Protocols of Zion," the author says that all opposition is controlled. If any state raises an objection to Rothschild domination, "it is only pro forma, at our discretion, and by our direction, for their anti-Semitism is indispensable to us for the management of our lesser brethren." (Protocol 9)

My current hypothesis is that there is a direct line between Hitler and the

Rothschild agenda, through a long line of "cut outs" (agents). Some of these cutouts were "useful idiots" like Erich Ludendorff who retired from politics when he realized Rothschild's Bank of England was financing Hitler.

Max Warburg, Chief of German Army Intelligence, member of the Rothschild-affiliated banking family, and Mayr's real boss in 1919, probably was the Rothschild point man in the "Hitler Experiment." Through the "secret masonry" the central bankers created both Communism and Nazism which, thanks to WWII, advanced the destruction of Western (Christian) civilization.

The human race is fast becoming the Rothschilds' ant farm. Thanks to their control over the media and education, information and entertainment are mostly tools for social control and behavior modification. Obscure documents like Captain Mayr's "I was Hitler's Boss" remind us we are being manipulated and betrayed in a most egregious way.

Was Hitler an Illuminati Agent?

Greg Hallett's book "Hitler Was A British Agent" depicts war as a ghoulish illusion conjured by occult magicians in order to degrade and eventually enslave humanity in a world government.

Hallett's claim that Hitler was a "British" agent is based on the testimony of a shadowy network of retired intelligence agents. While he fails to provide documentary proof, Hallett does offer persuasive circumstantial evidence.

For example, Adolph Hitler was in England in 1912-1913, a fact supported by his sister-in-law's book: "The Memoirs of Bridget Hitler"(1979). Many historians including Hitler biographer John Toland have ignored this startling information. (If Hallett is right, historians like Toland are guilty of sanitizing Hitler and building him up.)

Hallett says Hitler spent February to November 1912 being brainwashed and trained at the British Military Psych-Op War School at Tavistock in Devon and in Ireland. "War machines need war and [that means they need] funded, trained and supported double agents to be their patsies, their puppets and their puppet enemies," Hallett, a New Zealand-based architect, writes. (38)

Hitler's sister-in-law described him as completely wasted when he arrived at her Liverpool door baggage-less. "I had an idea he was ill, his color was so bad and his eyes looked so peculiar," she wrote. "He was always reading, not books, little pamphlets printed in German. I don't know what was in them nor exactly where they came from." (pp. 29,35) Hallett says these were Tavistock training manuals.

"Hitler was a British Agent" is useful as an alternative paradigm. (Usually we cannot recognize truth because we have the wrong paradigm, i.e. our "education" which acts as a filter.) When Hallett says "British", he means Illuminati, the Masonic cult of super rich bankers who control an interlocking network of cartels. This cult is based in the City of London but uses England and most nations and ideologies as sock puppets in a Punch and Judy show called history.

Hallett's claim would clarify many improbable events in the Second World War. For example, why did Hitler let 335,000 Allied soldiers escape at Dunkirk? This quixotic gesture was explained as a magnanimous peace overture, but surely England would have been more amenable if its army were in Nazi POW camps.

The Nazi triumph in May 1940 was like a knock-out in the first round. The Illuminati did not intend for the war to end so soon, nor for the Nazis to win.

In the summer of 1940, when Britain was prostrate, Nazi Military Intelligence Chief (Abwehr) Admiral Wilhelm Canaris told Romanian Foreign Minister Prince Michael Sturdza to stay neutral because England would win the war. He also gave this message to Spanish dictator Franco.

Hallett's theory also explains why Hitler, supposedly the arch enemy of Jewish bankers, acted like he didn't know the Rothschilds controlled England (and America) when this was practically common knowledge. (See Hillaire Belloc, "The Jews" 1922.) If Hitler were for real, he would have invaded England before Russia was attacked.

Hallett's hypothesis explains 1)Why Hitler was able to expand into the Rhineland etc. without fear of retaliation. 2) Why the Nazi war machine was financed and built by the Bank of England and a Who's Who of Anglo American corporations controlled by the Illuminati. 3) Why Hitler never sealed the Mediterranean at Gibraltar; and why the Spanish dictator Franco remained neutral, despite the huge debt he owed the Nazis from the Spanish Civil War. 4) Why I.G. Farben headquarters in Frankfurt was never bombed. This became CIA headquarters. 5) Why the Bank of England rewarded Hitler for taking Prague by giving him the Czech gold reserves in London.

It would explain why Hitler gave his ridiculous racial policies priority over actually winning the war. He could have enlisted millions of Slavs (and even many Jews) in overcoming Communist Russia. Instead, he made them implacable enemies.

We could question why German ally Japan attacked the U.S. instead of Russia; why the Nazis never figured out that their communications were compromised; why Hitler didn't conquer the oil fields of Russia and the Middle East when he had the chance etc. but you get the picture. The fix was in.

Hitler may have thought he was acting for Anglo American capitalists by invading Soviet Russia. Possibly he didn't realize he (and Germany) were being set up.

WHO WAS HITLER?

The biggest improbability is that an Austrian tramp, street cleaner and gay prostitute could become the Chancellor of Germany. Hitler joins a long list of obscure blackmail-able figures who have been catapulted to world prominence with the aid of an unseen hand.

Hallett writes that Hitler's grandfather was Nathan Meyer Rothschild. Maria Schickelgruber, Hitler's grandmother, was a maid in the Rothschild's Vienna mansion when his father, Alois was conceived "in fear" in a Satanic ritual rape. The Rothschilds could only marry within their extended family so they had illegitimate children who functioned as anonymous agents. (Apparently this is a pattern with the Illuminati. Bill Clinton is rumored to be a Rockefeller.)

His grandmother received child support from a Jewish businessman who probably was an intermediary for his grandfather. Bridget Hitler quotes Hitler's sister Paula:

"Since [Adolf] started the race laws we have no grandfather, Adolf and I. Certainly anyone who wished could make a good deal out of that." (Memoirs, p. 175)

Rothschild's son, Alois Hitler's third marriage was to his niece, Klara, who became Hitler's mother. His father was abusive and his mother over- compensated. Hitler became destitute at age 18 when his mother died, and he lived in a Vienna men's hostel that was a homosexual haunt.

According to German historian and professor Lothar Machtan, Hitler was a homosexual with a long police record for harassing men in both in Munich and Vienna. These records reached both Russia and England but were never used for propaganda, more evidence that the war may have been a charade. (Machtan,"The Hidden Hitler," 2001.)

MAKING OF A MADMAN

According to Hallett, Hitler travelled to England in 1912 for training which took place in German. This "training" ranged from imbibing a sense of his role in Germany's destiny to learning how to mesmerize audiences.

It also included trauma brainwashing. The "alter's" consciousness is shattered by witnessing savage atrocities and suffering sexual abuse, all of which is filmed. Then the various fragments of consciousness are programmed and can be accessed with special code words. (Read Fritz Springmeier and Cisco Wheeler for a detailed description of Illuminati mind control techniques.)

Hitler returned to Germany in May 1913 and enlisted in the German army. During World War One, he served as a runner and was captured twice by the English. On both occasions, he was spared execution by an "angel" in British intelligence.

According to Hallett, Hitler enjoyed having women defecate on him. He also had undersized genitals and only one testicle. (Many women whom he courted committed suicide. The love of his life was his 17-year-old half-niece Geli whom he murdered in 1931 when she got pregnant by his chauffeur. Machtan argues that Hitlers real affections were for the chauffeur.)

For more on Nazi Homosexuality, see the book, "The Pink Swastika" online.

IMPLICATIONS

History is unfolding according to the Illuminati's long-term plan. Wars are plotted decades in advance and orchestrated to achieve the destruction of nations and natural elites, depopulation, demoralization, and of course power and profit.

According to Hallett, Joseph Stalin was another Illuminati "agent of war" who attended the Tavistock Psyche Ops training school in 1907. Clifford Shack has suggested that Stalin was also an illegitimate offspring of a Rothschild.

Hallett says Hitler's death was faked (a double was killed) and Hitler escaped to

Barcelona where he lived until 1950, when he died of stomach cancer.

Greg Hallett is a maverick and his rambling book is full of repetition and digressions. I wouldn't swear by any of Hallett's claims as yet. But he deserves our thanks for advancing an alternative view of history that while far- fetched, is more plausible than what supposedly transpired. We should be able to entertain speculative views without feeling compelled to accept or reject them. (It's called "reserving judgement.")

Hitler must be seen in the perspective of this line from "The Protocols of the Elders of Zion," (9) : "Nowadays, if any States raise a protest against us it is only pro forma at our discretion and by our direction..."

World War Two achieved all of the Illuminati's goals. Germany and Japan were turned into a wasteland. Sixty million people were slaughtered. The Jewish holocaust motivated Jews to establish the Rothschild's world government headquarters in Israel. Idealists and natural leaders on both sides were slaughtered. Nations were laden with debt. The United Nations rose like a phoenix from the ashes. Hiroshima cast a pall of terror over the world. The U.S.SR was a superpower and controlled Eastern Europe. The stage was set for the next act in the play...the Cold War.

Given the bleak outlook for humanity, there is a tendency to actually idealize Hitler as an opponent of central banker hegemony. Hallett's book is an important reminder that like Stalin and Mao, Hitler was an agent. The Illuminati sponsor "enemies" in order to foment conflict, and keep humanity in its thrall.

Did the Illuminati Hire Hitler to Start WW2?

The ink wasn't dry on the Versailles Peace Treaty before the Illuminati started work on World War Two by building Adolf Hitler and the Nazi Party.

Before 1919, Hitler had been a political "gun for hire" who had many Jewish friends and had flirted with both Communism and Socialism. Overnight he became a virulent anti-Communist and anti-Semite. What happened? He became an army intelligence officer. Throughout the 1920's the German army (Reichswehr) secretly funded Hitler, his party and trained his SA "Brownshirts."

I suspect General Kurt Von Schleicher was a point man for Illuminati bankers like banker Max Warburg, whose Frankfurt I.G. Farben HQ was spared by Allied bombers, and whose Jewish mother lived in comfort in Hamburg throughout the war.

In the Protocols of Zion, the author, an Illuminati banker, boasts they create or sanction anti-Semitism when it serves their purpose. "Anti-Semitism is indispensible to us for the management of our lesser brethren...this matter has been the subject of repeated discussions amongst us." (Protocol 9). Hitler is an example of how anti-Semitism was created. The author continues:

"It is from us that the all engulfing terror proceeds. We have in our service persons of all opinions, of all doctrines, monarchists, demagogues, socialists, communists and utopian dreamers of every kind...striving to overthrow all established forms of order. All states are in torture... but we will not give them peace until they openly acknowledge our international Super government..."

There, in black and white, is the blueprint behind the NWO, UN, the EU and NAU, and every war until today. But the bankers have made us think it "racist" to pay heed. As if more than 1% of Jews were/are a conscious part of their heinous, diabolical conspiracy.

Modern history consists of this long-term plan to foment needless wars in order to enslave mankind by destroying our identity based on nation, religion, race and family. Most historians are paid to obscure the horrible fact that the people ultimately responsible for Auschwitz, the Gulag, Hiroshima and Verdun still run the world. They are responsible for 9/11 and Iraq.

Our leaders are chosen by their ability to lie and follow orders. Conflicts are charades between "antagonists" who actually serve the same masters.

VERSAILLES

Dr. E. J. Dillon of the London Daily Telegraph wrote in his book "The Inside Story of the Peace Conference," (1920): Many delegates deduced that "henceforth the world will be governed by the Anglo-Saxon people, who in turn are swayed by their Jewish elements..." (i.e. the central bankers and their factotums) p 497.

Germany was the major obstacle to using England and the U.S. to impose Illuminati rule upon the world. Thus, onerous reparations were imposed to prompt another much more devastating world war. Once it begin, the British vetoed attempts to assassinate or replace Hitler, and insisted on "unconditional surrender."

Hitler didn't come to power until 1933 but Germany started rearming in 1919 in contravention of Versailles provisions. The Allies turned a blind eye to a program that saw Communist and German soldiers train in Russia with the latest weaponry, including whole bases devoted to air force, armour and chemical warfare. When Hitler came to power in 1933, Germany already had an advanced air force.

Another way to evade Versailles was for the Reichswehr to fund and train paramilitary organizations like the Nazi SA which later could be incorporated into the regular army. General Kurt Von Schleicher and Captains Karl Mayr and Ernst Roehm were in charge of this "Black Werhmacht" program.

Sefton Delmer, who was the "Daily Express" correspondent in Berlin, describes this in his autobiography "Trail Sinister" (1961). He cites documents showing that Hitler was "acting under Mayr's orders when he joined the tiny German Workers Party and began to build it up..." (64) Delmer says Mayr also funded mass meetings and pamphlets in which Hitler railed against the Jews. "This anti-Jewish campaign ...was being promoted by no less a power than the Staff Officers of the Reichswehr." (63)

The Reichwehr's purpose was to create popular political support for WW2. According to Delmer, "Schleicher paid out no less than two million pounds from the Reichswehr's secret funds for the Nazi storm troopers..." (120) They were also funded by Illuminati industrialists and bankers.

(Born and raised in Berlin, Sefton Delmer knew Hitler personally, and had a wide range of confidential sources. During the war, he took charge of British "black propaganda" running a range of radio stations aimed at German soldiers.)

HITLER, "ANTI-COMMUNIST, ANTI-SEMITE"

Communism, Nazism and Zionism are triplets, movements conceived and nurtured by the Illuminati to dupe and manipulate humanity.

In his book "The Hidden Hitler" Lothar Machtan, a Professor of History at Bremen University says Hitler almost joined the Communists in 1918. He demanded a senior party post that would have exempted him from work but they refused. "Hitler did not set foot in the extreme right wing camp until he had been rejected by left wing groups," Machtan writes. (71)

According to Ian Kershaw, Hitler took part in pro Socialist and Communist demonstrations in 1918-1919 and served as a Socialist Soldiers' Council representative. ("Hitler: 1889-1936," p 118-120.)

According to Brigitte Hamann, Hitler's best friends in pre-war Vienna were Jewish. He benefited from Jewish charities and hospitality. Jews bought most of his artwork. For this reason, real anti-Semites shunned him. ("Hitler's Vienna: A Dictator's Apprenticeship," pp.347-352)

Hamann suggests that Hitler's ideas of Aryan racial purity and superiority were based on the Jews. She quotes Hitler:

"Through Moses the Jewish people received a rule for life and living one's life that was elevated to a religion which was entirely tailored toward the essence of one's race, and simply and clearly without dogmas and dubious rules of faith...contains what served the ...well being of one's people, nothing toward consideration of others." (351)

CONCLUSION

There is nostalgia for Hitler based on the belief that he represented resistance to the New World Order. In fact, he was created by the Illuminati to start another war.

People pin their hopes on leaders like Putin and Ahmadinejad but like Hitler, they were obscure figures who were raised to power by an unseen hand. We don't have real political (or cultural) leaders, just Illuminati pawns.

Human history is always the same: A minority wants to monopolize all power and wealth, at the expense of the many. Mass serial killers are in charge. No matter how long they make nice, eventually they will always revert to form.

Notes:

Some sources in this article were suggested by Jim Condit's fine documentary "The Final Solution to Adolph Hitler."

"Zionism was willing to sacrifice the whole of European Jewry for a Zionist State. Everything was done to create a state of Israel and that was only possible through a world war. Wall Street and Jewish large bankers aided the war effort on both sides. Zionists are also to blame for provoking the growing hatred for Jews in 1988." (Joseph Burg, "The Toronto Star," March 31, 1988)."

Major Robert H. Williams reported in his "Williams Intelligence Summary" for February 1950 about James P. Warburg's part in the plot against Christendom. He said: "Last November, the widow of the late General Ludendorff, on trial at Nuremberg, explained why her husband broke with Hitler, confirmed the reports in convincing detail.

She stated that, '...as early as the summer of 1929 James P. Warburg had undertaken an assignment from financial circles in America, which desired to exercise solitary influence on Germany in the unleashing of a national revolution. Warburg's task was to find the suitable man in Germany, and he entered into contract with Adolph Hitler who subsequently received sums of money amounting to 27 million dollars up to January 30, 1932, and still another seven million thereafter, enabling him to finance his movement.'"

Hitler Used Rothschild Banker's Typewriter (to Write "Mein Kampf")

Sometimes the symbolic details speak volumes.

Emil Georg von Stauss, the president of Germany's largest bank, the Deutsche Bank, lent Hitler a portable Remington so he could write his infamous anti-Jewish banker manifesto "Mein Kampf."

Von Stauss, a principal Nazi Party fundraiser, also was a long-time business associate of the Rothschilds.

Hitler dictated "Mein Kampf" to typists Rudolf Hess and Emil Maurice during his cushy eight-months stay at Landsberg Prison in April-December 1924. (His five-year sentence was commuted. He had a two-room suite with a view and was allowed to receive gifts and visitors.)

Von Stauss was part of a "Hitler support group" consisting of wealthy patrons. Helene Bechstein, the wife of the piano manufacturer pretended to be Hitler's adopted mother and smuggled out sections of the manuscript. She took care of all Hitler's expenses and hoped he would marry her daughter Lotte. Franz Thyssen, the chairman of United Steelworks sent Hitler a birthday gift of 100,000 gold marks.

This account is taken from Rudolf Hess' letters to his wife by Belgian author Stan Lauryssens, ("The Man Who Invented the Third Reich" 1999, pp.130-135.)

It contradicts the image we have of Hitler in 1924 leading a grass roots fringe party. In fact, he was a front man for the international bankers he pretended to oppose.

Both Nazism and Communism were fake opposition concocted by Illuminati bankers. As we sleepwalk into the next world war, let's recall that the people who issue our currency are behind every war and control both sides.

DEUTSCH BANK, VON STAUSS AND ROTHSCHILDS

The Deutsch Bank helped to create Hitler because he represented war profit. (Branch managers and executives belonged to the Nazi Party.) During the Second World War, the Deutsche Bank profited when it took over banks and industries in occupied countries, "Aryanized" Jewish-owned businesses, and Jewish bank accounts. (See Harold James, "The Deutsche Bank and the Nazi Economic War Against the Jews," 2001.)

Before becoming president of the bank, Von Stauss was General Director of Steaua Romana, a Romanian oil company owned by the bank. He was Managing

Director of the European Petroleum Union (EPU), an oil cartel. The E.P.U. was "an international association of industrialists whose object was to make the greatest possible profit on their products."

The EPU represented the Rothschild interests, the Nobel interests and the Deutsche Bank interests. The latter two probably included Rothschild interests.

After the Nazi seizure of power, Von Stauss co-ordinated the war build-up at major German corporations such as Daimler Benz and BMW, who were connected to Deutsch Bank.

One book describes him as "an enigmatic character of the Weimar and National Socialist periods, albeit one who has rarely been given his due in historical studies." While a major supporter, he never became a member of the Nazi Party and "always maintained good relations with prominent economic figures who were Jews such as his colleague Oscar Wassermann at the Deutsch Bank." (David Bankier ed. "Probing the Depth of German anti-Semitism," 2000, pp 256-257.)

Nevertheless he was instrumental in Aryanizing Jewish assets, even those of Jews who had long ago converted and intermarried. Clearly there were in-Jews and out-Jews, i.e. Illuminati or not.

WHY BANKERS CREATE WAR

War is the centrepiece of the bankers' long-term plan to decimate, degrade and enslave humanity, which is necessary to protect their fraudulent world monopoly over our credit. This logic explains the real meaning of "revolution," and why they consider war "revolutionary."

Mankind is stymied because a tiny clique usurped control of money making. This began when gold dealers realized they could issue receipts for gold they didn't have. They became bankers who figured they could also issue more loans than they had money, by a simple bookkeeping entry.

They used this Golden Goose to take control of the world's wealth and put their accomplices in charge of government, media and education. They arranged for our national governments to guarantee the paper they print.

War distracts us from this state of affairs, degrades, brutalizes, and increases debt and profits. (The bankers naturally put most faith in government debt.) Central bankers also love socialism. They buy people with their own money and indenture them at the same time.

Woodrow Wilson was a pawn of this "money power." But to save his soul, he said American industrialists are afraid of "a power somewhere, so organized, so subtle, so watchful, so interlocked, so complete, so pervasive" that they dared not speak above their breath.

Wilson actually identified this power:

"The great monopoly in this country is the monopoly of big credits. A great industrial nation is controlled by its system of credits. The growth of the nation, therefore, and all of our activities, are in the hands of a few men who chill and check and destroy genuine economic freedom." (Robertson, "Human Ecology," p. 166.)

CONCLUSION

War, including the "war on terror," is designed to create a world police state to protect the central banker monopoly on power and wealth. It doesn't really matter who gets elected. They all work for the central bankers.

Masons, Bilderbergers, Jesuits and Zionists are all empowered by the bankers. Mankind will never get on the right foot until bankers turn over their power to create money using our credit. In the meantime, our lives are shaped by a series of fantastic hoaxes, not the least of which is war.

Did Bormann
Run Hitler for the Illuminati?

The second most powerful man in Nazi Germany, Martin Bormann, was a "Soviet" (i.e. Illuminati) agent who ensured the destruction of both Germany and European Jewry.

Thus, he advanced two of the Illuminati's main goals: integrate Germany into a world government by annihilating its national, cultural and racial pretensions, and establish Israel as the Masonic banker's world capital by threatening European Jews with extermination.

The Illuminati are a loose alliance of Jewish finance and the British/America/European aristocracy joined by marriage, money and belief in the occult (Freemasonry). Winston Churchill, a Freemason whose mother was Jewish, fits this description.

They own vast interlocking cartels (banking, oil, pharmaceuticals, war, chemicals, minerals, media etc.) and control society and government through corporate and professional groups, the media, education, secret societies, think tanks, foundations and intelligence agencies. Their goal is "to absorb the world's wealth" (in Cecil Rhodes' words) and control its citizens using propaganda, "education" and social engineering.

Nations (Britain, US, Israel) movements (Zionism, Socialism, Nazism, Communism) and people (Americans, Germans, Jews) are their pawns to be sacrificed to their demented megalomaniac scheme for global dictatorship. Bormann's career illustrates how they orchestrate wars to advance this long-term objective.

Martin Bormann (1900-?) was the organizer, treasurer and paymaster of the Nazi Party and controlled its powerful machine. He was the contact with Illuminati bankers and industrialists who financed the Nazi Party and donated millions to Hitler. As Deputy Fuhrer and Hitler's Secretary, Bormann signed Hitler's paycheck and managed his accounts. He determined whom and what Hitler saw, and acted in his name.

Goering said "Bormann stayed with Hitler day and night and gradually brought him so much under his will that he ruled Hitler's whole existence." ("Martin Bormann" by James McGovern, p.160) Hitler made Bormann the Executor of his will. Bormann, not Hitler, owned the Berghof. "The entire complex on the Obersalzberg, consisting of 87 buildings and worth over one and a half million marks, was legally registered in Bormann's name. (McGovern, p.128)

In 1972 Gen. Reinhard Gehlen (head of Wehrmacht Soviet Intelligence) revealed that Bormann had been a Soviet spy, a view shared by many top Nazi generals and officials including Gottlob Berger, a SS Lieutenant General who knew Bormann well. "Bormann did the greatest harm of anyone," Berger testified at Nuremberg. (McGovern, 181)

The implications are staggering. Remember what Winston Churchill said. "This war is not against Hitler or National Socialism but against the strength of the German people, which is to be smashed once and for all, regardless whether it is in the hands of Hitler or a Jesuit priest." (Emrys Hughes, "Winston Churchill, His Career in War and Peace," p. 145)

The Nazi Party was created, and the Second World War staged in order to lead the German people into a diabolical trap, after fatally compromising them morally. In "The Bormann Brotherhood" (1972) William Stevenson says Bormann "gave the lowest priority to the fate of Germany..He was concerned instead with a future based on Nazi philosophy, financed by Nazi loot, supported by a personally loyal Brotherhood..." (62) Is this the Illuminati?

BORMANN

It is unlikely that Bormann perished in war-torn Berlin, as the Illuminati would like us to believe. A man who carefully prepared for the survival of the Reich by setting up 750 corporations in neutral countries would have provided for his own escape. There have been reports that the Russians rescued Bormann and set him up in Moscow. Other reports placed him in South America. Adolph Eichmann's eldest son, Horst claimed he had many conversations with him in Argentina. (McGovern, p.194)

Obviously Bormann was working for both the Soviets and the Nazis, i.e. he was working for the Illuminati. Two-time Pulitzer Prize winner Louis Kilzer makes the case that Bormann was a "Soviet" spy in his book "Hitler's Traitor" (2000). He examined the wire traffic between the spy known as "Werther" and Moscow and determined that only Bormann had access to this information. Bormann told Hitler he wanted a record for posterity and had stenographers transcribe Hitler's war conferences.

The Soviets were able to ask very detailed questions about Nazi defenses and intentions. The result was the decisive Nazis defeats at Stalingrad and Kursk. "Bormann had been as useful to Russia as fifty Red Army divisions," Kilzer writes. (61)

"His value to Stalin began early. In 1941, when Germany could have used millions of Ukrainian nationalists to defeat Soviet rule, Bormann decided that they deserved only, "enslavement and depopulation. ...Faced with ... genocide by the Germans or political domination by the Soviets, the Ukrainians chose to live and by so doing ruined German hopes for an easy conquest." (261)

Borman used the Nazi defeat at Stalingrad as an excuse to begin the extermination of Jews, the second Illuminati goal. In the words of the Nuremberg prosecutor, Bormann was a "prime mover in the program of starvation, degradation, spoliation and extermination." He shielded Hitler from the grisly details, forbidding Himmler from discussing the subject with Hitler and filing Himmler's reports. (261)

"Bormann's role with the Ukrainians and the Jews was only part of his devastating effect on the Third Reich," Kilzer writes. He blocked Albert Speer's attempt to move the economy to a "total war" footing until it was too late. "Bormann's influence," Speer concluded, "was a national disaster." (263)

Kilzer goes into great detail about Bormann's contacts with the Soviet espionage system, profiling many of his handlers. Even one of Bormann's mistresses, Marie Rubach Spangenberg, was active in the German Communist underground. (264)

Bormann encouraged Hitler to ignore the threat of encirclement at Stalingrad. Hitler's decisions "ceased to have anything in common with the principles of strategy and operations," General Halder noted in his diary. (McGovern, 82)

Bormann won Hitler's total allegiance by pretending to be his ruthlessly efficient instrument. When Bormann was criticized, Hitler replied, "Everybody has failed me but Bormann...who ever is against Bormann is also against the State! I'll shoot the lot of them..."(McGovern, 101.) And, "Bormann's proposals are so exactly worked out that I need only say yes or no..." (98)

The question remains, "Was Hitler himself a traitor?" Did he also serve the Illuminati? Kilzer remarks that Hitler was surprisingly lenient to dissent within the ranks and cultivated a "culture of treason." (Kilzer, 6) Was Hitler aware of Bormann's role and played along? I am still searching for this answer.

CONCLUSION

William Stevenson provides a suitable conclusion: "Bormann represented secret power; and in our disheveled human condition, we suspect that the trappings of democracy are more of a dangerous camouflage...that real power begins where secrecy begins. Martin Bormann ... possessed that secret power...to such a degree that he was able to escape the gallows." (9).

The lesson of this story is that the "news" upholds the "camouflage of democracy." Don't pay too much attention or invest your best energies. History is a play. The Illuminati control all the politicians who stand a chance.They control the mass media.

Louis Kilzer's book was published by a tiny publisher in Navato CA. This shows that the large banker-controlled New York publishers want to keep Bormann's secret as much as any Nazi.

We live in a world where the dominant elite has organized into a sinister secret society to plot against humanity. It is creating a "New World Order" symbolized by the unfinished capstone on the pyramid on the US Great Seal. Its symbols are everywhere but we are not allowed to protest them. Success depends on our willingness to betray our fellow citizens, nation and civilization and to allow this malignant power to grow in our midst.

Winston Churchill, Illuminati

After the first Nazi air raid on London Sept. 7, 1940 which killed 306 people, Winston Churchill remarked, "They cheered me as if I'd given them victory, instead of [purposely] getting their houses bombed to bits." (416)

Churchill is telling the truth. Unknown to Londoners, he had rejected Hitler's proposal to spare civilian targets. Quite the opposite, he goaded Hitler into bombing London by hitting Berlin and other civilian targets first.

Churchill told his Air Marshall: "Never mistreat an enemy by halves" and instructed his cabinet, "bombing of military objectives, increasingly widely interpreted, seems our best road home at present." He blocked the Red Cross from monitoring civilian casualties. (440)

Before the end of Sept. 1940, 7,000 Londoners including 700 children lay dead. By the end of the war, more than 60,000 British civilians and 650,000 German civilians died from "strategic" bombing.

In 1940, Churchill had to divert attacks from RAF airfields but he also wanted to start the bloodletting. A year had passed with little action. It was being called the "phoney war." Hitler was making generous peace offers that many Englishmen wanted to accept.

If Britain had made peace, there would not have been a Jewish holocaust.

Churchill described the Second World War as the "most unnecessary war in history." But he served bankers in the City who had made good his stock market losses and saved his beloved Chartwell estate from foreclosure. A manic-depressive, he thrived on the rush of war and cared little for ordinary people.

When he was flashing the "V" sign , people thought he was inspiring them. Instead he was signalling his true allegiance to Lucifer. The "V" sign is an occult sign for the upside-down or "broken" cross.

I realize this is not the saccharine history we are spoon-fed. What we term "history" is mostly propaganda, i.e. a cover-up.

My source for the above is David Irving's "Churchill's War " (Avon Books, 1987) which cuts through the sycophancy that characterizes most accounts of World War Two.

Churchill played a key role in starting the Second World War. This was a big step in a long-term program to enslave humanity in a world dictatorship run by the Illuminati (London-based monopoly capital.)

WHO WAS WINSTON CHURCHILL?

The essential fact about Winston Churchill is that his mother's father was Leonard Jerome (formerly Jacobson, 1818-1891) a speculator and business partner of August Belmont (nee Shoenberg 1813-1890) who was Rothschild's main American representative.

Jennie Jerome's marriage to Randolph Churchill, the second son of the Duke of Marlborough, appears to have been one of convenience, typical of many unions between daughters of Jewish financiers and spendthrift British aristocrats.

Apparently the Marlborough's objections were overcome by a dowry of 50,000 pounds, worth about five million dollars today. Nevertheless they did not attend the wedding in April 1874 and the Duchess referred to young Winston, born seven months later, as an "upstart."

Biographers tend to describe Churchill as not quite "English" and to use Jewish stereotypes. Of Churchill's "premature" birth, William Manchester says: "He never could wait his turn." ("The Last Lion," p. 108)

Beatrice Webb recorded sitting beside him at dinner: "First impression: restless, almost intolerably so...egotistical, bumptious, shallow minded and reactionary but with a certain personal magnetism...More of the American speculator than the English aristocrat. Talked exclusively about himself and his electioneering plans..." (John Pearson, "The Private Lives of Winston Churchill," p. 114)

Churchill's "driven" quality is attributed to the fact his parents neglected him and taught him to earn love by being successful. Winston became a successful author at age 24 and a cabinet minister at 33. His rise was assisted by his mother's connections with the Rothschild Syndicate, including the powerful banker Ernest Cassell. (Churchill also wanted to vindicate his father whose political career/life was cut short by syphilis.)

In the 1930's Churchill's banker friends made him the leading light in their lobby, "The Focus Group," led by the Zionist chairman of British Shell, Sir Robert Waley-Cohen. Churchill became the main opponent of "appeasement" and eventually the main barrier to making peace with Hitler.

In 1936, the Prime Minister Stanley Baldwin told a delegation led by Churchill, "If there is any fighting in Europe to be done, I'd rather see the Bolshies and Nazis doing it." But this policy was not what the Illuminati had in mind. (61)

According to the "Red Symphony" document, the Illuminati created Hitler to control Stalin and start a war. But it appears that Hitler alienated the bankers by printing his own money. This was a major threat to the "Revolution" (i.e. Illuminati world control.)

"Germany's unforgivable crime before the second world war," Churchill said, "was her attempt to extricate her economic power from the world's trading system and to create her own exchange mechanism which would deny world finance its opportunity to profit." (Churchill to Lord Robert Boothby, quoted in the Foreword,

2nd Ed. Sydney Rogerson, "Propaganda in the Next War" 2001, orig. 1938.)

UNANSWERED QUESTIONS

Hitler had no desire to fight Britain. He regarded the British as racial brothers and feared a two-front war. He made many peace overtures, promising to uphold the British Empire in return for a free hand in Europe where he promised considerable national autonomy (e.g. Vichy France.) He sent his Deputy Rudolph Hess to Britain to sue for peace in May 1941. Churchill had Hess locked away.

After Hitler's invasion of Russia in June 1941, his policy toward Jews shifted from expulsion to extermination. He regarded Russian Communism as a Jewish phenomenon. Increasingly, Germany was engaged in a genocidal death struggle.

This would not have been the case had Britain made peace, or allowed for conditional surrender. But abandoning Russia was never in the cards. FDR famously said that nothing in politics happens by accident. It is planned.

The Illuminati's purpose in World War Two was economic, political and occult: to enrich themselves while destroying the nation states of Europe (including Britain) while sacrificing millions of lives to their god Satan.

The Jewish holocaust was also part of the plan, to justify the creation of the Masonic "Jewish" state.

Bernard Wasserstein writes, "During the first two years of the war, when the German authorities bent their efforts to securing the exodus of the Jews from the Reich and from Nazi occupied territory, it was the British Government which took the lead in barring the escape routes from Europe against Jewish refugees." ("Britain and the Jews of Europe," 1939-1945, p.345)

The value of history is to remember that nothing is as it seems. It's all being orchestrated according to a plan that is centuries old. As the twilight rays of Christian civilization gradually fade, darkness and uncertainty spread over the Earth.

Lester Pearson, Illuminati Tool

"Treason doth never prosper: what's the reason?
For if it prosper, none dare call it treason."

No one likes to bring bad tidings or to disturb fellow citizens sleeping soundly.

So, with a heavy heart, I report that Lester Pearson (Canadian Prime Minister 1963-1968) provided confidential information to Russian Military Intelligence (GRU) while serving in Washington DC from 1942-1946, in his capacity ultimately as Canadian Ambassador.

Unfortunately, this is not an isolated case. Treason is the secret policy of the governing elite in the West. Wittingly or unwittingly, they serve the Illuminati plan for "world government," an Orwellian police state called the "New World Order."

The Illuminati is a secret Luciferian cult representing the highest rung of Freemasonry, which has members in key positions around the globe. The Illuminati control the central banking monopoly, (the Bank of England, the Federal Reserve) and a vast network of interlocking cartels (notably media, pharmaceuticals, defence, chemicals, food, minerals and oil.)

Illuminism believes that man (i.e. they) will define reality instead of God or nature. Thus, they have trouble with concepts such as objective truth or morality.

Communism was established by the Illuminati to undermine the basis of Western Civilization (religion, race, nation and family) while pretending to build a better world based on equality and social justice. They duped millions of people, opportunists and genuine idealists alike.

"Internationalism" which Lester Pearson advanced at the UN (winning a Nobel Prize in 1957) is a disguise for this occult tyranny of the super rich. Recent events (Sept. 11, the "War on Terror" Iraq and the Patriot Repression Act) must be seen in the perspective of this grotesque plan.

ELIZABETH BENTLEY

In August 1951, Elizabeth Bentley, a former GRU (Russian Military Intelligence) spy master, testified that Lester "Mike" Pearson was a primary source. He fed confidential information to Hazen Sise, a Soviet agent under her control, who worked for the National Film Board of Canada.

Bentley told the U.S. Senate McCarran Commission: "I understand from Hazen that Pearson knew Hazen was a Communist and was willing to help. Pearson by virtue of his position used to sit in on American functions, particularly British ones re. British policies, all of which was super hush-hush."

Pearson was Canada's Secretary of State for Foreign Affairs in 1951 so this testimony was kept quiet. It is included in Appendix A (p.186) of "No Sense of Evil/ Espionage: The Case of Herbert Norman" (1986) by James Barros, a political science professor at the University of Toronto.

Herbert Norman, the Canadian ambassador to Egypt, was an NKVD agent and Pearson colleague who came under investigation in 1957 and "committed suicide." Pearson protected and covered for him.

Pearson met with Benley's control officer, Anatoly Gorski ("Gromov") in Washington in Oct. 1944. Gorski was one of the KGB's top operatives, having run Blunt, Burgess, Maclean and Philby in England. Barros speculates "the unthinkable" that "Pearson was Moscow's ultimate mole." (169)

In 1957, the U.S. State Dept. held a meeting on whether to press this issue. It concluded: "Pearson is a hero. Right now he is co-operating to the fullest extent with our government in defence contracts." (206)

Lester Pearson may have been recruited while a Rhodes Scholar at Oxford University in 1923. From 1935-1941, he served at the Canadian High Commission in London and rubbed shoulders with the leaders of the world government plot. He helped to establish the North Atlantic Treaty Organization (NATO), and was the UN's point man during the Suez Crisis of 1956.

Canadian Navy Commander Guy Carr mixed with this clique of top civil servants in Ottawa in the 1930's and 1940's. They recognized each other by Masonic signals and indulged in "progressive" pursuits like wife-swapping. One told him: "Stop trying to save the human race. The vast majority aren't worth the time or trouble. Most will be better off under a totalitarian dictatorship; they will get what the government decides is good for them." ("Satan: Prince of this World," p. 101. See also his "Pawns in the Game" and "Red Fog Over America.")

Elizabeth Bentley's testimony was corroborated by decoded "Venona" messages between the Soviet Embassey and the KGB in Moscow which "assured American authorities of her veracity." ("Venona: Decoding Soviet Espionage in America", Yale University Press, 1999, p. 12)

MACKENZIE KING, GOUZENKO AND THE COLD WAR

Lester Pearson was the leader of the Liberal Party which dominated Canadian politics. He was sponsored by Mackenzie King, Prime Minister from 1921 until 1948, (except for 6 years.)

J.D. Rockefeller referred to Mackenzie King as "my best friend." King worked for Rockefeller from 1914-1918 developing company unions and "social reform" policies that ensnared the masses and created big government. The Rockefellers, who are the American agent for the Rothschilds, have controlled the Liberal Party ever since using the Quebec-based Paul Desmarais family (Power Corporation etc.) as intermediary. Former Prime Minister Paul Martin is a former employee who is beholden to Desmarais for selling him Canada Steamship Lines in a sweetheart deal.

In September 1945, three months before Elizabeth Bentley fled the GRU, a Soviet Embassy cipher clerk Igor Gouzenko defected in Ottawa with material documenting massive Soviet espionage in the West. Initially King ordered his officials to stall Gouzenko and his family in spite of the grave danger they were in. The heroic little family was referred from office to office, criss-crossing Ottawa with their incriminating documents. The Gouzenkos were actually told to return to the Russian embassy or commit suicide!

Why? Ostensibly King didn't want to offend the U.S.SR, a valued wartime ally. In reality, King, famous for being "inscrutable," was afraid that Gouzenko would reveal that the governing elite in the West was infested with Soviet (i.e. Illuminati) agents like Lester Pearson and himself.

It appears that Gouzenko was saved because the Illuminati quickly devised a use for him. A top operative, "the Man Called Intrepid" Canadian William Stephenson, Head of British Special Operations Executive suddenly appeared from New York and took the Gouzenkos under his wing.

He used Gouzenko's revelations to kick-start the phony "Cold War." The news that the U.S.SR had spies everywhere and was stealing atomic secrets caused a general panic that transformed public opinion of the U.S.SR from benign to hostile overnight. (See William Stevenson, "Intrepid's Last Case" p. 214.)

The trick was to create enough fear to justify the Cold War without exposing the top figures in the elite conspiracy, both in Canada and abroad. They sacrificed minor figures like atomic scientist Allan Nunn May, who was arrested for espionage and served six years. Meanwhile Lester Pearson and his high-ranking gang of elite traitors were unscathed.

Meanwhile Gouzenko was kept in limbo; records of his interrogations disappeared, and the volume of Mackenzie King's Diary pertaining to the case vanished from the National Archives. Gouzenko was subjected to the usual slander from liberal and left circles.

By the way, according to Peter Wright's "Spycatcher," Stephenson's deputy, Von Petrov was a Soviet agent, but then who wasn't working for the Illuminati? (327)

THE UNITED STATES

The same thing happened in the U.S. when Soviet agent Whittaker Chambers defected in 1938. In 1939, he saw Adolph Berle, FDR's Assistant in Charge of Internal Security and fingered dozens of Soviet spies in key positions, including Harry Dexter White, who later became Assistant Secretary of the Treasury. Nothing was done.

In 1948, to fan the flames of the Cold War, they let Chamber's charges against Alger

Hiss come to the forefront. Hiss was a Soviet agent and a senior State Department official who advised FDR at the Yalta Conference. He also drafted the UN Charter and served as its first acting Secretary General in 1945. When rumors about him began to circulate, he resigned to become President of Rockefeller's "Carnegie Endowment for World Peace."

Following Communist discipline, Hiss feigned outraged innocence and accused Chambers and his supporters of conducting a "witch hunt." He sued Chambers for libel and a 'who's who' of the Eastern Establishment came to his defence, including Felix Frankfurter and Adlai Stevenson.

Unfortunately for him, Chambers produced documents in Hiss's own handwriting and Hiss went to prison for three years and eight months for the relatively minor charge of perjury.

GREAT BRITAIN

The British bewail the five high ranking Soviet "moles" in their Diplomatic and Security services. But both the USSR (and Israel) were the creation of British Freemasonry. In other words, the British elite is at the heart of this world government conspiracy, which in reality is just "British" Imperialism repackaged. For heaven's sake, the fifth "mole," Anthony Blunt, was the Queen's personal art curator when he was "exposed" in 1979.

In 1945, there was another crisis when Konstantin Volkov the NKVD Chief in Istanbul, operating under the cover of Vice Counsel, inquired about defecting. He had worked at Moscow Centre and had information on 300 agents including two spies in the British Foreign Office and another "directing a counter espionage organization in London." (William Stevenson, "Intrepid's Last Case," p.187-8)

I don't know how many counter espionage directors they have in London but MI5 Chief Sir Stewart Menzies instructed his counter espionage director Kim Philby to "look after" the matter. He did. Volkov and his wife were heavily sedated and flown to Moscow for torture and execution. Philby later retired in Moscow on the pension of a KGB General. Similarly Guy Burgess, Donald Maclean and the other more obvious "moles" in the heart of the British Foreign Service eventually retired to dachas in Russia. The BBC continues to portray them as idealists and rogue heroes.

British atomic scientist Klaus Fuchs who betrayed the secrets of the Hydrogen Bomb to Moscow got all of 14 years in prison. He was released after just nine years and allowed to fly to East Germany where he became Deputy Director of Nuclear Physics Research.

CONCLUSION

The real battle is not between "left" and "right" but the age-old conflict between the super rich who want to monopolize all wealth, and the rest of humanity who seek a modicum to sustain a comfortable life.

The enemy is not capitalism but monopoly capitalism, not corporations but cartels that strive for the ultimate monopoly, world government.

Communism is a ruse by which the bankers co-opted the collective instincts of mankind and harnessed misplaced idealism to their diabolical agenda.

The true enemy is not Islam but an ancient Satanic cult gnawing at the heart of Western society, intent on hijacking humanity from its healthy natural path and enslaving it using sophisticated methods of social control.

Be Afraid: The New World Order's Fascist Pedigree

The Anglo American business elite was involved up to its ears in the Nazi Third Reich, an early attempt at a "New World Order." It is a reminder that the Illuminati is not just Jewish. It embraces both Jewish movements Communism and Zionism on one hand, and Aryan movements Fascism and Nazism on the other.

Economist Robert Brady defined the Nazi state as "a dictatorship of monopoly capitalism. Its 'fascism' is that of business enterprise organized on a monopoly basis, and in full command of all the military, police, legal and propaganda power of the state." (Richard Sasuly, "I.G. Farben," 1947, p. 128)

Communist Russia was the other half of the dialectic. It was also a dictatorship of monopoly capital, this time disguised as "public ownership." A Nazi general visiting Russia in the 1930's remarked that Communism was a "mirror-image" of Nazism. They were both socialist. The only difference was that one peddled race while the other peddled class. Indeed both were created by the central banking cartel.

A key to understanding the New World Order is the psychology of the cartel. They want it all. Cartels by definition are a conspiracy. Their purpose is to defraud the public by keeping prices high. They do this by controlling competition, markets, raw materials and new technology. They are by definition megalomaniacal, anti-national, and anti social.

One of the earliest cartels was J. D. Rockefeller's Standard Oil, which eliminated the competition by secretly fixing transportation costs. While pretending to profess Christianity, Rockefeller is famous for saying "the only sin is competition."

The largest German cartel was the chemical, film and pharmaceutical giant I.G. Farben. Max Warburg was a director of Farben from 1910 to 1938. Farben produced 85% of Germany's explosives in World War Two.

In 1926, Farben and Standard Oil entered into a cartel agreement in which Farben stayed out of synthetic oil in return for Standard representing Farben in the U.S.. The upshot was that Standard Oil supplied the Nazis with petroleum in spite of U.S. shortages. It supplied a rare lead additive without which the Luftwaffe could not fly. It suppressed the production of synthetic rubber in the U.S., which almost cost the Allies the war.

In turn, Rockefeller got a cut of Farben's other business, which included the many factories that employed slave labor from concentration camps like Auschwitz. (Farben- Rockefeller paid the SS for this labor at bargain rates. They paid the salaries of the SS guards.) They also supplied the poison gas that killed the laborers after their usefulness had ended.

This is the real reason the rail lines to Auschwitz were not bombed. Allied bombers hit within 5 miles of Auschwitz but the factories and death camp were off limits. In fact, German industry moved there for this reason. After the war, the CIA established its German headquarters in the undamaged Farben headquarters in Frankfurt.

The holocaust was very good business. Throughout the 1930's Wall Street investment banks participated in "aryanization" which meant getting Jewish owned breweries, banks, factories, department stores etc. for 30% of their true value. The gold from the teeth of holocaust victims ended up in their vaults.

The Nazi war machine was financed by the Bank of England (which, for example, transferred the Czech gold reserves to the Nazis), Wall Street and Jewish plunder. It was finessed by lawyer John Foster Dulles, and his law firm Sullivan and Cromwell. Dulles later became U.S. Secretary of State.

Nazi Germany was a capitalist paradise. There was a 60-hour workweek, low wages and no unions. German cartels began preparing for war long before they financed Hitler. As countries fell under the Nazi jackboot, they absorbed former competitors at fire sale prices. "For German big business, World War II was a chance to plunder on a scale without precedent in history," writes Sasuly (p.114).

After the war, Dillon Read banker General William Draper was put in charge of dismantling German industry and distributing it among the allies. Needless to say, this did not happen. His Wall Street cohorts owned too much of it. Nazi businessmen remained in positions of power. War criminals were transported to South America or went to work for the CIA.

The list of U.S. corporations that had the equivalent of $8 billion invested in Nazi Germany include Standard Oil, General Motors, IBM, Ford, the Chase and National City Banks, ITT and many others.

As a result, the men of "The Greatest Generation" didn't know that ITT built the airplanes that dropped bombs on them. They didn't know that Ford and General Motors built the Nazi trucks and tanks. They didn't know that ball bearings crucial to the Nazi war effort were manufactured in Philadelphia, yet were in short supply in the U.S.A. This was all done with the knowledge and permission of the U.S. government. (For details, I recommend Charles Higham's "Trading with the Enemy" 1983. Christopher Simpson's "The Splendid Blond Beast," 1993, and "Blowback," 1988 are also useful.)

"INTERNATIONALISM"

American convoys to England were reinsured in Nazi Germany. The German insurance companies had the details of cargoes and departure times; and these were passed on to Nazi Intelligence.

James Martin relates this anecdote in his book "All Honourable Men" (1950). Martin was head of the economic warfare branch with the U.S. Dept. of Justice and later with the Economics Division of the U.S. Military Government in Germany.

In the Munich Reinsurance Company files, Martin also found "bundles of photographs, blueprints and detailed descriptions of whole industrial developments in the U.S., many of them obtained through insurance channels. Together they made up the vital statistics of our war economy." (23)

Martin tells how in the 1920's New York bankers such as Dillon Read & Company and Brown Brothers Harriman (where Prescott Bush was President) helped consolidate German industry into giant cartels such as the United Steel Works and I.G. Farben. Less than 100 men linked with the Deutsche and the Dresdner Banks controlled 2/3 of Nazi industry and financed the Nazi Party.

"Prewar movies had pictured the goose stepping Nazis as the absolute masters of Germany," Martin writes. "Our...questioning of Alfred Krupp and his works managers erased that impression. Adolf Hitler and his Party had never been allowed quite to forget that they had depended on the industrialists to put them in office, and that in future they could go further with the industrialists' help than without it." (83)

The Nazi cartels were all linked to American corporations such as Du Pont, Standard Oil, General Motors, ITT and General Electric. In 1944, Martin found 3600 agreements between German and American companies that denied critical raw materials and patents to the United States in favor of the Nazi war effort. (13)

Martin realized that the enemy was not a political but an economic power. "We began to summarize our picture of an enemy that could survive a military defeat because it did not need or use military weapons." (13)

Martin concludes: "Except for its military outcome, the Nazi experiment appears to have been a success in the eyes of its original sponsors. The unity of German business and finance in backing the Nazis was matched only by the precision with which the Nazi government moved in to support the aims and interests of the dominant financiers and industrialists. They, in turn, have been waging a hard post-war fight to keep the economic lines of the Nazi system intact." (291)

The war was also a success for the Nazis' U.S. partners. During the five war years, the 60 largest corporations in the U.S. more than doubled their total assets. (296)

If the elite backed the Nazis, why didn't the Nazis win? As my readers know, I believe the German people were 'set up' to lose and be destroyed, and finally become the eunuchs they are today. The Nazi Party was a stalking horse designed to seduce and betray the German people. (Of course most Nazis were dupes.) All the while, the international business elite made money while the war degraded and demoralized humanity so it will accept banker world government. Like all wars, the Second World War was a war against humanity by a financial and occult elite.

In conclusion, the New World Order, and indeed modern history, is the product of the desire of the Illuminati central banking cartel to translate its monopoly over credit into a monopoly over all wealth, politics and culture. The ultimate goal is to wrest humanity from God's purpose, and deliver it hostage to Lucifer.

The "Ugly" Secret of World War II

Josslyn Victor Hay, 22nd Earl of Erroll, (1901-1941) a senior British colonial (Kenyan) official, knew the real cause of World War Two and had the stature to be heard.

Winston Churchill ordered the Secret Service (Special Operations Executive) to kill him. What "ugly secret" would make the British government go to so much trouble to murder a prominent British colonial politician?

Significantly the conspirators chose the code name "Operation Highland Clearance" for Erroll's murder. The brutal eviction of Scottish tenants from their farms in the early 1800's is a fitting symbol for the dispossession of the human race by the New World Order, which the Second World War did so much to advance.

The popular version of the Nairobi Kenya murder was depicted in the 1987 movie "White Mischief" starring Charles Dance as Lord Erroll and Greta Scacchi as Diana Broughton.

Erroll's body was found in the early morning Jan.24,1941 kneeling in the front passenger foot well of his car with a bullet wound behind the ear, murdered execution style. Erroll, 40, a widower, was having an affair with a married woman Diana Broughton and had brought her home after midnight.

Suspicion was cast on Diana's much older husband Sir Henry Broughton,who was tried but acquitted. The movie pins the blame on him and the decadence of the white settlers in general.

The murder would have remained unsolved but for a retired SOE insider who, informed of a terminal disease, gave the information to a colleague Tony Trafford who composed a 100-page memo. Trafford, since deceased, gave it to an author, coincidentally named Errol Trzebinski who was writing "The Life and Death of Lord Erroll: The Truth Behind the Happy Valley Murder." (2000)

At 6 foot 2" with chiselled Nordic looks, Lord Erroll was a natural leader, heir to an ancient Scottish lineage, organized and intelligent, an excellent speaker with a photographic memory. A member of the Kenyan colonial legislature, he held the post of Military Secretary with important military and intelligence duties.

SOE "Operation Highland Clearance" involved more than 100 people. In the early stages of the world war, why was it so important for the Churchill government to silence this man?

THE GREAT RUSE

Essentially, Hitler was not interested in a world war. His design was to conquer the U.S.SR in a loose "Nordic" alliance with England. Erroll belonged to the "Cliveden Set" a powerful section of the British elite that supported this alliance.

Churchill's backers, the privately-owned Bank of England set Hitler up as a means to menace Stalin, have a world war and destroy Germany all at once. War enables them to concentrate power and wealth in their hands and slaughter national elites who might interfere with world government.

The bankers used the Cliveden types to fool Hitler into thinking England approved of his plans. Like proud protégés, the Nazis entertained the English and gave them information on their military build-up. The Nazis were set up. This is the real meaning of the "Policy of Appeasement."

The Cliveden Set divided into two groups, those who were aware of the trap, and those who were not. Erroll was one of the latter who sincerely believed Hitler represented a bulwark to Communism. When the war broke out, Erroll did his patriotic duty. But he knew too much. He was aware of how Hitler and Churchill belonged to the same homosexual occult secret society and he may have spoken of it within range of MI-5 assets.

In May 1941, three months after Erroll's death, Rudolf Hess, the Deputy Fuhrer, flew to Scotland to present Hamilton with a generous peace proposal. Both men were homosexuals. Hess was Hitler's homosexual lover in the Landsberg Prison and helped him compose "Mein Kampf." Hamilton may have had an affair with Albrecht Haushofer, the son of Hitler and Hess' mentor Karl Haushofer, who originated the concept of lebensraum. A. Haushofer was part of the German Resistance who hoped to shunt Hitler aside and make peace with England.

(See the book by Kevin Abrams & Scott Lively, "The Pink Swastika", online Chapter "Homo-Occultism")

It is probable that Hitler was created by a largely homosexual occult secret society that spanned both British and Nazi elites. This was called the Thule Society in Germany and the Order of the Golden Dawn in England. Aleister Crowley's Ordo Templi Orientis was the common link.

Winston Churchill, a Druid and homosexual, was part of this homo-occult scene. (He was also a friend of Edward VIII, considered a Nazi sympathizer.) But the Nazi branch was not aware of the hidden English agenda. Erroll was probably silenced because he opposed Communism and the NWO. He could have discredited Churchill and the British war effort and possibly warned Hitler.

THE MURDER

On Sept 7, 1940, a highly placed group, including Douglas Douglas-Hamilton, the Fourteenth Duke of Hamilton, met in Scotland and decided to terminate Jocelyn Hay, Lord Erroll. The matter was to be handled by SOE Cairo station.

Jock and Diana Broughton were MI-5 assets who entered Kenya in Nov. 1940 to discover Erroll's intentions and involve him in a love triangle that would obscure the real purpose of his murder. In December, another agent-couple entered Kenya and on the night of the murder, pretended to have engine trouble. They requested a ride back to town for the female who shot Erroll. There were radio-controlled teams following Erroll.

Trezebinski's retired SOE contacts try to put a slightly different spin on events suggesting Erroll was murdered because "ex-appeasers " in the establishment including "the Duke of Hamilton, senior figures in Chamberlain's last cabinet, close friends of Edward VIII and Edward himself" would be embarrassed by what Erroll knew. (p.280.)

One insider said Rudolf Hess, Lord Moyne and Erroll shared knowledge of some "ugly" secret. Jewish terrorists ostensibly murdered Lord Moyne in 1944 for this reason. Other Cliveden members who died mysterious and premature deaths were Lord Lothian (1940), Lord Rothermere (1940), Sir Harry Oakes (1943) and the former Prime Minister Neville Chamberlain who died of "cancer" in Nov. 1940 just six months after leaving office. Hamilton conveniently died in action in 1944. The two SOE agents who executed Eroll also conveniently died in action.

According to this insider, the "ugly secret" is "not that Churchill had discovered the conspiracy [to make peace with Germany] ... but that he had been part of it." My hunch is that Churchill, Hitler, Stalin and FDR were part of the same Cabalistic secret society (the Illuminati) and Lord Erroll knew Hitler was set being up. This is why Lord Erroll had to be silenced.

CONCLUSION

The ultimate "ugly secret" is that the U.S.SR was a creation of British Freemasonry, financed by the Bank of England. They may have lost control of Stalin and created Hitler to menace him. But Stalin would have had to do something terrible for the British to have joined Hitler. Russian Communism was one half of their NWO Hegelian dialectic. We see it today in the form of arbitrary state power, repression and indoctrination. Nazism was also a dry-run for the New World Order but it was their Plan "B".

The real point is that history is a hoax, contrived by Cabalist central bankers, to advance world tyranny. They empower perverts and misfits to create war and mayhem. For example, Winston Churchill's suffered from chronic depression and thrived on mayhem. He confessed at the onset of WWI: "Everything is tending to catastrophe and collapse. I am interested, geared up, and happy. Is it not horrible to be built like this?"

These monsters are our leaders. Subverted by a Luciferian cult, the moral bankruptcy of Western society is masked by material prosperity but this cannot last. Thus, they are erecting a police state while the intelligentsia and masses can still be bought with their own money.

Surviving the New World Order

[Memo to Myself]

This isn't about storing silver coins or canned food or getting an AK-47.

It's about saving your soul, not your skin. It's about the tendency to obsess on the New World Order, get depressed and become unbearable.

The situation is depressing. A Satanic cult controls the credit of the world and rules through myriad proxies. It is determined to destroy civilization and institute an Orwellian police state.

You spend hours every day addictively watching for new developments. Your face is pressed up against the shop window of the world.

You are "externalized." You can't go into the kitchen without switching on the radio.

You try to squeeze your sustenance from the world. But much of what you imbibe is poisonous: depravity, corruption, duplicity and tragedy. (Is that the point of the mass media? To demoralize and brutalize?)

Mankind is in the grip of a diabolical force that constantly strives to legitimize itself through deception. You can't overcome this demon. But you still control your personal life. Ultimately, the battle is for the soul of humanity. Why not begin by defending your own soul?

This means erecting a wall between the soul, and the world, and establishing a balance between the sacred and the profane. You need to shut out the world (the profane) for set periods of time and focus on what inspires you. That means turning off the TV, Internet and media in general.

Just as you nourish your body with food, you feed your soul with thoughts, sights and sounds. Your soul reaches out for beauty, grace, harmony, truth and goodness. You become what you think about.

What lifts your spirit? It might be a long walk, nature, music, hobby, sport, or music. It might be time with your family or friends. It might be the Bible, religious writing or meditation.

"Do what you love," Henry David Thoreau said. "Know your own bone; gnaw at it, bury it, unearth it, and gnaw at it still."

You agree with the mystics who say happiness is within. It involves the possession of your soul, and not wanting anything else. By looking outside your self, you displace your soul and become attached to the thing you want. This is the source of addictive behavior and unhappiness.

The occult elite controls us with sex and money - the North-South of the mind. The courtship stage is a period when sexual feelings are strong so two people will bond and start a family. Sex/romance was not meant to become a lifelong preoccupation and panacea.

The same is true of money. The stock market is a giant casino addicting millions. The central banking cult has unlimited funds. To make us feel good, (while it trashes civil rights and wages senseless war) it makes the market go up. To fleece us, it crashes the market. Don't be a puppet.

The diabolical powers have been here for a long time. You have discovered their existence only because they signalled the beginning of their endgame on Sept. 11.

Don't let them stunt or degrade you by obsessing on their iniquity. Restore balance by attuning yourself to the things you love. Be an outpost of happiness.

Part Two: Making Your Own Heaven

The world often seems like a stuffy public toilet without ventilation. This is because Protagorus' dictum "man is the measure of all things" is the official religion.

Modern culture mostly consists of reflections of our degenerate selves, a "wilderness of mirrors" as T.S. Eliot said. We inhale our own fumes. The religion of man is "humanism "or "illuminism" which deifies man.

Plato tried to correct Protagorus. "God and not man is the measure of all things."

We didn't listen to Plato.

God is now banished from public life. When was the last time a Divine Standard was applied to anything? When is humanity's highest self ever celebrated? That would be like a breath of fresh air.

REMOVING THE NEW WORLD ODOR

This is about spiritual survival in a world gone insane.

We have a tendency to feel helpless, unable to affect faraway events. In fact, we are on the front lines. The New World Order wants our mind and soul. We fight back by dedicating ourselves to God instead.

First we have to short-circuit their two main control systems: sex and money. We can direct our sex drive by confining it to a monogamous relationship. We can escape the money compulsion by living within our means, and disciplining ourselves so money is a minor concern.

Henry David Thoreau said, "A man is rich in proportion to the number of things he can afford to leave alone." The truly rich man is the one who does not think about money.

By this standard many billionaires are paupers. In fact, the more money a person has, the harder it is to think of anything else.

REORIENTATION

Why should we obey God? God is really the principle of our own development and the path to our happiness and fulfillment. We serve ourselves when we serve God. God is synonymous with spiritual ideals: love, truth, justice, beauty.

Think life has no meaning? Life has intrinsic meaning when we fulfill God's purpose. We need to ask, "What does God want of me? What was I born to do?"

God speaks to us through our spirit and conscience. We don't hear Him because our minds are like mirrors facing the world. We need to turn the mirror around so it faces the soul inside and shows its back to the world.

Instead of blotting up the world, which makes us weary and sick, we focus on things that reflect our desire for purity, hope, beauty and goodness.

Instead of letting the world determine what we think (and therefore feel) we create our own world based on how we want to feel. That's what faith is all about, making spiritual reality paramount.

"I know of no more encouraging fact than the unquestionable ability of man to elevate his life by a conscious endeavor," Thoreau wrote in "Walden."

"It is something to carve a statue...but it is far more glorious to carve ...the very atmosphere and medium through which we look, which morally we can do. Every man is tasked to make his life, even in its details worthy of the contemplation of his most elevated and critical hour."

By making our thoughts conform to our soul, instead of the world, we create our own heaven.

All great religions teach us to control our thoughts. Our minds are altars and our thoughts are offerings to God.

"Muddied water, let stand, becomes clear," said Lao Tzu.

In the Hindu tradition, mind discipline is called "Raja Yoga." By learning to meditate, we learn to have constructive thoughts. The key is to treat your thoughts as though they were a stranger's, and edit them. If you master this skill of detachment, you will never be depressed, never go mad for the simple reason that you will not be identified with a negative mental complex.

Christians might maintain their vigilance by asking, " What would Christ do? What would Christ think?" Christianity, in a nutshell, is the imitation of Christ.

Prayer is another form of meditation. Whatever our opinion of Timothy Leary, he had the right idea in *"High Priest"*: "Prayer is the compass, the gyroscope, the centering device to give you direction, courage and trust..."

A CONCENTRATION CAMP IN THE MIND

How long has it been since you felt happy? Yes, it rankles that pathetic scoundrels control the world. But man is not the measure of all things. No matter what happens on earth, God is the only Reality. Look beyond man and focus on spiritual reality: beauty, goodness, justice and love.

We place ourselves in concentration camps before they're even built. The Illuminati is not likely to shatter the illusion of freedom. There is no better way to control people. But even if they did, we must be capable of joy even then. God is Joy and God is far greater than men.

The key is to ignore the crowd, which is manipulated by the Illuminati. It's good to be aware but we do not dance to tunes tapped out by degenerates. We do not gaze at mirrors made by midgets.

The words of poet Henry More (1614-1687) are also relevant. "When the inordinate desire after knowledge of things was allayed in me, and I aspired after nothing but purity and simplicity of mind, there shone in me daily a greater assurance than ever I could have expected, even of those things which before I had the greatest desire to know."

Retiring from the world periodically ensures that we don't forfeit the only sphere where we still have control. It enables us to make a wholesome contribution to society.

As Paul Elmer More (1864-1937) said, "A day that makes me happy makes me wise." Let's master the art of happiness.

ADDENDUM 1

Jewish Convert, Rev. Richard Wurmbrand Defined "The Spiritual War"

by Cornelius B

There are moments when we realize that we live in a world of merciless battles, and above all a world of spiritual battles. In those moments of lucidity, we may understand the deep meaning of Rimbaud's conclusion, which states that the spiritual battles are as terrible as any war, and the words of Christ - I did not come to bring peace, but a sword.

Yes, we live in a world of permanent battles between two opposed spiritual powers -- the subtle power of good and the rough power of evil. The first one is life creative, and works with truth, honesty, harmony, love, pardon, compassion, good will and altruism, abundance, joy and happiness, and all positive energies that feed the universe and the life we know here on earth. Opposed to this spiritual power is the evil, the father of deceptions and lies, the first revolutionary and father of tyrannical hierarchy in the universe, the spiritual power behind destruction of life, cruelty, tortures, greed, selfishness, robbery, lust and madness, all sorts of crimes, including suicide, suffering and diseases, hunger and thirst, poverty... The list could be a very long one... Just think of the crimes committed during the Bolshevik revolution, the Communist revolution of China, the first and second world wars, and all the wars and revolutions there since, including the war in Afghanistan or the absurd war between Israelis and Palestinians, the tortures and murder of millions and millions of innocent children, and people of all ethnic origins and ages. Just think of the deceptive power behind all these crimes against humanity, and how we, humans, accept lies in our lives, that cut us from the truth, from the positive spiritual power, with all the disastrous consequences ...

I consider myself a victim of the Conspiracy, being born in Romania, where Communism robbed the hard work of several generations of my ancestors. I faced the brutality and the tyrannical Communist regime, but what I suffered is nothing when my thoughts go to other Christians, true martyrs that suffered tortures, prison and untold persecutions.

It was in 1964, just few months after the assassination of John Kennedy, when I learned that Communism is a Satanic sect, a very evil religion tuned on the dark side of the spiritual powers, deceiving humanity with the struggle of social classes, the "champion of the poor, of the worker," for a better world, with more justice, on the way for the perfect human society. Yes, all these lies were the "worm on the hook to easy catch big fish". Marx was a priest of the Synagogue of Satan, and his mission and will was to destroy the Christian religion. He never attacked the Jewish credo in the Talmud and Kabala; nor did Lenin, Trotsky and even Stalin. Why? Because Communism is an offspring, a creation of the Talmudists, a tool intended to bring humanity into the net of the most racist, greedy, criminal and spiritually ugly concept, the people of Satan alias Sanat.

My parents were hosting for a few days in our house a legendary man, Reverend Richard Wurmbrand. I was only 13 years old, but I still have the vivid image of this tall man passing the gate of our courtyard and walking slowly and with difficulty. He was in company of a friend of my father, who few years later was murdered by the secret police, the sinister "securitate" for his Christian credo. Wurmbrand's whole body was covered with deep scars, reminders of the cruel tortures the Communists inflicted on this man for his Christianity during fourteen years of jail. The bones of his feet were all broken while he was severely tortured; this was the reason why this man had such difficulty to walk.

Wurmbrand was born in a Jewish family in Romania. He was in a family of four children and he was still a little boy when his father died. He had a rather harsh childhood, because his mother was a woman of modest condition, widow with the hard charge to raise four little kids. They even tried a better life for few years in Istanbul, Turkey. They returned to Romania, and by the age 16 he was brought to Paris by one of his uncles, a U.S.A citizen gone to Paris, France, for Communist activity. Wurmbrand was introduced by his uncle to the Soviet ambassador to France.

- Young man, said the ambassador, we need you for Romania. We shall send you to the Soviet Union to a special university to study politics. Once ready, you will receive missions of high importance for the International Revolution.

He went to Moscow, and during two years he was inculcated the Marxism-Leninism in the presence of people coming from all countries, preparing the Communist revolution for the whole world.

Thus, between 1930 and 1940, he was engaged in the Communist revolutionary subversive movement in Romania. He was arrested and condemned. He was jailed at Doftana together with other Communist comrades. Following one rebellion, Wurmbrand was isolated in a cold and dank cell. Here his heart was filled with despair, and he made a try with a prayer: "God, I know that You do not exist, but if You do exist, take me out of here." He was taken out unhurt, but his fanatic attitude of revolutionary Communist was still unchanged. In 1939 he contracted lung tuberculosis, and was released from jail. He lived for a while in the house of a Protestant family, where Wurmbrand had the opportunity to read the Bible and meet a Lutheran pastor of Jewish origin. This man gave to Wurmbrand the deep senses of what he read in the Bible. This was his conversion from Communism to Christianity, and he was baptized Lutheran. His wife, Sabina, Communist activist of Jewish origin also, after a short while became Christian too. Here is the mission of

Israel - Christ came, and through Christ shall be saved the Jewish people, concluded the new Jewish Christianized couple.

In 1940, Wurmbrand became the pastor of the Lutheran Jewish community in Bucharest, organized by the Norwegian Mission for the conversion of Romanian Jews to Christianity. Wurmbrand was introduced to the highest levels of the cults, and had access to the minister of the religious cults in Romania. In this period was born his son Mihai, and the couple adopted also an orphan Romanian boy who they named Sandu.

In Romania the Sabatean/Frankist credo was adopted by a large number of Jewish people. They, as the Talmudists and Kabalists do, proclaim that the Jewish people is the long awaited Messiah.

One of Richard Wurmbrand's brothers attained the highest ranks in the Jewish lodges of the Masonry and became grand master. One day the two brothers, one Christian, the other Freemason, had a very vivid discussion.

- How could you conceive that the few millions Jews take over and control and govern the almost five billions non Jews?

- We have enough adepts, answered his brother. Some of them know they are our men, others do not, but all of them are at our disposal, and we will be their god. We created the Freemasonry and Communism; and through Communism, Capitalism, Materialism and Humanitarianism we already gave a Jewish spirituality to the whole world. Day after day the world is more and more Jewish. We, the Jews, we are the ferment of the 20th century.

- Messiah already came for us, replied Richard.

- No, answered the Freemason brother. That one was a traitor to the chosen people.

- Why then the Messiah doesn't come?

- Because the Jewish people even is the Messiah!

- The Jewish people is full of sins and disobey to the commandments we received from the God of Abraham, Isaac and Jacob, therefore this people cannot be Messiah, the saint and perfect. That perfect and saint was and remains only Jesus Christ.

- We hate you, the Christians, and you, Richard, you are a traitor to our people. When we shall build again the Temple of Soloman, we shall build in the city of Jerusalem the highest monument in the world, and on it shall be written: "Never forget what the Christians did to you."

- Your destruction by yourself, Israel, replied Richard to his Satanist brother. There is no more heaven for you, because beyond your materialism you have no other aim, no ideal.

In 1946, in Bucharest took place a conference of the Confessions in Romania. This was arranged by Ana Pauker, a high ranked Communist of Jewish origins, promoted by the Soviets of Stalin. During this conference, the Rabin Safran accused the Christians of anti-Semitism and of crimes against the Jews, and he promised revenge according to the laws of the Jewish people. In the same while he started to negate the divine nature of Jesus Christ. The only chosen people is the Jewish People, concluded the Rabin.

The Christians were frozen of fright, and nobody defended Jesus Christ. At the conference were also present Richard and Sabina Wurmbrand. Sabina said to Richard:

- You must tell the truth to the Rabin. Ask to speak!

Because he was the representative of the ecumenical movement, he was allowed to speak. Richard started by describing his Jewish origin, and then explained how he became a Christian. Then, he started to address his speech to the Rabin, with power and without being afraid of being accused of anti-Semitism, as only a Jew can do that nowadays.

- You are the guilty ones, said Wurmbrand. Your sins went up to the sky. You hate, you conspire and lie against Jesus Christ and his church. You lost your right of chosen people through the murder of Messiah, Jesus Christ, and you should ask for pardon and become Christians, because the one that you oppose is the one foretold to the patriarchs and to the prophets. Without Him you have no mercy.

Ana Pauker asked to stop the radio casting. In the vast room was chorus and loud applause. Richard Wurmbrand was taken out through a lateral door by his people, and protected against Jews who were waiting at the main entrance with the intention to slay him.

Shortly after these events, Richard Wurmbrand was arrested on the way to his church, and his martyrdom started in the Communist jails, as he so well described in his books published in several languages.

One of the most interesting of his books is titled "Marx and Satan". All the knowledge he gathered in his life out of jail and in the jail, conducted this brilliant man to the conclusion that Marx was a priest of the Synagogue of Satan, and his chief aim was the destruction of the Christian religion and the Christian civilization. He made a thorough investigation on the subject, and the documents he could find concerning Marx and Engels show the trajectory of these two men of Jewish origin from a Christian credo to the Satanic credo. This is the best explanation for the deep hatred and genocides perpetrated by Communards and Communists against the Christians wherever they got in control. This is the hatred of evil powers against the positive good powers described at the beginning of this text. This hatred was also behind the massacre of the Tutsi Christians in Rwanda by the Utu animalists and pagans, programmed and assisted by high ranked personalities, such as the Satanist Madeleine Albright, and the leaders of the so called democratic western countries, deeply controlled by those who wish the destruction of a large part of humanity, and the total enslavement of the survivors.

There is a large number of Jews that gave up the teachings of the Torah and embraced the teachings of the Babylonian Talmud and of the Kabala, which perverted their spirit and acts. They want to dominate the whole world. They pretend to be the only ones the chosen of God, explained Richard Wurmbrand. They believe that their belonging to the Jewish people is sacred. Because the

Messiah they were waiting for did not come, they arrived at the theory that the Jews themselves, in their totality, represent the Messiah. Therefore, they refuse to consider their sins, and they prohibit to be criticized or accused of whatever, be it the most justified criticism or accusation, turning the accusation against the accuser, as anti-Semitism, with much propaganda and turmoil in the whole world.

Besides this they made the horrors perpetrated by the Nazis during the war on Jews, a "holocaust", forgetting to mention the much larger victims among other peoples. They pass under silence the much more murderous holocaust perpetrated against the Christians during the Bolshevik revolution, and during the Communist tyranny. There is no other known mass murder and genocide in the human history that can be compared with the holocaust they perpetrated on Christians. They accuse the Christians of anti-Semitism but they are not accused of being anti-Christians. They consider their blood to be sacred, and only their's, and to be revenged with hundred for one, as they did in 1930 with the genocide of more than ten million Christians in Ukraine, and of whom we hear practically nothing.

After the war, they believed that there came the time for the International Communist revolution, and grab in their claws the whole planet. They underestimated the reality and had to pull back. Now they are massed in America, while still keeping in their control the ex-Communist countries, and as well the capitalist countries, they dispose of much maneuverability. The Capitalist Jews, the International bankers and the Freemasonry financed the Communism. They controlled the Communism and what happened there. For example, the hate of Christianity is pure Jewish, and this hate was practiced under Communism. Only those Satanic Jews hate with such absurdity and totality Jesus Christ and his church. The Freemasonry is their creation and they have total dominion and control on it. They are arrogant, racist and excessive in all what they do. In these conditions it is hard to hope from them the humility necessary for the acceptance of Jesus Christ. The radical Talmudic Jews work to convert the whole planet to their credo and be installed as grand pontiffs over the peoples of the earth. They cultivate solidarity among them with the purpose to attain their final purpose. But they are dominated by the Satanic spirit of lies and deception, and they are the enemies of the whole humanity. Nevertheless, there are more and more Jews aware of this complot against the whole planet, and they feel concerned; they already organize the resistance against this madness. A significant number of Jews became Christians, and others get away from the Talmudists and return to the teachings of the Torah. It is probable that the last people to adopt the Christian religion are the Talmudists.

They accuse anyone that opposes their abuses of anti-Semitism and hatred, but in fact they are the real haters of the peoples of the earth.

These explanations of Richard Wurmbrand were taped on a TESLA tape recorder, so I could listen to it regularly before I managed to escape from the Communists of Romania swimming across the Danube in the night to Yugoslavia, and from there to Italy. I was only nineteen years old by then, but I never forgot the teachings of this man out of common, martyr of modern times.

Dec 2008

ADDENDUM 2

Illuminati Reveal Their Crazy Apocalyptic Agenda

by Henry Makow Ph.D.

"Thrust in your sickle and reap, for the time has come for you to reap, for the harvest of the earth is ripe." Revelations 14:15

The world may soon resemble Jonestown if a sick Illuminati plan to "harvest" souls in 2012 comes to pass. For a week in October 2008, a person claiming to be a "generational member of a Ruling Bloodline family" answered questions on abovetopsecret forum .

Using the moniker "Hidden Hand," he gave a convincing explanation of the demented Cabalistic beliefs motivating the Illuminati. He described how they find this world consciousness ("Third Density") to be "very constricting and uncomfortable" and want to be united again with Lucifer ("the One," the "Creator.") This will require them to stage an apocalyptic human sacrifice ("harvest of souls") in 2012.

The background according to "Hidden Hand" is this: Yahweh had been running a "benign dictatorship" in the Garden of Eden. He made a pact with the Luciferians (Illuminati) to introduce evil into the world so man will have Free Will to choose between right and wrong, and thus evolve spiritually. Yahweh didn't expect man would choose evil. As result, the Illuminati rule the world but now find it a tedious place. They intend to create the intense evil (selfishness, "negative polarity") required for them to rendezvous with their spaceship, as it were. Remember, this is an insane Satanic cult which just happens to control the planet.

At the "Harvest" evolved souls will enter the "Fourth Density" with the Illuminati and enjoy a "Golden Age," while everyone else's soul will be transported to a "replica earth" where they will continue to "work on themselves." The scenario is reminiscent of the "Left Behind" series where Christians suddenly disappear into heaven, and non-believers are left behind to face the Tribulation. I don't think this is a coincidence.

MANDATORY: NIKE RUNNING SHOES

In an excerpt from over 60 pages, "Hidden Hand" says:

"Yes, the noonday Winter Solstice Sun of December 21st, 2012 is the time when the Lord of The Harvest shall return. You might know him as "Nibiru. Read up on the Mayan Prophesies and Calendrical events for more detail upon how the actual Galactic and Universal Cycles work."

"There will be dramatic changes to your climate and weather conditions over the next few years, as the time of the Great Harvest approaches. You will see wind speeds surpassing 300 miles per hour at times. There will be raging tsunamis and widespread devastation; and a solar emission in late 2009 early 2010 that will cause major melting of the ice caps, and subsequent drastic rise in sea levels, leaving many (international) metropolitan areas underwater....San Francisco and Damascus, will be uninhabitable by the end of 2010, possibly even sooner. Again, it depends upon certain 'forces' at play, and which time lines are activated. Humanity, though utterly unconscious of the fact, has a significant part to play in this. You (as a collective consciousness of the planet) are choosing the Negative Polarization by default, by the quality of your thoughts and actions. Thought is creative energy, focused. You get exactly what you put out."

Decide for yourself whether this information is valid. It fits into the puzzle picture I have assembled about a long-term Cabalist plan to deliberately fulfill prophesy and initiate an apocalypse. For example, "Historian Demands Action on Powerful Doomsday Cults," "What Every Jew and Non-Jew Should Know," "Independent Historian Unveils Cabala Conspiracy," and "Illuminati Rebel Issues Dire Warning."

"Hidden Hand" explains:

"The End of this [26,000 year] Cycle, heralds literally, a New World Age, and a New Creation. A new Heaven, and a new Earth, and is the time of the Great Harvest. Smaller Cycles yield a Harvest, and then life continues on the planet as normal. Great Cycles yield a Great Harvest, and the end of current life on the 3rd Density. See it as a kind of 'Cosmic jet wash' and deep clean, while the planet takes a rest and regenerates herself.. When this Life-Cycle Ends, "All things will pass away, and All things shall be made new"."

"So, December 21, 2012 AD, is not the day where all of a sudden the lights go out, and everything will suddenly change, rather, we are NOW in the process of this transition, from one World Age to the next. The changes are underway and will continue steadily accelerating as we head towards the culminating date. The 26,000 year cycle is composed of 5 lesser cycles, each of which are 5,125 years in duration. Each of these 5 cycles is considered its own World Age or Creation Cycle. Our present great cycle (3113 B.C. - 2012 A.D.) is called the Age of the Fifth Sun."

"If we do not have a Negative Harvest, we are bound with you for another cycle.... We need a Negative Harvest, so that we can create our 4th Density Earth, and clear our Karmic Record..."

EVIL IS "FOR YOUR OWN GOOD" (i.e. EVIL IS GOOD)

"Hidden Hand" says the Illuminati create "War, Hatred, Greed, Control, Enslavement, Genocide, Torture, Moral Degradation, Prostitution, Drugs, all these things and more," for our own good.

"In all these Negative things, we are providing you with tools. But you do not see it. It is not what we do, but how you react to it, that is important. We give you the tools. You have the Free Will choice how you will use them. You have to take responsibility. There is only One of Us here. Understand that, and you will understand the Game."

"Understand, that we HAVE to be Negative. That's what we were sent here to be. It is our contract, and it has always been to help you, by providing the "Catalyst" I spoke of earlier. Being Negative is very hard for us, not on a physical level, (the characters we play enjoy our roles, as we're programmed that way), but on a Spiritual level, it is hard. We surpassed the lowly negative vibrations eons ago. We are Light, and we are Love. It is a very hard thing for us to do Spiritually, to create all this Negativity, but we do it because we love you, and it is for your highest good, ultimately. You could say, that it is our Sacrifice that we have made, in order to be of Service to the One Infinite Creator, and to you, our Brothers and Sisters in the One."

Just so there is no doubt whom the Illuminati worship: "Our Creator, is the one you refer to as 'Lucifer', "The Light Bearer" and "Bright and Morning Star". Our Creator is not "The Devil" as he has been spuriously portrayed in your bible. Lucifer is what you would call a "Group Soul" or "Social Memory Complex", which has evolved to the level of the Sixth Density, which in effect, means that he (or more accurately "'we") has evolved to a level sufficient that he (we) has attained a status equal or arguably 'greater' than that of Yahweh (we have evolved higher than him). In appearance, were you to gaze upon Lucifer's fullest expression of our Being, the appearance would be that of a Sun or a "Bright Star". Or, when stepping down into a 3rd Density vibration, we would appear as what you may term an 'Angel' or 'Light Being.'"

"Hidden Hand" says the media plays a major role in creating the negative meme and making us unwitting collaborators.

"Why do you think the Media is so important to us? You have (as a society), in your hypnotized comatose state, given your Free Will consent to the state your planet is in today. You saturate your minds with the unhealthy dishes served up for you on your televisions that you are addicted to, violence, pornography, greed, hatred, selfishness, incessant 'bad news', fear and 'terror'. When was the last time you stopped, to think of something beautiful and pure? The planet is the way it is, because of your collective thoughts about it. You are complicit in your inaction, every time you 'look the other way' when you see an injustice. Your 'thought' at the sub-conscious level of creation to the Creator, is your allowance of these things to occur. In so doing, you are serving our purpose."

CABALA

The Illuminati dogma is pure Cabalism (Occultism) which sees chaos and destruction as a prerequisite to change. The Creator as "sparks" trapped in our bodies which requires that the world be smashed in order to release Him. "Hidden Hand" tells forum members:

"You are indeed what you call "Divine Souls"; you are sparks or seeds of The One Infinite Creator. You are Life Itself (Light), remembering and learning who you really are (we came here to help you to do this) and yes, currently, you are trapped (or more accurately "Quarantined") within the 'matter' of this planet you call Earth."

"You can thank your Creator Yahweh for that. You are the 'offspring' or individuations of his Group Soul (or Social Memory Complex). Macrocosmically speaking, you ARE Yahweh. The 'Karmic' effect of his imprisoning us in his Astral Planes, also has an impact upon you. I cannot be more specific on this, without impinging on the Law of Confusion. You must work it out for yourselves."

For an evil do-er, "Hidden Hand" spent most of his time coaching forum members on avoiding the Illuminati traps and listening to their "inner voice" so they will be released from the wheel of reincarnation during the "Great Harvest."

"You will never be 'free', for as long as you are incarnating on this planet. The very nature of your being here, is indication of that. There is a reason why you are here, and 'here' is very likely not really where you think 'here' is. How do you become free? By working out where you are, and coming to an understanding, of why you are here. You are fast running out of time to do so, before the coming Harvest. Those that don't make it, will have to repeat the cycle."

By the end of the week, most of the forum members are eating out of the guru's hidden hand. The exceptions are, ironically, a "lower level mason" who accuses him of rehashing New Age Theology. The guru acknowledges that the "Ra Material" and "the Law of One" are 85-90% accurate. He says the "Ra Material" is "very similar to the knowledge my Family has, and have passed down for many many generations."

A Christian reader correctly sees "an elaborate ruse to 'make the devil look good.' I don't think there are many conservative Christians that would be able see the difference between the biblical Lucifer and the Lucifer you purport to be a part of."

But she asks for his advice in overcoming this obstacle.

NEW INFORMATION ABOUT THE ILLUMINATI

"Hidden Hand" claims to belong to one of 13 Bloodlines that have ruled the world from the dawn of time. They are "Houses" performing functions like organs in a body, which is the "Family" united in the common cause. They all have an area of specialty: Military, Government, Spiritual, Scholarship, Leadership, and Sciences. They hold key positions in all of these main areas. With the addition of a complicit Media machine and ownership of Financial establishments, all bases are covered.

Writing in Oct, he said a certain faction wanted to call off the U.S. election. "If nothing happens to Obama, he will win. Remember, behind the scenes, there is only One Party. Our Party. 'Democracy' is an illusion which is created to uphold your slavery. Whichever side 'wins'; the Family wins. There are many possibilities and alternative 'scripts'. All of them lead toward the ultimate implementation of the overall blueprint of our Creator" [i.e. Lucifer.]

He says he is only a "regional" leader (as opposed to national or international) but his information is that, barring "unforeseen disruptions" there will be "a new currency by the end of 2008 / early 2009, along with a new Union of nations. January has been spoken of in some circles, as the latest, though there are plans underway which could even bring this to fruition much earlier than initially hoped for. It depends upon the results of other upcoming events as to how this will play out."

Asked if "911" was the creation of a "star gate," he replied, "No, it was a Ritual Human Sacrifice. That, and the obvious catalyst for the so-called 'War on Terror.'"

He confirms that "Svali" was "a part of the Family, at the lower levels, from the German Lines I believe. As I understand, she did reveal a lot of truth about the lower levels, but she was only Regional Level in the Earth Lines, so not that high. She certainly would not have had anything like the "bigger picture."

He says the Rothschilds etc. belong to "earth-based" bloodlines. "The Earth lines are not aware of the entire picture. They themselves are not of our Lucifer Group Soul, and as far as they are aware, they are out to 'rule the world', to Control and Enslave, and create as much Suffering and Negativity as is humanly possible. That's what they 'get out of the deal'. World Domination. You'd have to say with that in mind, they're doing a great job. But one of the things they don't know or understand, is that our (Venusian Power Lines) agenda, is ultimately for the Highest Good of all concerned, in providing you with the Catalyst. If they were aware of this Truth, there is a slight risk that they would not have done their jobs properly, and they would miss out on joining us in our 95% Negative Harvest. They are aware of the Harvest, and the need for them to attain the 95%, to get out of 3rd Density, and that is all the motivation they need to help us achieve our ultimate aims".

ILLUMINATI STRUCTURE

"Starting at the bottom level, you have what we call "Local Cell Groups" or "Family Clusters". There will be anything from say five to thirty or so of these, depending upon the size of the town or city in question. Each Local area has it's own Council, comprised of Local Leaders representing the Six Disciplines of learning. There is also either a High Priest or High Priestess of The Order, who Serves their local community."

"Above this, you have the Regional Council, with the Leader of each Local Council representing their specific areas. Then the National Council, in the same vein, with the Leaders of the Regional Councils sitting to represent their Regions."

"Then you have the Supreme World Council above them all, with the National Leaders representing their Countries. Above this, is another group I cannot mention, who liaise with the "Hidden Hands.""

"Then above this, there are many other levels of Leadership, purely from the Power Lines (the ones that are not of this planet.) The Supreme World Council, only know as much as is "Handed" down to them from us."

"In our Power Lines, we have a similar structure, with Local and Regional groups etc, though most of us are living in entirely 'different' types of communities than you would understand. All I shall say is that we are not "surface dwellers.""

CONCLUSION: OUR SURVIVAL IS AT STAKE

In his own terms, "Hidden Hand" is credible but I regard him as insane, pretending to purity and talking about "service to others" while wreaking incalculable misery and mayhem on humanity. He offers invaluable insight into the hypocritical Illuminati mindset, always dressing their evil in pretensions of public service. For example, Communism is Satanism posing as working class rebellion.

To inflict so much suffering and depravity under the pretext of "testing" mankind and furthering evolution is preposterous. Aren't there enough tests in life without the Illuminati's hidden hand on the scale? If instead the Illuminati had exercised a positive influence, spiritual evolution would have taken place at an amazing pace. Retarding human evolution, not advancing it, is their real agenda. They want us to be their cattle.

I believe the harbor is best reached by setting your course and avoiding the rocks. In contrast, the Illuminati steer the vessel onto the rocks, as many times as it takes to sink it. This sick Cabalistic dogma is behind the blank gaze of our politicians and newscasters.

It's time to admit that humanity is under constant stealth attack by a sadistic and dangerous Satanic cult. Obviously, it is well organized and funded and has subverted every institution.

It's time we set aside occultism and used common sense. It's time we adopted simple morality, as in "Do Unto Others as You Would have Them do Unto You."

Unless we wrest control of this planet from the Illuminati, we are doomed, like Rev. Jones' followers at Jonestown. And we will deserve our fate. Hidden Hand is right. "You are complicit in your inaction, every time you 'look the other way' when you see an injustice." Let's be "Service Oriented" and reject the Illuminati -- their phony terror, fascist government and Satanic religion.Let's throw their kool-aid in their face.

Note:

Two years ago (Jan. 2007) Illuminati defector Leo Zagami issued this warning:

"The cosmic alignment on the 21st of December 2012 gives you 6 years to prepare... So its about time you all wake up and fight for your right to stay free under one God before they take complete control and start persecuting the true believers in the one God. ...Get your swords and get ready to fight to defend your faith or perish...This is a war against Satan so please wake up in the western countries or you might wake up in a nightmare one morning in December 2012."

"From 2010 you will start feeling the big changes in the air more and more but in 2012 you will have the clear evidence of the end of this civilization in front of your eyes....the total NAZIFICATION of the western countries by 2010 before the economic situation starts to badly crack for everyone. Then social tension will hit a peak never seen before and internal conflicts could eventually become in 2012: CIVIL WAR!"